THE NORTON GUIDE TO AP®

Literature

WRITING & SKILLS

First Edition Update

W0006414

THE NORTON GUIDE TO AP®
Literature
WRITING & SKILLS

First Edition Update

Susan G. Barber
MIDTOWN HIGH SCHOOL,
GEORGIA

Melissa Alter Smith
LAKE NORMAN CHARTER HIGH SCHOOL,
NORTH CAROLINA

W. W. NORTON & COMPANY
Independent Publishers Since 1923

W. W. Norton & Company has been independent since its founding in 1923, when William Warder Norton and Mary D. Herter Norton first published lectures delivered at the People's Institute, the adult education division of New York City's Cooper Union. The firm soon expanded its program beyond the Institute, publishing books by celebrated academics from America and abroad. By midcentury, the two major pillars of Norton's publishing program—trade books and college texts—were firmly established. In the 1950s, the Norton family transferred control of the company to its employees, and today—with a staff of five hundred and hundreds of trade, college, and professional titles published each year—W. W. Norton & Company stands as the largest and oldest publishing house owned wholly by its employees.

Copyright © 2024 by W. W. Norton & Company, Inc.

All rights reserved

Printed in the United States of America

First Edition Update

Director of High School Publishing: Christina Magoulis
Project Editor: Melissa Atkin
Assistant Editor, High School: Katelyn Taylor
Managing Editor, College: Marian Johnson
Associate Director of Production, College: Benjamin Reynolds
Media Editor: Alicia Jimenez
Media Project Editor: Diane Cipollone
Managing Editor, College Digital Media: Kim Yi
Ebook Production Manager: Kate Barnes
High School Marketing Manager, Language Arts: Claire Molk
Design Director: Rubina Yeh
Designer: Juan Paolo Francisco
Director of College Permissions: Megan Schindel
Permissions Specialist: Josh Garvin
Composition: Westchester Publishing Services
Illustration Studio: Dragonfly / Craig Durant
Manufacturing: LSC Communications—Crawfordsville, IN

Permission to use copyrighted material is included in the credits section of this book, which begins on page 239. AP® is a trademark registered by the College Board, which is not affiliated with, and does not endorse, this product.

Library of Congress Cataloging-in-Publication Data

Names: Barber, Susan G., author. | Smith, Melissa Alter, 1980– author.
Title: The Norton guide to AP literature : writing and skills / Susan G. Barber, Melissa Alter Smith.
Other titles: Norton guide to Advanced Placement literature
Description: First edition. | New York, NY : W. W. Norton & Company, [2022] | Includes index.
Identifiers: LCCN 2021054508 | ISBN 9780393886412 (paperback) | ISBN 9780393886443 (epub)
   ISBN 978-1-324-08722-9
Subjects: LCSH: English literature—Examinations—Study guides. | English philology—
   Examinations—Study guides. | Advanced placement programs (Education)—Examinations—
   Study guides. | College entrance achievement tests—Study guides. | LCGFT: Study guides.
Classification: LCC PR87 .B256 2022 | DDC 808/.042076—dc23/eng/20220111
LC record available at https://lccn.loc.gov/2021054508

W. W. Norton & Company, Inc., 500 Fifth Avenue, New York, NY 10110
   wwnorton.com
W. W. Norton & Company Ltd., 15 Carlisle Street, London W1D 3BS

1 2 3 4 5 6 7 8 9 0

Contents

About the Authors

SUSAN G. BARBER teaches AP® English Literature at Midtown High School in Atlanta, Georgia, and serves English teachers on the National Council of Teachers of English Secondary Steering Committee and on the Test Development Committee for AP® Literature. She is the editor of and frequent contributor to the online resource AP Lit Help and has been an AP® Reader for the past eight years. Susan, along with Carlos Escobar, instructed thousands of students (and teachers) through the College Board's AP® Live videos after schools went remote during the spring of 2020; she was also an instructor for AP® Daily that fall. She has offered training at NCTE, Georgia Council of Teachers of English, the Folger Shakespeare Library, and AP® Summer Institutes through the College Board, and frequently leads English language arts workshops across the country. Susan is most proud, however, of the work she does on a daily basis at Midtown; she never tires of the beauty and chaos of the classroom.

MELISSA ALTER SMITH teaches at Lake Norman Charter High School in Huntersville, North Carolina, and was the 2017 District Teacher of the Year. She is an AP® Reader, the creator of the #TeachLivingPoets hashtag and https://teach livingpoets.com, and the coauthor of *Teach Living Poets* (2021). A frequent presenter, she has facilitated conversations with poets on behalf of the National Council of Teachers of English for several years.

Preface for Students

We commend you for taking AP® Literature and Composition, a class that is both extremely challenging and deeply rewarding. This book will guide you through improving the skills you will need to be successful in this course. Whether you feel comfortable and ready to take the exam in May or confused and wondering if taking this class was a mistake, our aim is to build your confidence, advance your writing skills, and improve your score on your exam essays.

Understanding that every student learns differently, all having their own individual approaches to writing and analyzing literature, we want to share with you up front that some of the strategies in this book will work for you while others may not. That is why we try to offer an array of methods to achieve the ultimate goal of a successfully written essay. With that in mind, whether you plan on taking the AP® Exam or not, working through this book will help improve your close-reading, analytical thinking, and writing skills overall.

If you are planning on taking the AP® Literature and Composition Exam, or are at least considering taking it, here's what you can expect: a three-hour adventure in literature divided into two parts. The first part is a one-hour multiple-choice section with fifty-five questions on short prose fiction passages and poems spanning from the fifteenth century to the present day. The second part is a two-hour essay portion consisting of three different types of essays:

Question 1: Poetry Analysis essay
Question 2: Prose Analysis essay
Question 3: Literary Argument essay

This book will first introduce the skills identified by College Board as the focus of the course, which will guide you as you read various texts. Next this book will provide instruction for writing each of the different types of essays. The writing chapters will be structured around the six-point rubric used to assess student essays:

Essay Rubric

Reporting category	Points possible	Scoring criteria
Row A	1	Thesis Statement
Row B	4	Evidence and Commentary
Row C	1	Sophistication

Perhaps you're worried that you will read a passage or poem on the exam, or even in class, and not understand it at all. This is a common fear some of our students have and it's completely normal. Here's what we suggest: instead of thinking of a text as something "to figure out," think of it as a human story. We're all human and share the same experiences and emotions, whether we are living today or in the sixteenth century like Shakespeare. Our humanity connects us through space and time, and literature is a perfect vehicle to illustrate this phenomenon.

You have just as much right as a student to share your thoughts on humanity as adults do. In fact, we desperately need your voice in today's society. Choosing to take the AP* Literature and Composition Exam is an opportunity for you to show others that you can respond to literature with your thinking and in your voice. Our hope is this book will provide resources and ideas to build your confidence and supplement the instruction you are receiving in class. Thank you for allowing us to play a small role in your journey as a thinker and writer.

Cheering you on,
Susan and Melissa

Preface for Teachers

The Norton Guide to AP® Literature was written to give students and teachers the tools to succeed with the course's fundamental skills and writing portion of the AP® Literature and Composition Exam. We hope that you will find this book useful as an addition to the *Norton Introduction to Literature*, another anthology, or as a stand-alone resource. While this text will be a useful resource for any ELA educator, we have written it specifically with AP® Literature and Composition teachers in mind. Whether you are new to teaching the course or a seasoned veteran, we believe this book will offer you valuable guidance for teaching, as well as preparing students for the exam.

What sets this book apart from many other course guides out there is that we both are currently AP® Literature teachers in the classroom, every day, same as you. What you will find in this book is student tested, tried and true. Furthermore, as experienced AP® Readers, we openly share our knowledge of the essential skills as well as the little things students can do to impress their scorers. You'll see our advice referred to as "pro tips" interwoven contextually within the chapters.

Finally, it is important to remember that *you* know what is best for your students. While we offer teaching strategies and ideas for improving students' writing, you know your students' needs. Please use this guide as exactly that—a guide. Use what works in your classroom—with your scholars, with your teaching style. We hope this book will affirm what you are already doing in the classroom, and help to elucidate the intricacies and nuances of writing for the exam. We wholeheartedly agree with David Miller, a former AP® Literature Chief Reader, whose sentiment is that every essay we grade is representative of a student putting forth their best effort, and that they should be rewarded for what they do well; our approach to scoring their writing is with care and attention. We encourage you to keep the mantra "reward them for what they do well" in mind as you evaluate student work, especially timed writings. And remember to be kind to yourself, too; you deserve it.

Acknowledgments

We would like to thank the W. W. Norton team of Jenna Bookin Barry, Quinn Fusting, Christina Magoulis, Claire Molk, Rose Paulson, Katelyn Taylor, Thea Goodrich, Melissa Atkin, Josh Garvin, and Ben Reynolds. We would also like to thank Roy Smith of Round Rock High School, who authored the two full AP® Exams in this book. Thank you to our colleagues and friends in #APLitChat and our educator colleagues and friends. Without your fellowship, we would not be the teachers we are today: Julie Adams, Matt Brisbin, Brian Hannon, Karla Hilliard, Kelly Herrera, Jori Krulder, Jill Massey, Tia Miller, Adrian Nester, Kristin Runyon, Sarah Soper, Jennifer Stuckey, Brian Sztabnik, and Melissa Tucker. Finally, we extend our thanks to the following teachers and reviewers whose feedback helped to shape this project:

Yael Abrahamsson, Cherry Creek High School
Noelle Ackland, Interboro High School
Kelly Barnes, Munster High School
Amy Biancheri, Batavia High School
Laura Bryson, Northwest Cabarrus High School
Lisa Camera, Woodside High School
Kelly Castillo, Middle Creek High School
Asani Charles, John Horn High School
Marilena Ferraiuolo, Ridgefield Memorial High School
Mary Hardin, Verona Area High School
Carolyn Harrod, Ryan High School
Lisa Hollins, Hazelwood East High School
Kathryn Jacobi, Our Lady of Providence High School
Gina Kortuem, New Life Academy
Jori Krulder, Paradise High School
Kellie Lentz, Knoch High School
Sara Magalli, Valley Park High School
Steve Miles, Arapahoe High School
Mary Parry, Bishop England High School
Brenda Paxton, Idaho Arts Charter School
Liberty Phillips, Knoxville Catholic School
Lisa Picardi, Council Rock South
Jill Pinard, John Stark Regional High School
Jacqueline Pinchot, Riverside High School
Charles Preacher, Woodrow Wilson High School
Jose Ramirez, Marine Leadership Academy at Ames
Brandon Runyon, Berean Christian High School
Kristin Runyon, Charleston High School
Whitney Sharp, Sallisaw High School

Michelle Summers, Dunmore Junior High School
Jeremy Voigt, Burlington Edison High School
Johnny Walters, Heritage High School
Jim Wickes, Dalton High School
Justin Williams, Montgomery High School

Susan would like to thank her family, Scott, Bethany, Nathan, Brandon, Katie, and Brooke, who have all listened to far more conversations about English ed than any non-educator should. Thank you also to the teachers in the #APLitHelp community who challenge and inspire me on a daily basis. I am especially grateful for Melissa Smith who partnered with me on this project; she is smart, kind, and a good friend. Of all the work I do, I am most proud of what occurs on a daily basis in my classroom at Midtown High School. This book is a testament to the resilience of the classes of 2021 and 2022; thank you!

Melissa would like to thank her family, Craig, Payson, and Chase, for their support and love. You are my world. Thank you to my parents, Don and Carol, to the poets who share their work in this book and with the #TeachLivingPoets movement, and to my students who inspire me every day. Susan Barber, you are a mentor, a friend, and I am beyond grateful for you; thank you for being my partner on this project. And finally, thank you, Lake Norman Charter's Class of 2021 AP° Lit seniors, for writing this book with me.

1

Close Reading Skills

INTRODUCTION

Ten lanes wide, I-75 and I-85 run through the heart of Atlanta, and traffic either moves quickly or stands at a dead gridlock. Entering onto the interstate can be difficult, but at each on-ramp, a traffic light alternates between red and green signaling motorists to merge in traffic and staggering the number of cars trying to get on the interstate at one time.

Reading can be like navigating heavy traffic. Readers may feel the words are either speeding by at a blinding pace or stuck at a standstill while they read paragraphs over and over. But much like entry ramps and traffic lights aiding us onto interstates, readers have a variety of avenues into a text. In AP® Literature specifically, the skills presented in this chapter provide ways into texts allowing readers to understand and appreciate works at a deeper level.

Following the interstate analogy, what would happen if once we successfully navigated onto an interstate, we stopped? That would be ridiculous, as the whole point of taking an entry ramp and proceeding through the green light onto the interstate is to move through the city. Yet many readers stop as soon as they find a way into a text. We are quick and often fairly successful at identifying literary devices and elements but then fail to allow them to bring us all the way through the text.

Learning what to do once we have navigated our way into a text is where the real work lies. Self-questioning, breaking down thoughts, and reading between the lines are habits that good readers learn and develop over a lifetime. This chapter will provide basic frameworks for thinking more deeply about literature. Use them to train your mind. Initially this process may seem cumbersome and slow, but it will become easier the more you use it. Soon this type of thinking will become second nature.

The basic framework for thinking about literature in the AP® English Literature and Composition course is broken down into Big Ideas and Enduring Understandings. The Big Ideas—characterization, setting, structure, narration, figurative

AP® English Literature and Composition Skills

BIG IDEAS

CHR Character	SET Setting	STR Structure
ENDURING UNDERSTANDINGS		
Characters in literature allow readers to study and explore a range of values, beliefs, assumptions, biases, and cultural norms represented by those characters.	Setting and the details associated with it not only depict a time and place, but also convey values associated with that setting.	The arrangement of the parts and sections of a text, the relationship of the parts to each other, and the sequence in which the text reveals information are all structural choices made by a writer that contribute to the reader's interpretation of a text.
Skill Category 1	**Skill Category 2**	**Skill Category 3**
Explain the function of character.	*Explain the function of setting.*	*Explain the function of plot and structure.*
SKILLS		
1.A Identify and describe what specific textual details reveal about a character, that character's perspective, and that character's motives. Units 1, 2, 3, 4, 6	**2.A** Identify and describe specific textual details that convey or reveal a setting. Units 1, 3	**3.A** Identify and describe how plot orders events in a narrative. Units 1, 4, 6, 7
1.B Explain the function of a character changing or remaining unchanged. Units 3, 7, 9	**2.B** Explain the function of setting in a narrative. Units 4, 7	**3.B** Explain the function of a particular sequence of events in a plot. Units 1, 6, 7
1.C Explain the function of contrasting characters. Units 4, 6	**2.C** Describe the relationship between a character and a setting. Units 4, 7	**3.C** Explain the function of structure in a text. Units 2, 5, 8
1.D Describe how textual details reveal nuances and complexities in characters' relationships with one another. Units 4, 7		**3.D** Explain the function of contrasts within a text. Units 2, 4, 6, 8
1.E Explain how a character's own choices, actions, and speech reveal complexities in that character, and explain the function of those complexities. Units 6, 9		**3.E** Explain the function of a significant event or related set of significant events in a plot. Units 3, 9
		3.F Explain the function of conflict in a text. Units 3, 9

BIG IDEAS

NAR Narration	**FIG** Figurative Language	**LAN** Literary Argumentation

ENDURING UNDERSTANDINGS

A narrator's or speaker's perspective controls the details and emphases that affect how readers experience and interpret a text.	Comparisons, representations, and associations shift meaning from the literal to the figurative and invite readers to interpret a text.	Readers establish and communicate their interpretations of literature through arguments supported by textual evidence.

Skill Category 4	Skill Category 5	Skill Category 6	Skill Category 7
Explain the function of the narrator or speaker.	*Explain the function of word choice, imagery, and symbols.*	*Explain the function of comparison.*	*Develop textually substantiated arguments about interpretations of part or all of a text.*

SKILLS

4.A Identify and describe the narrator or speaker of a text. Units 1, 4	**5.A** Distinguish between the literal and figurative meanings of words and phrases. Unit 5	**6.A** Identify and explain the function of a simile. Units 2, 7	**7.A** Develop a paragraph that includes (1) a claim that requires defense with evidence from the text and (2) the evidence itself. Units 1, 2, 3
4.B Identify and explain the function of point of view in a narrative. Units 1, 4	**5.B** Explain the function of specific words and phrases in a text. Units 2, 5, 8	**6.B** Identify and explain the function of a metaphor. Units 2, 5, 8	**7.B** Develop a thesis statement that conveys a defensible claim about an interpretation of literature and that may establish a line of reasoning. Units 3, 4, 5, 6, 7, 8, 9
4.C Identify and describe details, diction, or syntax in a text that reveal a narrator's or speaker's perspective. Units 4, 6, 9	**5.C** Identify and explain the function of a symbol. Units 6, 7, 8	**6.C** Identify and explain the function of personification. Units 5, 7	**7.C** Develop commentary that establishes and explains relationships among textual evidence, the line of reasoning, and the thesis. Units 3, 4, 5, 6, 7, 8, 9
4.D Explain how a narrator's reliability affects a narrative. Units 6, 7	**5.D** Identify and explain the function of an image or imagery. Units 5, 7	**6.D** Identify and explain the function of an allusion. Units 5, 8	**7.D** Select and use relevant and sufficient evidence to both develop and support a line of reasoning. Units 3, 4, 5, 6, 7, 8, 9
			7.E Demonstrate control over the elements of composition to communicate clearly. Units 3, 4, 5, 6, 8

Source: 2020 AP® English Literature and Composition Course and Exam Description (CED), p. 19.

language, and literary argumentation—help us make connections to the text. The first five of these will be explored in this chapter while literary argumentation will be discussed in subsequent chapters. The Big Ideas discussed in this chapter will not only help you think more deeply about literature but will also serve as the basis of your writing about literature. We read closely, think deeply about our reading, and push those thoughts out onto the paper when we write, so the reading and understanding of these Big Ideas are the foundation for our writing.

CHARACTERIZATION

Characters in literature allow readers to study and explore a range of values, beliefs, assumptions, biases, and cultural norms represented by those characters. (CED 15)

Frankenstein. Starr Carter. Bigger Thomas. Lizzie Bennet. These characters allow us to step into another person's life and invite us to view the world differently. Sometimes we see ourselves in characters and can easily relate to their thoughts, actions, and environment; other times characters are strikingly different from us. Every time we encounter a character, however, their role is far more than entertaining readers. Characters ultimately invite readers to consider different ideas and ways of thinking. Learning to read and unpack characters in a way that takes us beyond the character as a person in the story is essential to discovering and understanding central ideas in literature. We should consider the values and beliefs characters represent as well as biases they may have. Often **cultural norms** can also be explored through characters. *The goal is to advance from identifying character traits in a single character to exploring relationships and roles of characters within a text.*

Think about your life. Can you be described in one word? No, and the same applies for a character. Characters—like people—are complex and cannot be described simply. Learning about characters begins by looking at specific details and drawing conclusions, then constructing a 3D mental image of them. Characterization includes physical description but also personality, emotions, and mental

WORKSHEET 1

Text evidence			
Adjective			
Text evidence			
Adjective			

traits as well as motivations and desires. Consider the categories in Worksheet 1 as a tool to use for thinking about character complexity. By filling in quotes that highlight different character traits, we can shift to thinking of characters multidimensionally instead of simplistically. (You can replicate this worksheet on a blank sheet of paper or download it from this book's digital landing page.)

We find information about characters through direct description, but other times we need to draw assumptions based on characters' actions or speech. Most of the time we know a character's actions and speech—and sometimes their thoughts, but we must think about what drives a character. Thinking about the unseen or what is not obvious is just as important as what we know directly. Character motivation is highly important. Use Figure 1 to consider aspects of a character that are not easily seen.

FIGURE 1

Character Complexity

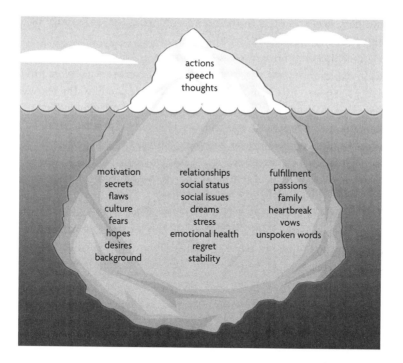

After we have a basic understanding of who a character is, we should think about how a character grows. In our own lives, relationships, significant events, and maturing as we age often result in different thinking; the same is true for characters. Characters' emotional and psychological growth—or lack thereof—is significant because *these changes highlight values and beliefs* and invite us to think differently as well. The most obvious way to note these changes is by examining the textual details of a character's perspective and motivation; relationships with others; and choices, actions, and speech. However, central **conflicts** and significant scenes are also important as they often highlight change in characters. Taking time to consider *the conflicts characters face and how the character responds (or doesn't respond) to these conflicts sheds light on central ideas of a text.* Other ideas to note concerning change and growth include:

- Change can be physical, psychological, or emotional.
- Change can occur in an instant or slowly.
- Change can be positive, negative, or both.
- Characters will either submit to or resist a central or secondary conflict in the story which highlights their values and beliefs.

After we have an understanding of an individual character, *exploring that character through a contrasting character opens a broader context of central ideas, beliefs, and values in the text.* Often **protagonists** and **antagonists** represent opposing values while **foils** also magnify differences. Not all contrasting characters are as clear-cut as foils or protagonists and antagonists; characters may share some traits but have others unique to themselves, showing the wide range of understanding of controlling ideas in a text.

Relationships among characters do more than highlight differences—they allow us to explore perspectives, ambiguity, and inconsistencies which reinforce central ideas in a text. Just as individual characters are complex, the relationships characters have and pursue can also be complex. When characters in relationships start making inconsistent and conflicting choices, the relationships and the plot become more complicated. This tension moves the plot forward and pulls readers into the story. Sometimes a group of people can act as a character (for example when a character is in conflict with society or a segment of society), or an external force such as a storm can be seen as one.

Finally, we should remember that characters have flaws and inconsistencies that appear in speech, thought, and action and can reveal tension. Does a character think or say one thing but act in a totally different way? Inconsistencies make characters relatable but also invite us to further explore their motives. These contradictions and inconsistencies can affect not only our understanding of the character but also our interpretation of a text and point us to central ideas in the text.

Quick Guide: Questions about Characters

- How is the character described physically, emotionally, and psychologically?
- Is the character's name significant?
- How does a character's background, motivation, or desires affect what they do and say?

- What do conflicts reveal about characters and central ideas in a text?
- How does a contrasting character highlight values and beliefs addressed in a text?
- Are there contradictions in how characters behave or between how they think and act?
- Can you identify a conflict or conflicts that involve the character? What does the nature of these conflicts reveal about the possible deeper meanings of the story?

Key Terms

cultural norms shared rules and expectations that members of society adhere to

conflict struggle between opposing forces. A conflict is *external* when it pits a character against something or someone outside himself or herself—another character or characters or some impersonal force (e.g., nature or society). A conflict is *internal* when the opposing forces are two drives, impulses, or parts of a single character.

protagonist most neutral and broadly applicable term for the main character in a work, whether male or female, heroic or not heroic

antagonist a character or a nonhuman force that opposes or is in conflict with the protagonist

foil character that serves as a contrast to another

Your Turn

Read this passage from *The Great Gatsby* for the literary elements the author F. Scott Fitzgerald uses to characterize Tom Buchanan in chapter 1.

The front was broken by a line of French windows, glowing now with reflected gold and wide open to the warm windy afternoon, and Tom Buchanan in riding clothes was standing with his legs apart on the front porch.

He had changed since his New Haven years. Now he was a sturdy straw-haired man of thirty with a rather hard mouth and a supercilious manner. Two shining arrogant eyes had established dominance over his face and gave him the appearance of always leaning aggressively forward. Not even the effeminate swank of his riding clothes could hide the enormous power of that body—he seemed to fill those glistening boots until he strained the top lacing, and you could see a great pack of muscle shifting when his shoulder moved under his thin coat. It was a body capable of enormous leverage—a cruel body.

His speaking voice, a gruff husky tenor, added to the impression of fractiousness he conveyed. There was a touch of paternal contempt in it, even toward people he liked—and there were men at New Haven who had hated his guts.

"Now, don't think my opinion on these matters is final," he seemed to say, "just because I'm stronger and more of a man than you are." We were in the same senior society, and while we were never intimate I always had the impression that he approved of me and wanted me to like him with some harsh, defiant wistfulness of his own.

We talked for a few minutes on the sunny porch.

"I've got a nice place here," he said, his eyes flashing about restlessly.

Turning me around by one arm, he moved a broad flat hand along the front vista, including in its sweep a sunken Italian garden, a half acre of deep, pungent roses, and a snub-nosed motor-boat that bumped the tide offshore.

After reading through the passage once to get a general idea about Tom, read back through it again and underline some words and phrases that stand out to you. Circle and look up any words you aren't familiar with. How is he described physically, emotionally, and psychologically? Consider his dialogue. What adjectives would you use to describe him based on your noticings? What can we tell about the way the narrator and Tom interact with each other? Here's an example of what your notes might look like:

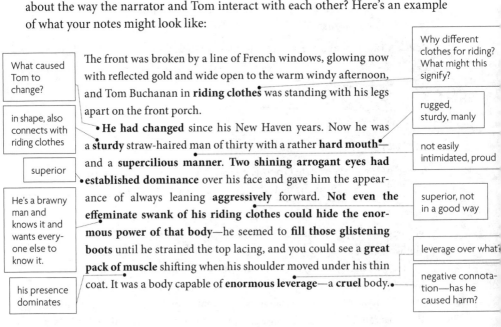

Why different clothes for riding? What might this signify?

What caused Tom to change?

The front was broken by a line of French windows, glowing now with reflected gold and wide open to the warm windy afternoon, and Tom Buchanan in **riding clothes** was standing with his legs apart on the front porch.

in shape, also connects with riding clothes

He had changed since his New Haven years. Now he was a **sturdy** straw-haired man of thirty with a rather **hard mouth**— and a **supercilious manner. Two shining arrogant eyes had established dominance** over his face and gave him the appearance of always leaning **aggressively** forward. **Not even the effeminate swank of his riding clothes could hide the enormous power of that body**—he seemed to **fill those glistening boots** until he strained the top lacing, and you could see a **great pack of muscle** shifting when his shoulder moved under his thin coat. It was a body capable of **enormous leverage**—a **cruel** body.

rugged, sturdy, manly

not easily intimidated, proud

superior

superior, not in a good way

He's a brawny man and knows it and wants everyone else to know it.

his presence dominates

leverage over what?

negative connotation—has he caused harm?

His speaking voice, a **gruff husky tenor**, added to the **impression of fractiousness he conveyed**. There was a touch of paternal contempt in it, even toward people he liked—and there were men at New Haven who had <u>hated his guts</u>.

"Now, don't think my opinion on these matters is final," **he seemed to say**, "just because I'm stronger and more of a man than you are." We were in the same senior society, and while we were never intimate I always had the impression that he approved of me and wanted me to like him with some harsh, defiant wistfulness of his own.

We talked for a few minutes on the sunny porch.

"I've got a nice place here," he said, his eyes flashing about **restlessly**.

Turning me around by one arm, he moved a broad flat hand along the **front vista, including in its sweep a sunken Italian garden, a half acre of deep, pungent roses, and a snub-nosed motor-boat that bumped the tide offshore.**

Margin annotations:

- again—negative connotation—not welcoming
- He has enemies—why?
- Narrator is imagining him saying this to him just from his appearance and presence.
- What's causing the restlessness?
- Is he unruly or just giving this impression? Why might he be unruly?
- He's got money—is this what makes him superior?

In asking these questions and using the text as evidence, we can determine that Tom is a stereotypical arrogant man. Fitzgerald's negative **diction** to describe Tom's physical attributes, such as his "arrogant eyes," "cruel body," and "gruff husky" voice, characterize Tom as "harsh, defiant" and someone who isn't shy to aggressively establish his alpha-male "dominance." Tom even goes so far as to forcefully "[t]urn" the narrator "around by one arm" and pretentiously claim he's "got a nice place here," referring to his own house. From this initial description, it is clear that Tom is a man who revels in his superiority and power over others.

WORKSHEET 1 SAMPLE

Text evidence	"sturdy"	"Two shining arrogant eyes had established dominance"	"restlessly"
Adjective	Tough	Superior	Impatient
Text evidence	"gruff husky tenor"	"fractiousness"	"cruel body"
Adjective	Harsh	Out of control	Overpowering

SETTING

Setting and the details associated with it not only depict a time and place, but also convey values associated with that setting. (CED 15)

Hogwarts. The South Side of Chicago. The valley of ashes. Sweet Home. These settings are so much more than the place where a story occurs. Settings shape characters and provide important information not only about characters but about central ideas in the text. Since elementary school, readers have been asked to identify the setting of a work, but as more advanced readers, we must go beyond identification and think about the values associated with that particular time and place.

Before readers can think about how setting shapes characters, advances plot, or influences an interpretation of a text, we need to go beyond details of time and consider the time of day, specific seasons, aspects of geography, and cultural and historical details. Think about the inferences that can be made from these details. As readers, we should question everything in regard to setting. What is the significance of the time? The physical location? Implications of the weather? Juxtaposition of multiple settings? It's also important to note whether the time period of a text is the same one that the author wrote in. You may not be able to make inferences immediately, but record details on Worksheet 2 and revisit this chart as you continue to read and develop an interpretation of the text.

WORKSHEET 2

Setting	Textual evidence	Inferences	Function

After training our minds to look for details about setting, we next move to thinking about its function. Settings can serve a variety of purposes. They can establish the atmosphere or mood, affect character action or motivation, illustrate **irony**, mirror the plot, provide symbolism, and reveal the nature of characters. Sometimes the setting acts as a character itself manipulating the plot or forcing a character to act. The goal is to think beyond the literal setting and learn to draw inferences about its function in the work as a whole.

In addition to thinking about the function of the setting, readers should also consider how the setting affects characters. Are there values and cultural norms characters are wrestling with throughout the story? The relationship between setting and character can serve as an avenue to explore larger ideas in the text.

Quick Guide: Questions about Setting

- What is the significance of the location? Are there contrasts in locations?
- What is the significance of the time of day or time of year?
- What does the weather add?
- Are there historical or cultural implications of the setting that affect characters, plot, or central meaning?
- How does the setting reinforce what happens to a character?

Your Turn

Read this passage from chapter 2 of *The Great Gatsby* and consider how the valley of ashes is described and how that might reflect central ideas in the text.

About half way between West Egg and New York the motor road hastily joins the railroad and runs beside it for a quarter of a mile, so as to shrink away from a certain desolate area of land. This is a valley of ashes—a fantastic farm where ashes grow like wheat into ridges and hills and grotesque gardens; where ashes take the forms of houses and chimneys and rising smoke and, finally, with a transcendent effort, of ash-gray men who move dimly and already crumbling through the powdery air. Occasionally a line of gray cars crawls along an invisible track, gives out a ghastly creak, and comes to rest, and immediately the ash-gray men swarm up with leaden spades and stir up an impenetrable cloud, which screens their obscure operations from your sight.

But above the gray land and the spasms of bleak dust which drift endlessly over it, you perceive, after a moment, the eyes of Doctor T. J. Eckleburg. The eyes of Doctor T. J. Eckleburg are blue and gigantic—their retinas are one yard high. They look out of no face, but, instead, from a pair of enormous yellow spectacles which pass over a non-existent nose. Evidently some wild wag of an oculist set them there to fatten his practice in the borough of Queens, and then sank down himself into eternal blindness, or forgot them and moved away. But his eyes, dimmed a little by many paintless days, under sun and rain, brood on over the solemn dumping ground.

The valley of ashes is bounded on one side by a small foul river, and, when the drawbridge is up to let barges through, the passengers on waiting trains can stare at the dismal scene for as long as half an hour. There is always a halt there of at least a minute, and it was because of this that I first met Tom Buchanan's mistress.

After reading through the passage once to get a general idea about the valley of ashes, read back through it again and underline words and phrases that stand out to you. Look up any words you aren't familiar with. What specific textual details describe the valley of ashes? What inferences can we draw from these details? What effect does the setting have on the narrator? on other characters? What thematic ideas might the setting reinforce? Here's an example of what your notes might look like:

Notes (left)	Passage	Notes (right)
in the middle, doesn't identify with one of the places more than the other	**About half way between West Egg and New York**, the motor road hastily joins the railroad and runs beside it for a quarter of a mile, so as to shrink away from a certain **desolate** area of land. This is a **valley of ashes**—a fantastic farm where **ashes grow like wheat into ridges and hills** and **grotesque** gardens; where ashes take the forms of houses and chimneys and rising smoke and, finally, with a transcendent effort, of ash-gray men who move **dimly** and **already crumbling** through the **powdery air**. Occasionally a line of **gray** cars crawls along an invisible track, gives out a **ghastly creak**, and comes to rest, and immediately the **ash-gray men** swarm up with leaden spades and stir up an **impenetrable cloud**, which screens their **obscure operations from your sight**.	Why is this area deserted?
valley—low place, and ashes—burned		Enormous amounts of burning have occurred to produce so much ash.
not typical to describe a movement		as opposed to a beautiful
They are wasting away already.		the ash is pervasive
everything is ash colored		the color of ash
the ashes cannot be moved	But above the **gray** land and the spasms of **bleak dust** which drift **endlessly** over it, you perceive, after a moment, **the eyes of Doctor T. J. Eckleburg**. The eyes of Doctor T. J. Eckleburg are **blue** and **gigantic**—their retinas are one yard high. They look out of no face, but, instead, from a pair of enormous **yellow** spectacles which pass over a **non-existent nose**. Evidently some wild wag of an oculist set them there to fatten his practice in the borough of Queens, and then sank down himself into eternal blindness, or forgot them and moved away. But his eyes, dimmed a little by many paintless days, under sun and rain, brood on over the solemn dumping ground. The valley of ashes is **bounded** on one side by a **small foul river** and, when the drawbridge is up to let barges through, the passengers on waiting trains can stare at the **dismal scene** for as long as half an hour. There is always a halt there of at least a minute, and it was because of this that I first met **Tom Buchanan's mistress**.	old, connects with moving dimly and already crumbling
and they hide secret happenings		more prevalence of ashes
no relief		more gray
contrast to the gray		the only thing that penetrates the ashes
only eyes—no face		Huge eyes? Does this mean they see all?
water but not enough to make a difference and it's contaminated		more color
he's also been portrayed negatively, why is a man of money here?		has distinct limits
		evokes sympathy from others
		"Mistress" has a negative connotation in a place of death—ominous tone, foreshadows something bad here.

WORKSHEET 2 SAMPLE

Setting	Textual evidence	Inferences	Function
Valley of ashes	"About half way between West Egg and New York"	The valley of ashes does not belong to either West Egg or New York—both places that represent wealth in this novel.	The poor do not fit in the wealthy society, but the rich cannot ignore their society.
Valley of ashes	"ashes grow like wheat into ridges and hills and grotesque gardens"	The personification of the ashes shows they have a life and will of their own, and the use of the word "gardens" shows that this place has become accepted even though it is "grotesque."	Destruction—even though confined to this one place—cannot be eliminated and will do its work and have its effect even on the people who travel through.
Valley of ashes	"But above the gray land and the spasms of bleak dust which drift endlessly over it, you perceive, after a moment, the eyes of Doctor T. J. Eckleburg."	The eyes are overlooking the dreary valley even though it seems to be forgotten by the rest of society.	Nothing goes unseen.

Located between West Egg and New York City, the valley of ashes is a place of oppression and impending doom. As the wealthy travel from their homes to work, they quickly pass through the "fantastic farm where ashes grow like wheat into ridges and hills and grotesque gardens." The images of a farm and garden are contrasted with the ashes growing and covering everything. The **imagery** extends from the setting to the "ash-gray men" who live there; they "move dimly and are already crumbling through the powdery air." No one or nothing can escape the ashes. Overlooking this valley, however, are "the eyes of Doctor T. J. Eckleburg," painted on a billboard towering above all. These eyes "brood on over the solemn dumping ground" as a reminder that what happens here is seen. This scene serves as the backdrop for introducing Tom Buchanan's mistress, foreshadowing destruction and death.

STRUCTURE

The arrangement of the parts and sections of a text, the relationship of the parts to each other, and the sequence in which the text reveals information are all structural choices made by a writer that contribute to the reader's interpretation of a text. (CED 15)

Just as buildings have a framework for support, writers make structural choices in both poetry and prose for a variety of reasons. The way in which a story or poem unfolds is a choice which allows the reader to discover information in a certain way. Analyzing structure requires higher-level thinking skills and is one of the most difficult concepts in literary analysis and is probably an area where readers feel least confident drawing conclusions. The arrangement of the parts of a text, the relationship of the parts to each other, and the order of events in a text are structural choices that contribute to central ideas in a text.

Plot in prose passages can occur in either a linear or nonlinear order. Stories told in chronological order can allow readers to focus more on characterization and conflict or set up a shock with a twist at the end. Stories told in a nonlinear way can create a surreal atmosphere, point to the unreliability of a narrator, or complicate a complex theme even further. Recognizing the basic plot line and structural choices such as **flashback, flashforward,** *in medias res,* and use of a **frame narrative** position us to consider not only how information is being presented but also the effect it has. Scenes occurring in the exposition and rising action build suspense and push readers to the climax of a work while scenes in the falling action and resolution confirm or complicate conclusions reached before the climax and allow us to think about central ideas, as illustrated in Figure 2.

FIGURE 2

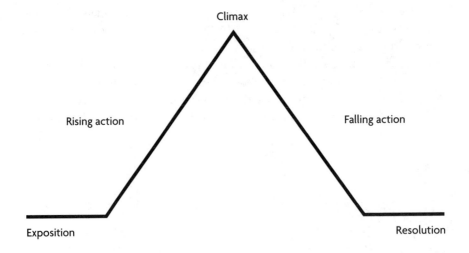

Climax

Rising action

Falling action

Exposition

Resolution

Summarizing the plot is not the same as analyzing the plot. The story and the plot are different, and recalling a story is not the same as understanding the cause and effects and motivations that the plot allows the reader to understand. An author may choose to give us the backstory of a character first to build empathy before the character does something that might otherwise be considered shocking. Or the author may drop the reader right into the action such as Donna Tartt does in *The Secret History*, whose first sentence reads, "The snow in the mountains was melting and Bunny had been dead for several weeks before we came to understand the gravity of our situation." Thus the reader is left to wonder the entire novel how Bunny died. Each choice holds the reader's attention but in a different way and for a different purpose.

Contrasts in literature show much more than how something is different from something else. Contrasts expand ideas and themes allowing us to see ironies, nuances, and complexities that we might miss if exploring an idea through a single lens. Exploring contrasts requires a reader to examine specific aspects of characterization, setting, structure, figurative language, or anything else that is highlighted—not in isolation but through comparison of how it differs from an equal counterpart. In poetry, contrasts are often seen in words, ideas, or the structure of a poem. Once these contrasts are identified, readers can use them to think about their importance in the text as a whole.

First identify the contrasts in the text according to the different headings in Worksheet 3. List the characteristics of each item being contrasted, then compare them to think about what the author may be communicating through showing the contrast. (Adapt or add to the elements listed in the top row.)

WORKSHEET 3

	Character	Setting	Structure	Figurative language	Ideas
Contrast item A					
Contrast item B					

The relationships among character, conflict, and plot are always in motion. Conflict often causes characters to take action (or not make a choice, which is still choosing), and the action characters take affects the plot. Events in the plot often force characters to respond, causing more conflict. This is a cycle that can repeat itself multiple times. All three parts can stand alone but also work together. As readers we must continually zoom in to look at specific scenes and small details in them, then zoom out to see how these small details and scenes work together to create meaning.

Conflict is tension between competing values either within a character, known as internal or psychological conflict, or with outside forces that obstruct a character, known as external conflict. Identifying types of conflict can help us understand the purpose the conflict has in a text. External conflicts often arise from tensions with other characters who have different values or with society, nature, or technology. Internal conflicts arise from tension within and highlight growth or stagnation in characters; these may be conflicts over identity, change, fear, or incidents from the past. Consider what values are being highlighted and what statement the author is making about society through those values.

Quick Guide: Questions about Structure

- Is the structure chronological or nonlinear? Why would the author choose to structure the story this way? How does this choice relate to the setting, characterization, or a controlling idea? How does the order of the events affect our interpretation of them?
- How does conflict push the plot forward? Does it represent opposing motivations or values?
- Does the author use flashbacks or flashforwards? How do they affect the reader's understanding of the events and emotional reactions to them (e.g., suspense, frustration, confusion)?
- What is the relationship of a section of a text to the text's setting, character, plot, conflict, point of view, thematic idea, or other literary elements?
- If reading an excerpt specifically for the AP® Exam, what does the beginning of the passage emphasize? Why might this be important?
- If reading an excerpt specifically for the AP® Exam, why might the passage end where it does? Can this be used when writing a conclusion?

Key Terms

in medias res "in the midst of things" (Latin); refers to opening a plot in the middle of the action, and then filling in past details by means of exposition and/or flashback

flashback plot-structuring device whereby a scene from the fictional past is inserted into the fictional present or is dramatized out of order

flashforward plot-structuring device whereby a scene from the fictional future is inserted into the fictional present or is dramatized out of order

frame narrative a narrative that recounts and thus "frames" the telling of another narrative or story

Your Turn

Read this passage from chapter 6 of *The Great Gatsby* and consider structural choices and their effect. In this excerpt Nick, the narrator, moves from the present to the past to provide more information about Gatsby.

About this time an ambitious young reporter from New York arrived one morning at Gatsby's door and asked him if he had anything to say.

"Anything to say about what?" inquired Gatsby politely.

"Why—any statement to give out."

It transpired after a confused five minutes that the man had heard Gatsby's name around his office in a connection which he either wouldn't reveal or didn't fully understand. This was his day off and with laudable initiative he had hurried out "to see."

It was a random shot, and yet the reporter's instinct was right. Gatsby's notoriety, spread about by the hundreds who had accepted his hospitality and so become authorities upon his past, had increased all summer until he fell just short of being news. Contemporary legends such as the "underground pipe-line to Canada" attached themselves to him, and there was one persistent story that he didn't live in a house at all, but in a boat that looked like a house and was moved secretly up and down the Long Island shore. Just why these inventions were a source of satisfaction to James Gatz of North Dakota, isn't easy to say.

James Gatz—that was really, or at least legally, his name. He had changed it at the age of seventeen and at the specific moment that witnessed the beginning of his career—when he saw Dan Cody's yacht drop anchor over the most insidious flat on Lake Superior. It was James Gatz who had been loafing along the beach that afternoon in a torn green jersey and a pair of canvas pants, but it was already Jay Gatsby who borrowed a rowboat, pulled out to the *Tuolomee*, and informed Cody that a wind might catch him and break him up in half an hour. . . .

He told me all this very much later, but I've put it down here with the idea of exploding those first wild rumors about his antecedents, which weren't even faintly true. Moreover he told it to me at a time of confusion, when I had reached the point of believing everything and nothing about him. So I take advantage of this short halt, while Gatsby, so to speak, caught his breath, to clear this set of misconceptions away.

After reading through the passage once to get a general idea about the structure, read back through it again and note its structural elements. Is this passage linear or nonlinear? Are there structural shifts? How are these significant? Why might the author use flashback? What effect does the structure have on the reader? Let's reread the excerpt with a focus on structure.

> marking this moment in the present tense before a shift

About this time an ambitious young reporter from New York arrived one morning at Gatsby's door and asked him if he had anything to say.

> pulls the reader into the scene by using dialogue

"Anything to say about what?" inquired Gatsby politely.

"Why—any statement to give out."

It transpired after a confused five minutes that the man had heard Gatsby's name around his office in a connection which he either wouldn't reveal or didn't fully understand. This was his day off and with laudable initiative he had hurried out "to see."

It was a random shot, and yet the reporter's instinct was right. **Gatsby's notoriety, spread about by the hundreds who had accepted his hospitality and so become authorities upon his past, had increased all summer until he fell just short of being news. Contemporary legends such as the "underground pipe-line to Canada" attached themselves to him, and there was one persistent story that he didn't live in a house at all, but in a boat that looked like a house and was moved secretly up and down the Long Island shore.** Just why these inventions were a source of satisfaction to James Gatz of North Dakota, isn't easy to say.

> Elaborating on current theories about Gatsby's past provides a contrast to what his past really was and sets Nick up to tell the real story.

> All of this is Nick retelling Gatsby's past. Why was this information saved until now?

James Gatz—that was really, or at least legally, his name. He had changed it at the age of seventeen and at the specific moment that witnessed the beginning of his career—when he saw Dan Cody's yacht drop anchor over the most insidious flat on Lake Superior. It was James Gatz who had been loafing along the beach that afternoon in a torn green jersey and a pair of canvas pants, but it was already Jay Gatsby who borrowed a

rowboat, pulled out to the *Tuolomee*, and informed Cody that a wind might catch him and break him up in half an hour. . . .

back to present—but when is the "much later" Nick is referring to?

•He told me all this very much later, but I've put it down here with the idea of exploding those first wild rumors about his antecedents, which weren't even faintly true. Moreover he told it to me at a time of confusion, when I had reached the point of believing everything and nothing about him. So I take advantage of this short halt, while Gatsby, so to speak, caught his breath, to clear this set of misconceptions away.

Do the past and the present somewhat run together and skew reality?

Nick uses the break to set the record straight.

Nick recognizes that he's breaking in the story.

WORKSHEET 3 SAMPLE

	Character	Setting	Structure	Ideas
Contrast item A	"Gatsby's notoriety ... had increased all summer until he fell just short of being news."	Present tense—one morning at Gatsby's door (West Egg)	Chronological order of story	Rumors and mystery around circumstances of Gatsby's current life—hundreds who had accepted his hospitality considered themselves authorities on his past
Contrast item B	"who had been loafing along the beach that afternoon in a torn green jersey and a pair of canvas pants"	Past tense: "the age of seventeen ... when he saw Dan Cody's yacht drop anchor over the most insidious flat on Lake Superior."	Shift to Gatsby's past	Specific details about Gatsby's past: loafing on beach, borrowed a rowboat

The Great Gatsby follows a chronological line; however, a few breaks occur in the forward-moving account of Gatsby's life. Chapter 6, which provides a good example of this break, offers an opportunity to explore contrasts. The chapter opens with a journalist seeking information on Gatsby which sets Nick up to tell about Gatsby's past. Since readers already know Gatsby's opulent present with its extravagant parties, the narrator feels we are now ready to know his past, which includes a very poor childhood. The New York reporter knows the mystery and rumors surrounding Gatsby while Nick's recounting of his past is anchored in facts and concrete details. These contrasts show the two lives that Gatsby has lived. After establishing the wealthy and ostentatious Gatsby first, the shift to his background elicits sympathy for him and helps the reader understand some of the roots of Gatsby's aloofness and love of pageantry.

NARRATION

A narrator's or speaker's perspective controls the details and emphases that affect how readers experience and interpret a text. (CED 15)

A cliff looks completely different if you're at the top staring down a drop-off or at the bottom looking up a large granite wall. A marathon feels completely different if you're running by the twenty-mile mark or handing out water. Perspective matters in a text. As readers, we need to be aware of different types of narrators and what they bring—or fail to bring—to a story. Thinking about the narrator's perspective, we can understand how events in the text and their interpretations are shaped by the narrator. The details a narrator chooses to give a reader and the events recounted all affect how we experience and interpret a text.

Understanding point of view is important in perspective. One point of view is not better than another, but all have different advantages and disadvantages. The **first-person point of view** can put us in the middle of a story while a **third-person point of view** can provide a much broader picture. Point of view can shift throughout a story causing the reader to question the perspective and position of the narrator.

Here's a brief summary of the most frequently used points of view.

First-Person Point of View—I, We

Advantages:

- Provides the perspective of an *important character*
- Can help readers better *understand the main character*

Disadvantages:

- May use an **unreliable narrator**—for example, one who's insane, naïve, deceptive, or narrow-minded
- Gives only *one perspective*

Third-Person Point of View—He, She, They

Advantages:

- Knows *everything*—past, present, and future
- Equal access to *all* characters
- Provides more objectivity for readers to draw their own conclusions about characters

Disadvantage:

- Can feel *impersonal*

Perspective is the way a character views the world based on a narrator's personal experiences and background; this is important because the perspectives of the characters open readers to consider different views as well as central ideas in the text. Just as you were raised in an environment unique to you with personal experiences that shaped who you are, in first-person narratives the perspective of events and characters is colored by the narrator's personal experiences and background. Our job as readers is to consider how the narrator's perspective shapes our understanding of the text. *A narrator's perspective and attitude are revealed to the reader through* **tone**, *which is conveyed through a narrator's diction,* **syntax**, *and selection of details.* Analyzing tone not only gives insight to the perspective of a narrator but also shapes our interpretation of the story.

Readers enter a text trusting the narrator or speaker to tell us what we need to know. What if, however, a narrator cannot be trusted? How might that affect our understanding of a story? A large part of the reader's job is to determine the degree to which a narrator is reliable. One narrator may reveal events in a way to win our sympathy; another may be a child who is too immature to process what is happening around them. Sometimes narrators intentionally deceive readers. Unreliable narrators invite us to view someone else's notion of truth or perception of reality.

You can use Worksheet 4 when reading a text to track all these elements of narration and their significance.

WORKSHEET 4

	Point of view	Details, diction, and syntax	Reliability	Tone and shifts in tone
Identification and description				
Textual evidence				
Author's purpose				

Quick Guide: Questions about Narration

- What advantages or biases does the narrator or speaker have?
- Can the narrator or speaker be trusted? If so, to what extent?
- Why may a narrator or speaker choose to provide certain information? withhold information?
- Are there shifts in perspective? What contrasts can be observed in the different shifts?
- How does the perspective highlight or reinforce the meaning of the text?
- What would the text lose if it were told from a different perspective?

Key Terms

first-person point of view mode in which an internal narrator consistently refers to himself or herself using the first-person pronouns *I* or *we*

third-person point of view mode in which a narrator uses third-person pronouns such as *she*, *he*, *they*, *it*, and so on; third-person narrators are almost always external narrators

unreliable narrator a narrator who encourages us to view the account of events with suspicion; unreliable narrators are almost always first-person

diction choice of words. Diction is often described as either *informal* or *colloquial* if it resembles everyday speech, or as *formal* if it is instead lofty, impersonal, and dignified.

irony situation or statement characterized by a significant difference between what is expected or understood and what actually happens or is meant

syntax word order; the way words are put together to form phrases, clauses, and sentences

tone attitude a literary work takes toward its subject or that a character in the work conveys, especially as revealed through diction

Your Turn

Read this opening passage of *The Great Gatsby* thinking about Nick Carraway, the narrator, and his role in telling this story.

In my younger and more vulnerable years my father gave me some advice that I've been turning over in my mind ever since.

"Whenever you feel like criticising any one," he told me, "just remember that all the people in this world haven't had the advantages that you've had."

He didn't say any more, but we've always been unusually communicative in a reserved way, and I understood that he meant a great deal more than that. In consequence, I'm inclined to reserve all judgments, a habit that has opened up many curious natures to me and also made me the victim of not a few veteran bores. The abnormal mind is quick to detect and attach itself to this quality when it appears in a normal person, and so it came about that in college I was unjustly accused of being a politician, because I was privy to the secret griefs of wild, unknown men. Most of the confidences were unsought—frequently I have feigned sleep, preoccupation, or a hostile levity when I realized by some unmistakable sign that an intimate revelation was quivering on the horizon; for the intimate revelations of young men, or at least the terms in which they express them, are usually plagiaristic and marred by obvious suppressions. Reserving judgments is a matter of infinite hope. I am still a little afraid of missing something if I forget that, as my father snobbishly suggested, and I snobbishly repeat, a sense of the fundamental decencies is parcelled out unequally at birth.

After reading through the passage once to get a general idea about Nick, read back through it again and underline some words and phrases that stand out to you and note how they describe the narrator. Then consider the point of view (abbreviated in notes here as POV). Do you think the narrator can be trusted? Does he have any biases? What may we not know with the story being told through his perspective?

Annotations (left)	Passage	Annotations (right)
1st-person POV	In **my** younger and more vulnerable years **my father gave me some advice that I've been turning over in my mind ever since.**	Entire story will be framed through the advice his father gave him.
Will Nick want to criticize someone? Will that make us want to criticize them as well?	**"Whenever you feel like criticising any one,"** he told me, "**just remember that all the people in this world haven't had the advantages that you've had.**"	
What advantages has Nick had? How will this impact his telling of the story?	He didn't say any more, but we've always been unusually communicative in a reserved way, and **I understood that he meant a great deal more than that.** In consequence, **I'm inclined to reserve all judgments, a habit that has opened up many curious natures to me and also made me the victim of not a few veteran bores.** The abnormal mind is quick to detect and	What else could this mean?
Does that mean this story is told objectively?	attach itself to this quality when it appears in a normal person, and so it came about that in college I was unjustly accused of	This quality has both advantages and disadvantages.

being a politician, because I was **privy to the secret griefs of wild, unknown men**. Most of the confidences were unsought—frequently I have feigned sleep, preoccupation, or a hostile levity when I realized by some unmistakable sign that an intimate revelation was quivering on the horizon; for the intimate revelations of young men, or at least the terms in which they express them, are usually plagiaristic and marred by obvious suppressions. **Reserving judgments is a matter of infinite hope.** I am still a little afraid of missing something if I forget that, as my father snobbishly suggested, and I snobbishly repeat, a sense of the fundamental decencies is parcelled out unequally at birth.

> Will we be privy to these same secrets?

> Is he reminding us to withhold judgment?

Nick Carraway begins *The Great Gatsby* with some advice his father gave him early in life: "Whenever you feel like criticising any one [. . .] just remember that all the people in this world haven't had the advantages that you've had," establishing him as a narrator who will recount Gatsby's story without judgment. Fitzgerald continues to reassure readers that we can trust Nick when he claims, "I'm inclined to reserve all judgments." By noting that his habit "has opened up many curious natures to me and also made me the victim of not a few veteran bores," Nick shows his self-awareness. By admitting that he's continuing to turn over this advice his father gave him, we as readers will be working out our judgment about Gatsby as he recounts the story.

WORKSHEET 4 SAMPLE

	Point of view	Details, diction, and syntax	Reliability	Tone and shifts in tone
Identification and description	1st-person POV	Nick is self-intuitive	Nick tells us he's reserving judgment, but how do we know this is true?	Elitist
Textual evidence	"In my younger and more vulnerable years my father gave me some advice that I've been turning over in my mind ever since."	"a habit that has opened up many curious natures to me and also made me the victim of not a few veteran bores."	"In consequence I'm inclined to reserve all judgments, a habit that has opened up many curious natures to me and also made me the victim of not a few veteran bores."	"I snobbishly repeat, a sense of the fundamental decencies is parcelled out unequally at birth."
Author's purpose	Establish intimacy with the narrator; insiders look to Gatsby through Nick's personal relationship	Builds our trust in Nick	Fitzgerald wants to assure the reader that we can trust Nick to give an accurate representation of Gatsby.	By showing us Nick's elitism, Fitzgerald causes some question of his reliability.

FIGURATIVE LANGUAGE

Comparisons, representations, and associations shift meaning from the literal to the figurative and invite readers to interpret a text. (CED 16)

"Hope is the thing with feathers." "The wind howls in disbelief." "Buzzing is the sound of bees perforating the air." Phrases like these can bring a text to life. Figurative language goes beyond making a poem sound good or "painting a picture" with words. Figurative language not only adds depth and meaning to specific sections of a work but reframes the way we think about ideas and invites readers to think more deeply about a text as a whole. Specific figurative language as well as comparisons, contrasts, and associations lead us to our interpretation of a work. Literary analysis not only requires constructing thematic ideas, tracing character development, and considering the impact of structural choices, we must also look closely at words and phrases and consider them from every angle.

Words have two types of meanings: **denotative**, or literal meanings, and **connotative,** or emotional or possibly cultural meanings (see Figure 3). If words seem out of place or repeated, our job as a reader is to consider all potential meanings and nuances of the word.

FIGURE 3

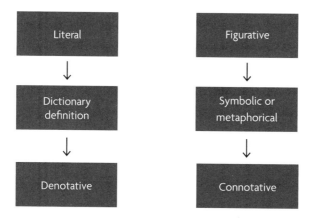

The next step after identifying and considering all possible meanings of specific words and phrases is to explain their function. Thinking about how words and phrases emphasize, minimize, or qualify subjects and ideas allows us to move from the sentence level to a broader perspective. Repetition, **alliteration**, adjectives, adverbs, **hyperboles**, and **understatements** are all invitations to explore larger ideas and meanings (see Figure 4). Repetition, especially in poetry, which is based on an economy of words, begs to be further explored (see chapter 3).

In addition to an emphasis on words and phrases, imagery and **symbols** are also a way for a writer to emphasize ideas. Imagery is words and phrases that

FIGURE 4

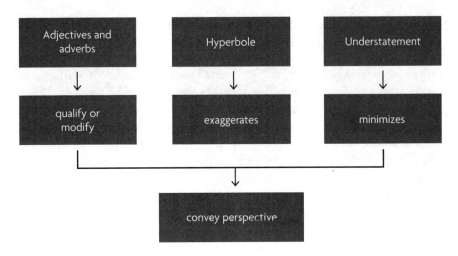

appeal specifically to the senses. By relating images and sensations of sight, sound, smell, touch, and taste, authors create experiences for the reader to feel what the speaker is experiencing. Imagery can also be a form of comparison causing the reader to make associations with different parts of the text. The sensations emphasized through imagery directly affect our interpretation of a text.

Symbols are a way for an author to extend a meaning beyond an original object allowing the reader an opportunity to reimagine and explore ideas in nontraditional ways and provide a connection to central ideas in a work. Sometimes symbols are obvious, such as a plane representing escape or a rose representing love. Other times symbols such as light and water are a bit more vague, allowing for multiple interpretations. Think of symbols, especially recurring symbols, not in isolation but as a part of the text as a whole. To help analyze a symbol in a text, consider the categories in Worksheet 5.

In addition to words and phrases having literal and figurative meanings, some figurative language forces us to make comparisons in order to reframe our thinking of perspective and ideas. **Similes** and **metaphors** draw a comparison between two things that are not usually compared. Through this comparison, the qualities or attributes of one subject are transferred to another making us think of it in a different way. **Personification** and **allusion** draw comparisons. These comparisons add layers of meaning and new understanding to the text and establish tone.

WORKSHEET 5

Important object	
Description of the object	
What the object represents	
Character's response to the object	
Connection to a central idea	

Quick Guide: Questions about Figurative Language

- What are the literal and figurative meanings of a word or phrase? How do these meanings establish both a literal meaning of the text and invite readers to form their own interpretation of a text?
- How do specific words and phrases emphasize or minimize controlling ideas in a text?
- How does figurative language shape perspective and add to tone?
- When figurative language draws comparisons, how do the specific comparisons open new meaning and understanding of central ideas in a text?

Key Terms

denotation a word's direct and literal meaning, as opposed to its connotation

connotation what is suggested by a word, apart from what it literally means or how it is defined in the dictionary

alliteration the repetition of usually initial consonant sounds through a sequence of words

hyperbole exaggerated language

understatement language that makes its point by self-consciously downplaying its real emphasis

symbol person, place, thing, or event that figuratively represents or stands for something else. Often the thing or idea represented is more abstract and general, and the symbol is more concrete and particular.

imagery any sensory detail used to evoke a feeling, to call to mind an idea, or to describe an object

simile figure of speech involving a direct, explicit comparison of one thing to another, usually using the words *like* or *as* to draw the connection

metaphor figure of speech in which two unlike things are compared implicitly

personification figure of speech that involves treating something nonhuman, such as an abstraction, as if it were a person by endowing it with humanlike qualities

allusion brief, often implicit and indirect reference within a literary text to something outside the text, whether another text or any imaginary or historical person, place, or thing

Your Turn

Read these excerpts from *The Great Gatsby* that pertain to the green light. Consider how the green light is used as a symbol.

[H]e [Gatsby] stretched out his arms toward the dark water in a curious way, and, far as I was from him, I could have sworn he was trembling. Involuntarily I glanced seaward—and distinguished nothing except a single green light, minute and far away, that might have been the end of a dock. (ch. 1)

"If it wasn't for the mist we could see your home across the bay," said Gatsby. "You always have a green light that burns all night at the end of your dock."

... Possibly it had occurred to him that the colossal significance of that light had now vanished forever. Compared to the great distance that had separated him from Daisy it had seemed very near to her, almost touching her. It had seemed as close as a star to the moon. Now it was again a green light on a dock. His count of enchanted objects had diminished by one. (ch. 5)

And as I sat there brooding on the old, unknown world, I thought of Gatsby's wonder when he first picked out the green light at the end of Daisy's dock. He had come a long way to this blue lawn and his dream must have seemed so that he could hardly fail to grasp it. He did not know that it was already behind him, somewhere back in that vast obscurity beyond the city, where the dark fields of the republic rolled on under the night.

Gatsby believed in the green light, the orgastic future that year by year recedes before us. (ch. 9)

After reading through these quotes once to get a general idea about the green light, read back through them, making notes on the description of the light and its function. How is the green light literally described? What are the connotations in the words and phrases used to describe the green light? What could the green light represent? What central ideas could this reinforce in the novel?

[Nick observing Gatsby:]

> [H]e [Gatsby] **stretched out his arms toward the dark water in a curious way**, and, far as I was from him, I could have sworn **he was trembling**. Involuntarily I glanced seaward—and distinguished nothing except **a single green light**, minute and far away, that might have been the end of a dock. (ch. 1)

| affects him to his core |
| The green light pulls on Gatsby like a magnet. |
| like a traffic light signaling go |

[Gatsby talking to Daisy:]

> "**If it wasn't for the mist we could see your home across the bay**," said Gatsby. "You always have a **green light that burns all night** at the end of your dock."
>
> . . . Possibly it had occurred to him that the **colossal significance** of that light had now vanished forever. Compared to the great distance that had separated him from **Daisy** it had seemed very near to her, almost touching her. It had seemed as close as a star to the moon. Now it was again a green light on a dock. His count of enchanted objects had diminished by one. (ch. 5)

| green represents money, always present |
| His ability to see is clouded. |
| extremely important to him |
| the light is Daisy |

> And as I sat there brooding on the old, unknown world, I thought of Gatsby's wonder when he first picked out the green light at the end of Daisy's dock. He had come a long way to this blue lawn and **his dream must have seemed so close** that he could hardly fail to grasp it. He did not know that it was already behind him, somewhere back in that vast obscurity beyond the city, where the dark fields of the republic rolled on under the night.
>
> **Gatsby believed in the green light**, the orgastic future that year by year recedes before us. (ch. 9)

| Daisy seemed as close as the distance across the bay initially. |
| Daisy was his guiding light. |

WORKSHEET 5 SAMPLE

Important object	Green light
Description of the object	Across the bay, burns all night, one single light
What the object represents	Daisy, money
Character's response to the object	Literally causes Gatsby to tremble—deeply affects him emotionally
Connection to a central idea	Love for Daisy, American dream

The green light at the end of Daisy's dock serves as a recurring symbol throughout *The Great Gatsby*. From the first chapter Nick swears that Gatsby "was trembling" as he stood with his arms stretched "toward the dark water in a curious way" while the green light shone across the bay. Gatsby later refers to the green light in a conversation with Daisy noting, "If it wasn't for the mist we could see your home across the bay." Here the light is blocked by the mist, signifying the light—or Gatsby's dream—is clouded and not clearly attainable. "Gatsby believed in the green light"—this dream not only of Daisy but of him being in the same class as her—until the final moments of his life as this symbol provides the hope he needs to keep dreaming.

Close reading is work which requires us to learn how to look at specific details, ask questions, and draw conclusions which all work together and lead to a deeper understanding of the text. Much like exercising a muscle, the more we as readers practice reading closely, the better we get at reading. Sometimes we will consciously stop and think about very specific skills and their function within a work. Other times we will read with different Big Ideas in our mind simultaneously making meaning of what's happening in regard to character development, structure, narration, etc. Finally, there will be times we are actively reading with our trained minds processing and making meaning without us fully acknowledging the process in motion. The mature reader understands when and where to slow down and look for deeper meaning, when to look at a prior portion of the text as our understanding changes with more knowledge, and when to keep moving on in a text.

CHAPTER REVIEW

Let's do a quick recap of what you've learned in this chapter.

- Reading is an active process of training the mind how to self-question ideas in order to develop an interpretation of the text.
- Practicing close reading over time is essential to grow as a reader.
- The Big Ideas—Characterization, Setting, Structure, Narration, and Figurative Language—invite readers to think deeply about specific parts of the text.
- The Big Ideas also provide ways for readers to connect different elements of a text and consider their relationship.
- Close reading is a combination of zooming in to look at small details and zooming out to think about central ideas in a text.
- Close reading almost always requires reading a passage more than once.

2

General Writing Strategies

INTRODUCTION

In this chapter, we will move from close-reading skills to learning how to put your noticings into writing. We'll cover questions you should ask while reading a text to produce insightful analyses and provide you with some templates for writing. Remember that templates are just guides; they only represent one of the many ways to write, and we encourage you to move beyond using templates as you grow in your writing. We'll pay close attention to crafting insightful **thesis statements** and developing a **line of reasoning**. Then, we'll give you some pointers on how to select and effectively incorporate evidence from the text to support your ideas, as well as how to successfully organize an essay. This chapter primarily serves as an introduction to the general writing skills you will need to be successful on the AP® Literature Exam, with individual chapters to follow that go into more detail for each of the three types of essays.

Key Terms

Before we dive into strategies for writing, let's make sure we are all on the same page with the key terminology from the AP® Literature Course and Exam Description (CED) that we will use throughout the book.

thesis statement the overall guiding argument for your essay. According to the AP® Exam rubric, an acceptable thesis must both be defensible *and* provide an interpretation of the text.

- **defensible** able to be argued against; takes a position
- **interpretation** an idea of your own that is not just a summary of the passage, but an observation of the meaning you derive from the passage. Your interpretation may also suggest or include how that meaning is created, which you will develop further in your essay. There are many possible interpretations of any given text.

textual evidence the selected portions of the text you include in your essay to support your claims

commentary your explanation of how the textual evidence and literary devices in the text work to create meaning and support your claims. Commentary should be explicit; don't make your AP® Exam Readers have to connect the dots on their own. Successful commentary thoroughly explains connections among literary elements, textual evidence, and your reasoning. And, yes, you must always explain. You can't just say a metaphor helps to create tone and call it a day—you need to explicitly explain *how*.

topic sentence the first sentence of each body paragraph that guides the direction of the paragraph. Ideally, a topic sentence should contain an element of analysis and provide one of your claims in support of your thesis statement. It may or may not include a literary device.

line of reasoning your layout of claims that all help to support your thesis. This includes topic sentences, textual evidence, and commentary. Essentially, it's your list of reasons to show how you arrived at your thesis statement. A line of reasoning should be organized and logical and should include smooth transitions from one idea to the next.

QUESTIONS TO ASK WHEN WRITING ABOUT LITERATURE

When approaching a text you'll be analyzing and writing about, enter the text with intention. Read the text with focus and purpose. You aren't reading just for comprehension, but for opportunities to analyze and explore how an author's message is developed through craft and style choices. In other words, we aren't reading a novel for the plot alone, or a poem for its story, but to discover how the elements of the text are working together to create meaning in the work. Here are some general questions you can ask upon your initial reading of any type of work on the exam: a poem (AP® Exam question 1), a prose passage excerpted from a longer work (AP® Exam question 2), or a full-length work (AP® Exam question 3).

Questions to Ask When Writing about Literature

Upon initial read	What to look for	Opportunity for further analysis
What stands out to me as being important?	The author might focus on a particular image, symbol, event, or character.	Why is the author focusing on this? How does it work to create meaning in the overall work?
Are there any patterns?	Patterns might be created by diction, use of detail, figurative language, or structural elements.	What does the author want you to notice? What is being signaled by the pattern?
Is there conflict or tension?	Juxtaposition, tone, and character relationships may create tension.	How does the conflict work to create or magnify the theme or message of the work?
Where/when is the setting?	Setting is most often described through details and imagery.	How does the setting affect the characters, plot, or theme?
Who is the narrator?	The speaker of the text can be determined through the use of pronouns as well as the speaker's relationship to other characters and the setting.	Does the point of view affect how the story is told? What are the narrator's motivations?
How is the text structured?	Where does the author place shifts? How does the author chunk together or separate elements in the text?	How does the form or structure of the work reflect its meaning?

SUMMARY VERSUS ANALYSIS

By reading with intention and considering the questions in the table above as you work your way through a text, you are moving beyond surface-level summary and into analysis. Sure, you still need to know what is happening in a passage or a poem, but that is only the first step. Being able to identify the subject of a poem or retell the basic plot of a passage or novel is like getting into position at the starting line on a running track. Clearly the race does not end at the starting line; it's only the beginning. If staying at the starting line gets a runner nowhere, then so does just summarizing a text. You need to go beyond retelling and paraphrasing.

Perhaps the best way to demonstrate the difference between summary and analysis is to provide an example. Please read Tiana Clark's poem "My Therapist Wants to Know about My Relationship to Work."

My Therapist Wants to Know about My Relationship to Work

TIANA CLARK

I hustle
            upstream.
I grasp.
            I grind.
5   I control & panic. Poke
balloons in my chest,
always popping there,
always my thoughts thump,
thump. I snooze — wake & go
10   boom. All day, like this I short
my breath. I scroll & scroll.
I see what you wrote — I like.
I heart. My thumb, so tired.
My head bent down, but not
15   in prayer, heavy from the looking.
I see your face, your phone-lit
faces. I tap your food, two times
for more hearts. I retweet.
I email: *yes* & *yes* & *yes*.
20   Then I cry & need to say: *no-no-no*.
Why does it take so long to reply?
I FOMO & shout. I read. I never
enough. New book. New post.
New ping. A new tab, then another.
25   Papers on the floor, scattered & stacked.
So many journals, unbroken white spines,
waiting. Did you hear that new new?
I start to text back. Ellipsis, then I forget.
I balk. I lazy the bed. I wallow when I write.
30   I truth when I lie. I throw a book
when a poem undoes me. I underline
Clifton: *today we are possible*. I start
from image. I begin with Phillis Wheatley.
I begin with Phillis Wheatley. I begin
35   with Phillis Wheatley reaching for coal.
I start with a napkin, receipt, or my hand.
I muscle memory. I stutter the page. I fail.
Hit delete — scratch out one more line. I sonnet,
then break form. I make tea, use two bags.
40   Rooibos again. I bathe now. Epsom salt.
No books or phone. Just water & the sound

of water filling, glory — be my buoyant body,
bowl of me. Yes, lavender, more bubbles
& bath bomb, of course some candles too.
45 All alone with Coltrane. My favorite, "Naima,"
for his wife, now for me, inside my own womb.
Again, I child back. I float. I sing. I simple
& humble. Eyes close. I low my voice,
was it a psalm? Don't know. But I stopped.

Now that you have read the whole poem, go back and reread lines 1–20. Below you will see two paragraphs, one of which is a summary of these lines and the other, an analysis. See if you can spot the difference.

Paragraph 1:
The speaker's anxiety over her workload is mirrored by the short, abrupt phrasing. Each choppy phrase, broken up consistently by punctuation, reflects the speaker's panic, which she describes as balloons popping in her chest, racing thoughts, and shortened breath. She has an inability to focus on anything for a length of time before the next thing calls for her attention, reflected in the first four lines bouncing from side to side. Feeling overworked seems to be self-induced as an obsession or need for acceptance, as she doles out infinite "likes" on social media. Agreeing to email requests stems from this desire for recognition; even though they are only going to further overwhelm her, she can't help herself.

Paragraph 2:
The speaker is panicking from grinding away constantly at work and relentlessly scrolling through social media profiles. Her panic feels like balloons popping in her chest, her thoughts are always racing through her mind, and her breathing is short. Taking rests to snooze, then waking up, she is immediately back at it. She looks through her social media daily, liking people's posts and pictures of their food. Her thumb is tired and her head feels heavy from looking down at her device all day as she scrolls and scrolls, tapping the heart icon to like a picture. She sees her friends' faces on her phone and responds "yes" to many emails but then cries because she wishes she had said "no."

Both paragraphs are the same length and discuss the same lines, but only one of them connects what is literally happening in the poem to the poem's features and devices. Only one of them includes **defensible interpretations** that go beyond the speaker's literal actions. The other paragraph simply paraphrases what is literally happening in the poem. Can you tell which one is the summary and which one is the analysis?

Hopefully, you identified Paragraph 1 as the analysis and Paragraph 2 as the summary. So what makes Paragraph 1 more than just a summary? Notice where Paragraph 1 notes the line lengths and short phrases, and how the abruptness caused by the quick phrasing mimics the speaker's actions and thoughts. It provides a reason for the opening lines bopping back and forth, which the writer claims is to emphasize the speaker's diverted concentration. Paragraph 1 makes inferences about the speaker: The need for acceptance and recognition causes her to overwork. Paragraph 2 does none of these things and only repeats what is happening on a surface level in the poem.

To help get yourself out of the summary zone and into analysis, consider the questions provided on page 33.

WRITING A LITERARY ANALYSIS THESIS STATEMENT

> **Pro Tip**: While your thesis can appear anywhere in the essay, we *highly* suggest you place it in your introduction paragraph. This is where AP® Readers expect it, and you probably don't want to make your Reader spend extra time searching around your essay for your guiding argument.

The most important reason for placing your thesis in the introduction is to create a foundation for your line of reasoning. If all your **topic sentences**, evidence, and **commentary** are meant to tie back to and support your thesis, it's kind of hard to do that if a thesis does not exist to tie back to. Furthermore, your introduction can even just be your thesis. Plenty of high-scoring essays have a solid one-sentence thesis. Since the majority of your essay score comes from the evidence and commentary found in your body paragraphs, the body is where you want to focus most of your time and effort. Once you have a strong thesis, that's all you really need as your introduction. Don't spend extra time trying to come up with a fancy attention-grabber—there are no criteria on the exam rubric for quality of introductions (or conclusions, for that matter). The best use of your time is to craft a solid thesis statement and launch right into your analysis.

A successful thesis statement does more than just repeat the prompt or summarize the text. If you regurgitate the prompt as your thesis, you will not earn the Thesis Statement point on the essay rubric. A thesis also needs to find an appropriate scale—not being so general that it could be applied to *any* text, but not so specific that it only covers a portion of the text.

Think of a thesis statement as answering the *what, how,* and *why* of a text.

What?	What is the text's title? Who is the author? What topic is the prompt asking you to consider? What literary elements will you choose to discuss?
How?	How are the literary elements developed? Through which literary devices?
Why?	Why are these elements developed? What is the author trying to show us?

The *why* part is usually the most difficult for students. It requires consideration, analysis, and invention of an original interpretation of the text. For this part of the thesis, think about what the author is trying to say about life or humanity. Think of all those thematic ideas your teacher has shared with you for the texts you read in class. Perhaps you read *Frankenstein* and discussed the effects of alienation and isolation. Maybe you examined the disillusionment of the American Dream in *The Great Gatsby*. These thematic ideas are the author's message—and are exactly what we are looking for in this last part of your thesis. Furthermore, we would argue that the *why* is the most important part of your thesis. The thematic idea you identify posits your interpretation of the work, considers the entire text in all of its complexity, and serves as the foundation for your line of reasoning.

Read the following prompt and poem, which we will use to examine sample thesis statements written by students.

In "A House Divided" by Kyle Dargan, the speaker considers different groups of people in the United States. Read the poem carefully. Then, in a well-written essay, analyze how Dargan uses literary elements to develop his complex view of the current state of American society.

A House Divided

KYLE DARGAN

On a railroad car in your America,
I made the acquaintance of a man
who sang a life-song with these lyrics:
"Do whatever you can/ to avoid
5   becoming a roofing man."
I think maybe you'd deem his tenor
elitist, or you'd hear him as falling
off working-class key. He sang
not from his heart but his pulsing
10   imagination, where every roof is
sloped like a spire and Sequoia tall.
Who would wish for themselves, another,
such a treacherous climb? In your America,
a clay-colored colt stomps, its hooves
15   cursing the barn's chronic lean.
In your America, blood pulses
within the fields, slow-poaching a mill saw's
buried flesh. In my America, my father
awakens again thankful that my face
20   is not the face returning his glare
from above eleven o'clock news
murder headlines. In his imagination,

the odds are just as convincing
that I would be posted on a corner
25   pushing powder instead of poems—
no reflection of him as a father nor me
as a son. We were merely born
in a city where the rues beyond our doors
were the *streets* that shanghaied souls.
30   To you, my America appears
distant, if even real at all. While you are
barely visible to me. Yet we continue
stealing glances at each other
from across the tattered hallways
35   of this overgrown house we call
a nation—every minute
a new wall erected, a bedroom added
beneath its leaking canopy of dreams.
We hear the dripping, we feel drafts
40   wrap cold fingers about our necks,
but neither you or I trust each other
to hold the ladder or to ascend.

Let's take a look at some example thesis statements—some which are successful and some which do not meet all the criteria—and commentary as to why they would or would not earn the Thesis Statement point on the exam rubric.

Thesis statement	Commentary
In "A House Divided" by Kyle Dargan, the speaker considers different groups of Americans and develops a complex view of the current state of American society.	This thesis statement is unsuccessful because it only repeats the prompt. A couple words have been changed, but it does not provide any defensible claims or interpretations.
In "A House Divided" Kyle Dargan uses metaphor, juxtaposition, and imagery to develop a complex view of the current state of society in America.	This thesis statement is also unsuccessful and would not earn the Thesis Statement point on the essay rubric. It may provide a list of literary devices, but it still does not include any defensible claims or interpretations.
In "A House Divided" by Kyle Dargan, the speaker compares two different Americas, illustrating that because people have different experiences it is hard to agree and trust each other, which prevents us from moving forward as one society.	This thesis statement is successful because it provides both a defensible claim and an interpretation that will guide a line of reasoning. Notice that this thesis does not list literary devices, which is optional.

In "A House Divided" Kyle Dargan uses metaphor and structural elements to reveal the divide in American society, and the distrust that prevents both sides from annexing into a unified people as they are unable to relate to the others' experiences.	This thesis statement is successful because it offers a defensible claim, an interpretation, and includes literary devices that will be discussed in the essay.

If you want to have the best thesis statement possible, it will actually contain *two* original ideas: your answer to the *what* and *how* the prompt is asking *and* the *why*—an overall bigger meaning for the entire passage, that is, a *thematic idea* (see Figure 5). Putting this all into one sentence might end up producing one really long sentence, which can get messy, so you can divide these two ideas into two different sentences. It is better to have a clean thesis than one that sounds convoluted, and if that means breaking it up into two sentences, that is absolutely appropriate.

FIGURE 5

Basic Thesis Statement Template

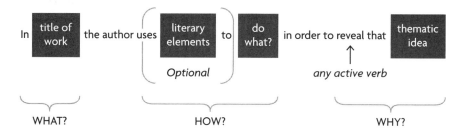

There are lots of options when it comes to the *Do what?* box in the template above. That's mostly because it depends on what the prompt is asking you to do. This box is where you answer the prompt specifically with your defensible interpretation. Some possibilities are that you may answer how a protagonist is characterized (e.g., vindictive and manipulative yet lacking self-confidence), how a setting influences a character, or whatever it is that the prompt is asking.

Here is a successful thesis for a question 3 Literary Argument essay that focuses on a villain as a character. Note that this thesis removes the optional portion of literary elements from the thesis template.

> In *The Crucible,* Arthur Miller characterizes Reverend Parris as a greedy, vain, and corrupt leader in order to illustrate how quickly people can become a gullible mob, easily manipulated into panic and paranoia.

And here is an effective thesis that keeps the optional portion of literary elements:

> In *The Handmaid's Tale* Margaret Atwood uses a regime set-
> ting, juxtaposition of characters' morals, and point of view to
> explore how language can be used as a tool of power to
> maintain one's identity in the face of oppression.

Remember: A successful thesis statement answers the prompt, provides a defensible claim, and includes an interpretation of the work.

LINE OF REASONING AND TOPIC SENTENCES

A line of reasoning is defined as a set of reasons used in order to reach a conclusion. It may seem backwards to think of your thesis statement as your conclusion. But that's pretty much what it is—the overall claim you come to about a text after reading, considering, and analyzing it. So, if your thesis is the conclusion you come to about a text, a line of reasoning is a list of all of the reasons that led you to that conclusion. Your essay will lay these reasons out in a logical, organized way, so that the person reading it can follow along on the ride with you through all your points, which all support and help to form your overall claim in your thesis.

A line of reasoning is basically an outline of your argument. The clearest way to lay out your line of reasoning is through your topic sentences, with each topic sentence offering a new sub-claim that supports your overall thesis. Here's an oversimplified example to show you what we mean:

Thesis statement (overall claim)	Payson's Ice Cream Palace is the best ice cream shop.
Reason 1	It has the greatest variety of flavors made from natural ingredients.
Reason 2	The price per scoop is lower than that of its competitors, but the quality of the product is not compromised.
Reason 3	The cozy furniture, welcoming environment, and excellent customer service allow guests to feel comfortable while enjoying a special treat.

Obviously, these examples are way too simplistic for any AP® Literature essay, but they serve to show the line of reasons, or sub-claims, as to why Payson's Ice Cream Palace is the best. Your topic sentences should do the same—they should all provide a new reason that supports your overall thesis statement. They should be organized in a logical way so that they build off each other and transition from one idea to the next, ultimately advancing the argument to the conclusion (your thesis).

Along with the topic sentence, each paragraph provides specific **textual evidence** and commentary that explains how the evidence and your analysis connect back to the thesis.

Let's take a look at a prose prompt from the 2017 AP® Exam to see how various students constructed thesis statements and topic sentences to form a line of reasoning. (Note: This is a prompt from before the course redesign. Newer prompts will no longer have a list of literary techniques like you see here.)

Question 2

(Suggested time—40 minutes. This question counts as one-third of the total essay section score.)

In the passage below, from *The Adventures of Peregrine Pickle* (1751) by Tobias Smollett, Mr. Pickle encounters Godfrey Gauntlet, the brother of his beloved Emilia. Consider how the two men confront their own uncontrolled emotions and yet attempt to abide by their social norms. In a well-developed essay, analyze how the author explores the complex interplay between emotions and social propriety in the passage. You may wish to consider such literary techniques as dialogue, narrative pace, and tone.

"Mr. Pickle, you have carried on a correspondence
with my sister for some time, and I
should be glad to know the nature of it." To this
question our lover replied, "Sir, I should be glad to
5   know what title you have to demand that
satisfaction?"—"Sir," answered the other, "I demand
it in the capacity of a brother, jealous of his own
honour, as well as of his sister's reputation; and if
your intentions are honourable, you will not refuse
10   it."—"Sir," said Peregrine, "I am not at present
disposed to appeal to your opinion for the rectitude of
my intentions: and I think you assume a little too
much importance, in pretending to judge my
conduct."—"Sir," replied the soldier, "I pretend to
15   judge the conduct of every man who interferes with
my concerns, and even to chastise him, if I think he
acts amiss."—"Chastise!" cried the youth, with
indignation in his looks, "sure you dare not apply that
term to me?"—"You are mistaken," said Godfrey; "I
20   dare do anything that becomes the character of a

gentleman."—"Gentleman, God wot!" replied the other, looking contemptuously at his equipage,[1] which was none of the most superb, "a very pretty gentleman, truly!"

25 The soldier's wrath was inflamed by this ironical repetition, the contempt of which his conscious poverty made him feel; and he called his antagonist presumptuous boy, insolent upstart, and with other epithets, which Perry retorted with great bitterness.

30 A formal challenge having passed between them, they alighted at the first inn, and walked into the next field, in order to decide their quarrel by the sword. Having pitched upon the spot, helped to pull off each other's boots, and laid aside their coats and waistcoats, Mr.

35 Gauntlet told his opponent, that he himself was looked upon in the army as an expert swordsman, and that if Mr. Pickle had not made that science his particular study, they should be upon a more equal footing in using pistols. Peregrine was too much incensed to

40 thank him for his plain dealing, and too confident of his own skill to relish the other's proposal, which he accordingly rejected: then, drawing his sword, he observed, that were he to treat Mr. Gauntlet according to his deserts, he would order his man to punish his

45 audacity with a horsewhip. Exasperated at this expression, which he considered an indelible affront, he made no reply, but attacked his adversary with equal ferocity and address. The youth parried his first and second thrust, but received the third in the outside

50 of his sword-arm. Though the wound was superficial, he was transported with rage at the sight of his own blood, and returned the assault with such fury and precipitation, that Gauntlet, loath to take advantage of his unguarded heat, stood upon the defensive. In the

55 second lunge, Peregrine's weapon entering a kind of network in the shell of Godfrey's sword, the blade snapped in two, and left him at the mercy of the soldier, who, far from making an insolent use of the victory he had gained, put up his Toledo with great

60 deliberation, like a man who had been used to that kind of rencounters, and observed that such a blade as Peregrine's was not to be trusted with a man's life:

1. Carriage and horse.

65

> then advising the owner to treat a gentleman in
> distress with more respect for the future, he slipped on
> his boots, and with sullen dignity of demeanour
> stalked back to the inn.

Before we can create a defensible claim, let's pause and make sure we understand the literal story of this passage, which is where you need to begin with any text—that runner's starting line we mentioned earlier. Let's start with who's who since this passage can be a little confusing.

Godfrey Gauntlet	Peregrine Pickle
• Soldier	• Lover
• Brother to Pickle's love interest	• Youth
• Expert swordsman	• Lets anger get the better of him, can't even talk (45–47), loses control (50–53)
• Remains in control (for the most part)	
• Chooses to walk away (66)	• Gets hit (49–50)
• Warns Pickle to be more respectful (63–64)	• Sword snaps (56–57)
• Winner	• Loser

The prompt specifically asks you to explore "the complex interplay between emotions and social propriety." Ah yes, there's a version of that familiar word we see in every prompt: *complexity*. As we discuss further in chapter 3, complexity means that there are several literary elements working together to create meaning in a text. Your job is to identify some of these parts (out of many combinations of options) and explore how they operate together. To explore the complexity in this prompt, you might make a chart of where you see the features they are asking you to explore in the prompt (in this case, uncontrolled emotions and social propriety) occur in the passage, then consider how literary elements work to enhance these features.

Uncontrolled emotions	Social propriety
• Insults (23–24, 27–29)	• "Sir" and "Gentleman" to address each other (used throughout)
• "wrath was inflamed" (25)	
• "Exasperated" (45)	• "formal challenge" (a duel) (30)
• "he made no reply, but attacked his adversary with equal ferocity" (47–48)	• They help each other with their boots
	• "laid aside their coats and waistcoats" (34)
• "he was transported with rage" (51)	
• "returned the assault with such fury" (52)	• Gauntlet attempts a fair fight
• "his unguarded heat" (54)	• Last sentence: "respect," "dignity," "treat a gentleman"

Now that you've pulled some textual evidence, you can look over it all and see what connections can be made and what meanings can be derived. Think back to the table of questions to ask when writing about literature on page 33 and the *what, how, why* table on page 36 to craft a thesis statement, and then craft your main reasons as topic sentences.

To create a logical and organized line of reasoning, there are four main ways to lay out your topic sentences, and therefore your essay.

1. Organize by insights.
2. Organize chronologically within the passage, like a walkthrough of the text from beginning to end.
3. Organize by literary devices. (Note: If you choose this method, be extra careful that your topic sentences say something analytical about the device and how or why it is used.)
4. Organize by insights, chronology, *and* literary devices.

1. Organize by Insights

Student 1

Thesis statement	In this excerpt from *The Adventures of Peregrine Pickle*, Tobias Smollett creates a comedic atmosphere through the battle between the rage the two opposing men feel towards each other and the respect that is ingrained in them, displaying how anger and cordiality do not bode well together and usually end up causing complications.
Topic sentence 1	Even though Godfrey Gauntlet and Peregrine Pickle are aware of their differences, they initially address each other in a respectful way despite their tension to show that they are trying to avoid any unnecessary battles.
Topic sentence 2	Smollett utilizes a duel, a valid and respected event in the time period, as the setting for the men to have an outlet to express their true emotions under societal expectations.
Topic sentence 3	The peak of the conflict between Gauntlet and Pickle amplifies the extreme tension between the two main characters, and causes one of them to finally lose control.

2. Organize by Chronological Walkthrough of Text
Student 2

Thesis statement	In *The Adventures of Peregrine Pickle* Tobias Smollett creates tension between Peregrine and Godfrey, revealing how society shapes social norms in order for people to maintain a reputable appearance.
Topic sentence 1	In the opening of the passage, the characters' conversation demonstrates their propriety and civility.
Topic sentence 2	As the author begins the second paragraph, the characters pause to help one another, even as they are about to fight.
Topic sentence 3	In concluding the passage, the characters chose to show mercy and manners to one another, rather than giving in to their desires for harm.

3. Organize by Literary Devices (with Analysis)
Student 3

Thesis statement	In the excerpt from *The Adventures of Peregrine Pickle*, Tobias Smollett uses formal diction, juxtaposition, and imagery to imply that upholding society's expectations of propriety is more valuable than revealing one's true emotions.
Topic sentence 1	Mr. Pickle and Gauntlet use formal language, showing how societal expectations are prioritized regardless of how one feels towards another.
Topic sentence 2	The author uses juxtaposition between Mr. Pickle and Gauntlet to contrast the characters' fundamentally different approaches to their emotions, which leads to different outcomes for each character.
Topic sentence 3	The vivid imagery of the sword fight reveals how each character displays different behaviors in the fight, and Gauntlet's more socially acceptable behavior of controlling his emotions is what ultimately makes him win.

4. Organize by Insights, Chronology, and Literary Devices

Finally, we offer the best option—a mixture of all three ways. Topic sentences contain an insight *and* are in chronological order and may even contain literary devices.

Student 4 (No Literary Devices)

Thesis statement	In the passage, both Pickle and Gauntlet attempt to act with social decency towards each other despite their feelings of disrespect and mistrust. Through their moderately respectable conversation to their brief duel, the author conveys how those with less control over their emotions ultimately fail when compared to those who remain calm and collected.
Topic sentence 1	At the beginning of the passage both men attempt to remain cordial as they question each other's relationship with Emilia, which highlights the proper manners of the time.
Topic sentence 2	However, as their conversation continues the men challenge each other to a duel when their feelings of disrespect and mistrust towards each other boil over, signaling that even the most controlled men have strong emotions.
Topic sentence 3	In the end, Gauntlet, with his ability to remain calm under adversity, wins the duel with Pickle when Pickle loses control of his emotions and succumbs to his rage.

Student 5 (Includes Literary Devices)

Thesis statement	In *The Adventures of Peregrine Pickle*, Mr. Pickle and Mr. Gauntlet struggle to maintain a facade of composure while battling intense animosity towards each other, creating a humorous tone throughout the passage that comments on the absurdity of politeness in certain situations.
Topic sentence 1	The author utilizes dialogue to emphasize the proper and polite diction the characters display in the passage, which points out the absurdity of the social norms that get in the way of direct communication between Mr. Pickle and Mr. Gauntlet.
Topic sentence 2	The additional names used for the two characters create confusion during the scene, which heightens the drama of the conflict and draws more attention to the hidden and repressed emotions of the two adversaries.

Topic sentence 3	Tone is an important strategy within the passage because the humorous tone allows the reader to clearly see the silly pettiness of the situation and the ridiculous tactics that the characters use to mask their true feelings.

SELECTING AND INTEGRATING TEXTUAL EVIDENCE

Selecting Evidence

To select appropriate evidence, find *short* phrases from the text to work into your body paragraphs. Pick out phrases that illustrate the literary techniques you notice, as well as specific words or details that seem important to you. Let's use Student 5's Topic sentence 1 as an example:

> The author utilizes dialogue to emphasize the proper and polite diction the characters display in the passage, which points out the absurdity of the social norms that get in the way of direct communication between Mr. Pickle and Mr. Gauntlet.

Look back in the passage and find some instances where we see this dialogue and polite diction happening and record them. We make a bulleted list here, but given the time constraints on exam day, you could speed up this process by underlining, circling, or otherwise annotating the passage. You might want to use a different style of annotation for each body paragraph so you know which evidence goes with which topic sentence.

- "Sir" and "Gentleman" to address each other (throughout)
- "I am not at present disposed to appeal to your opinion for the rectitude of my intentions" (10–12)
- "'You are mistaken,' said Godfrey" (19)
- "I dare do anything that becomes the character of a gentleman" (19–21)
- "Helped to pull off each other's boots" (33–34)

Quote only the portions of the text specifically relevant to your point. Think of the text in terms of units—words and phrases—and use only the units you need. If it is particular words or phrases that prove your point, you do not need to quote the sentences they appear in; rather, incorporate the words and phrases into sentences expressing your own ideas. Now that we've identified some evidence from the passage that demonstrates the use of dialogue and polite and proper diction, we can write the rest of our body paragraph, integrating the evidence into our analysis.

Integrating Evidence

We ask you to find *phrases* as evidence instead of entire sentences so that you can more smoothly integrate textual evidence into your own insights and analysis. We like to refer to these short little phrases you pull from the text as *sprinkles*. A *sprinkle* is a word or phrase up to ten(ish) words long that is going to be embedded within your own sentence. Like a scoop of ice cream with rainbow sprinkles, a perfect sundae would have a smattering of sprinkles spread evenly over the top of the ice cream. Pretend your body paragraphs are the scoops of ice cream and the phrases that you've selected as evidence are the rainbow sprinkles.

> **Pro tip:** Do your best to distribute your chosen phrases—and you should have *multiple* phrases—throughout your paragraphs to avoid sprinkle clumps. Long quotations (clumps), such as a whole sentence from a passage or several lines from a poem, feel heavy, weigh down your analysis, and most often are unnecessary. AP® Readers are looking for *your* insights and interpretations of a text, not to read the whole passage again quoted in your essay.

Continuing with Topic sentence 1 from Student 5, and using the evidence we've identified for it, a body paragraph might look like this:

Topic sentence	**The author utilizes dialogue to emphasize the proper and polite diction the characters display in the passage, which points out the absurdity of the social norms that get in the way of direct communication between Mr. Pickle and Mr. Gauntlet.**

Topic sentence — **The author utilizes dialogue to emphasize the proper and polite diction the characters display in the passage, which points out the absurdity of the social norms that get in the way of direct communication between Mr. Pickle and**

Evidence — **Mr. Gauntlet.** The heavy **repetition of "Sir"** to address each other throughout their initial exchange sets up a satirical sense of formality between the two characters. **Even though** *(Commentary)* **the conversation is based in jealousy and anger, the words the characters use remain formal and polite.** A tone of sophistication oozes from Peregrine as he claims he is **"not at**

Evidence — **present disposed to appeal to your opinion,"** instead of more rudely telling his opponent to bugger off. Godfrey

Evidence — responds in kind with **"You are mistaken."** Both men are so caught up in the pretense of social propriety that they **"dare**

Evidence — **do anything that becomes the character of a gentleman."** Even going as far to help "to pull off each other's boots," **emphasizes the absurd nature of their social norms**. The *(Commentary)* duelers attempt to keep their composure even as they are getting ready to fight each other, and **with such ridiculous acts as helping each other take off their boots, the author pokes fun at the silly practices of social interaction.**

> Commentary; connects back to thesis statement

Notice that this body paragraph includes all five bullets of textual evidence we made note of previously, which are smoothly integrated into the analysis and commentary. Furthermore, they all support the claim stated in the paragraph's topic sentence. We know that the quotations are effectively integrated because if you close your eyes and have someone read the paragraph out loud to you, you would not be able to tell where the quoted excerpts fall. Notice there are no introductory phrases to each quote, such as "when the author says" or "the author writes." Moreover, you don't see the dreaded phrase "this quote shows that..." anywhere in the paragraph.

> **Pro tip**: "This quote shows that" weakens your writer's voice. While your ideas might be insightful and your analysis spot-on, starting your commentary sentences with "This shows that..." diminishes the quality of your writing—it's sophomoric. A quick fix for this is to either just cut "This shows that" and say what you were going to say, or replace it with "The author reveals that...," making sure to switch up the verb each time, and using a mixture of the author's last name and "the author" to avoid being repetitive.

The paragraph also embeds sufficient textual evidence smoothly, avoiding clumps and allowing the syntax to read seamlessly. In the following body paragraphs, we would go through the same steps with each topic sentence. Remember: A line of reasoning is the arrangement of claims and evidence that supports your overall claim in your thesis statement. A line of reasoning should connect your sub-claims in your topic sentences, textual evidence, and commentary in a logical and organized way. It is important to note that there is no one correct way to write your essay, and this template is only a guide. Within each body paragraph box, the order of the bullets is interchangeable. You may lead into textual evidence with commentary or analyze the literary device after your evidence and commentary; there are options. We encourage you to structure your essay and your paragraphs however feels most natural and offers the most confident and effective draft.

If you feel like you need a road map to follow for organizing your essay, Figure 6 is a basic essay structure template you may follow. Of course, not every essay will look exactly like this, but it is a decent starting place to anchor your writing.

FIGURE 6

Essay Structure Template

Thesis statement: Defensible and includes an interpretation that answers the prompt		
Body paragraph 1 • Topic sentence 1 • Literary element • Textual evidence • Commentary • More evidence and commentary if possible • Tie back to thesis	**Body paragraph 2** • Topic sentence 2 • Literary element • Textual evidence • Commentary • More evidence and commentary if possible • Tie back to thesis	**Body paragraph 3** • Topic sentence 3 • Literary element • Textual evidence • Commentary • More evidence and commentary if possible • Tie back to thesis
Conclusion: Link back to thematic idea in thesis statement		

IMPROVING VOICE AND STYLE

Students often get so caught up in *what* they are writing that they forget to pay attention to *how* they are writing, especially when they are under a time limit. But it's *how* you write that may help you to earn the extra point given for the overall sophistication of the essay.

Sentence Variety

One of the most effective ways to improve your writing style is to check for sentence variety, which means that your sentences are a mixture of lengths and grammatical arrangements. What happens when you *don't* have sentence length variety is that your writing sounds choppy and elementary. Aim for a mixture of short, medium, and long sentences that follow different grammatical patterns so that your syntax is not repetitive and dry. Check to see where you might be able to combine sentences—to create compound, complex, or compound-complex sentences. For a tutorial on how to effectively combine sentences, check out the AP® Classroom Daily videos for Skill 7.E in Units 5 and 6.

> **Pro tip:** One particularly effective move we encourage our students to utilize is finding an opportune spot in your essay to use a *shorty*, what we like to call extremely short sentences. A two- or three-word sentence well placed for emphasis can really pack a punch. Use a shorty when you really want something to stand out.

A syntax trap our students often fall into is starting too many sentences with "This shows that..." when writing their commentary. Having a couple sentences in your essay that start this way is acceptable, but when almost every sentence of commentary starts with "This shows that" it is repetitive and detracts from your quality of writing. *It's amateur.* Not only do we encourage you to switch up the grammatical order of your sentences, but also the verbs that you use.

Strong Verbs

Shows. Every student's favorite go-to verb. The author shows this; the narrator shows that. And we get it—you are in a time crunch—you don't have time to think of extraordinary verbs when you are trying to explain an extended metaphor in a poem. So we encourage you to practice throughout the school year experimenting with different verbs. The more you use them, the more naturally they will come to you when writing on the exam. Here are some verbs you could use to replace the notorious "show":

reveal	*suggest*	*indicate*
highlight	*imply*	*prove*
demonstrate	*provide*	*underline*
illustrate	*assert*	*expose*
claims	*infer*	*establish*

Transitions

Finally, to improve fluidity in your writing and the cohesiveness of your line of reasoning, try to use transitions to connect body paragraphs. Allow one paragraph's idea to lead into the next one, by connecting both ideas into the same sentence at the end of the first paragraph or the beginning of the next paragraph. You can also use transitional words and phrases such as:

furthermore	*next*	*in a similar manner*
moreover	*unlike*	*conversely*
in addition to	*consequently*	*on the other hand*
similarly	*besides*	*however*
in contrast to	*likewise*	*in other words*

STUDENT SAMPLE ESSAY

To tie together the elements of successful writing we discussed in this chapter, let's look at this prose prompt from the AP® Exam (2019) and a student's response to it.

AP® English Literature and Composition Free-Response Questions

Question 2

(Suggested time—40 minutes. This question counts as one-third of the total essay section score.)

Carefully read the following excerpt from William Dean Howells' novel *The Rise of Silas Lapham* (1885). Then, in a well-constructed essay, analyze how the author portrays the complex experience of two sisters, Penelope and Irene, within their family and society. You may wish to consider such literary elements as style, tone, and selection of detail. [Note: Remember that you won't see a list of literary devices like this on prompts from 2020 or later.]

> They were not girls who embroidered or
> abandoned themselves to needle-work. Irene spent her
> abundant leisure in shopping for herself and her
> mother, of whom both daughters made a kind of idol,
> 5 buying her caps and laces out of their pin-money,[1]
> and getting her dresses far beyond her capacity to
> wear. Irene dressed herself very stylishly, and spent
> hours on her toilet[2] every day. Her sister had a
> simpler taste, and, if she had done altogether as she
> 10 liked, might even have slighted dress. They all three
> took long naps every day, and sat hours together
> minutely discussing what they saw out of the window.
> In her self-guided search for self-improvement, the
> elder sister went to many church lectures on a vast
> 15 variety of secular subjects, and usually came home
> with a comic account of them, and that made more
> matter of talk for the whole family. She could make
> fun of nearly everything; Irene complained that she
> scared away the young men whom they got
> 20 acquainted with at the dancing-school sociables.
> They were, perhaps, not the wisest young men.

1. Pin-money: money used for small expenses and incidentals.
2. Toilet: dressing and grooming.

The girls had learned to dance at Papanti's;[3] but
they had not belonged to the private classes. They did
not even know of them, and a great gulf divided them
25   from those who did. Their father did not like
company, except such as came informally in their
way; and their mother had remained too rustic to
know how to attract it in the sophisticated city
fashion. None of them had grasped the idea of
30   European travel; but they had gone about to mountain
and sea-side resorts, the mother and the two girls,
where they witnessed the spectacle which such resorts
present throughout New England, of multitudes of
girls, lovely, accomplished, exquisitely dressed,
35   humbly glad of the presence of any sort of young
man; but the Laphams had no skill or courage to make
themselves noticed, far less courted by the solitary
invalid, or clergyman, or artist. They lurked helplessly
about in the hotel parlors, looking on and not knowing
40   how to put themselves forward. Perhaps they did not
care a great deal to do so. They had not a conceit of
themselves, but a sort of content in their own ways
that one may notice in certain families. The very
strength of their mutual affection was a barrier to
45   worldly knowledge; they dressed for one another;
they equipped their house for their own satisfaction;
they lived richly to themselves, not because they were
selfish, but because they did not know how to do
otherwise. The elder daughter did not care for society,
50   apparently. The younger, who was but three years
younger, was not yet quite old enough to be ambitious
of it. With all her wonderful beauty, she had an
innocence almost vegetable. When her beauty, which
in its immaturity was crude and harsh, suddenly
55   ripened, she bloomed and glowed with the
unconsciousness of a flower; she not merely did
not feel herself admired, but hardly knew herself
discovered. If she dressed well, perhaps too well, it
was because she had the instinct of dress; but till
60   she met this young man who was so nice to her at
Baie St. Joan,[4] she had scarcely lived a detached,
individual life, so wholly had she depended on her

---

3. Papanti's: a fashionable social dance school in nineteenth-century Boston.
4. Baie St. Joan: a Canadian resort.

65

mother and her sister for her opinions, almost her sensations. She took account of everything he did and said, pondering it, and trying to make out exactly what he meant, to the inflection of a syllable, the slightest movement or gesture. In this way she began for the first time to form ideas which she had not derived from her family, and they were none the

70

less her own because they were often mistaken.

ANNOTATED STUDENT SAMPLE ESSAY

The primary agent in human socialization is the family. Some are more impacted by this factor more than others. Irene and Penelope embody this sociological concept because nearly every part of Irene's identity was crafted by or as a response to her family. Despite this dedication to family, both of the sisters long to be a part of the wealthy social circles that exclude them. **Howell utilizes techniques such as diction, tone, and contrast to exemplify the sisters' lack of identity outside of the family as a response to exclusion from the high society they want to be a part of. Imagery is also an important element that Howell employs to characterize the sisters and draw more attention to their desire to expand their horizons.**

> Introduction includes a multi-sentence thesis statement that is defensible and contains an interpretation.

Much of the passage is spent contrasting the two sisters. They have different interests, styles of dress, and passions. The author utilizes diction and tone to exacerbate the contrast of the two characters. One example of this is words used to describe Irene. **She is characterized as "stylish", "exquisitely dressed", and "beautiful." Meanwhile Penelope has much more practical words ascribed to her that contain less drama and flair. Penelope's taste is described as "simple" and her dress is "humble." These words help characterize the sisters and create different perceptions of them in the mind of the reader.** Irene is more impressionable by her peers, while Penelope is more interested in religion and education than socializing with those other than her family. **This contrast between them in many ways makes it more surprising that the family as a whole still desperately tries to insert themselves into the world of the upper class. No matter how different they are in their interests or style,**

> First topic sentence provides an insight that will be explored in the paragraph.

> Textual evidence is integrated using quote sprinkles and is explicitly explained with commentary.

> Ties back to overall claim in thesis statement.

they are still influenced by their family's desire to be part of high society despite not belonging.

Topic sentence provides claim for paragraph, a literary device, and analysis.

There are some striking examples of imagery in the passage, one of which is used to describe Irene's beauty. It is compared to a flower because it was "crude and harsh, suddenly ripened, she bloomed and glowed with the unconsciousness of a flower." This quote perfectly describes Irene's change in priority as she grows up. It is normal for one's main factor of socialization to become peers rather than family as a child grows up. Irene is still very influenced by her family, but she has a growing curiosity and attraction to her peers and the upper class culture she is surrounded by. At the same time, both sisters are trying to please their family social circle. The sisters see their mother as "a kind of idol" they buy her "caps and laces out of their pin money" as well as extremely fancy dresses. This desire for acceptance and attention from both their family, and from the outside world creates a complexity in each sister because each of the social circles have different interests.

Textual evidence commentary is provided, with a connection back to the thesis at the end of the paragraph.

Howell's passage exemplifies a family's desire to be a part of upper class society because of the perceived social advantages. Interest and attraction to the upper class is a common theme in American culture and around the world today. The obsession with celebrities and the British royalty point to a desire to be involved in the lives of those in the upper echelons of society. It is almost voyeuristic in the ways that people try to gain information about celebrities to be like them and learn the newest trends. This passage also discusses how different factors of socialization create complexity in the lives of the daughters. They are at once trying to please their family and their peers, which is no easy task. This results in the daughters having complex lives and interests that change over time.

Passage connects to a broader context in modern-day society and ends with a return to the claim in the thesis.

A Note on Scoring

Your AP® Readers will follow scoring guidelines to award points from each of these three scales for each of your three essays:

- Row A, Thesis: 0–1 points
- Row B, Evidence and Commentary: 0–4 points
- Row C, Sophistication: 0–1 points

Each essay can thus receive a minimum of 0 points and a maximum of 6 points. We have followed this rubric when providing scores and feedback for the sample essays in this book.

Score: 1-3-1

This student sample essay would earn the point on the exam rubric for the thesis statement. The thesis spans two sentences to avoid being convoluted. ("Howell utilizes techniques such as diction, tone, and contrast to exemplify the sisters' lack of identity outside of the family as a response to exclusion from the high society they want to be a part of. Imagery is also an important element that Howell employs to characterize the sisters and draw more attention to their desire to expand their horizons.") In the thesis, the student sets up a line of reasoning for the essay, makes claims that are defensible, and makes an interpretation of the sisters' experience. Each body paragraph is nicely framed with an introductory topic sentence, which is then followed with relevant selected evidence and thoughtful commentary, helping to create and support a line of reasoning. The student discusses contrast, diction, tone, and imagery as the literary elements of focus. The paragraph on imagery could be improved by adding more explicit explanation of the connection between the image of the flower and the analysis, which puts this essay at a 3 out of 4 for textual evidence and commentary. We would award this essay the point for sophistication due to the use of elevated vocabulary, consistency in maintaining the line of reasoning, and making a broader context comparison to modern American culture.

CHAPTER REVIEW

Let's do a quick recap of the process you've learned in this chapter in order to be successful in writing for the AP® Exam.

1. Analyze a text instead of summarizing or paraphrasing it. To help you glean insightful analysis, ask yourself the guiding questions on page 33.
2. Write a defensible thesis that answers the prompt and includes an interpretation of the text.
3. Establish a line of reasoning through strong topic sentences, aptly selected evidence, and quality commentary.
4. Embed evidence smoothly into your own sentences using integrated quotations.
5. Enhance your writing by utilizing sentence variety, strong verbs, and transitions.

In the following chapters, we will break down each individual exam essay (question 1: Poetry Analysis, question 2: Prose Analysis, and question 3: Literary Argument). You will see the information and skills from this chapter built upon and refined specifically for each type of essay.

3

Question 1: Poetry Analysis Essay

INTRODUCTION

On the AP® Literature and Composition Exam, the first of three essay questions you will see in your exam booklet is the Poetry Analysis essay. Before we dive into what that essay looks like, we'd like to say a brief word about poetry. This essay tends to daunt students the most, and this stems from a fear of not "getting" the poem. But here's the thing. Poetry is open to interpretations. Yes, that is a *plural—interpretations*—because there are many ways to understand a poem. There is no one right way to derive meaning from a poem. What AP® Readers are looking for in your essay is *your* thoughts on a poem; what *you* see in it.

When approaching poetry, we must accept its ambiguity. That's part of the beauty of poetry, after all—its ability to morph and reconstitute itself in different readers' hands. We as readers bring ourselves into a poem, whether consciously or subconsciously, and our life experiences and personal identities affect the way we receive a poem. Reading a poem is not about unlocking its secret meaning or an Easter egg hunt for literary devices, but rather exploring it for what it means to you. And while we can't say there are absolutely no wrong answers, there are probably more right answers than you imagine. If a poem is about nature or love, but you claim it's about pink aliens, then yes, you are probably wrong. But if you can read a poem, and start with one thought about one line that stands out to you, that is your entrance, like a door, into the poem. Walk through that door and walk around the poem; explore it like a house. What else do you see? Once you've walked around the whole house, what conclusions can you make that pertain to the essay's prompt? The great thing about these conclusions is that there are a million ways to form them.

A poem offers us so much to work with as students of literature: language, **tone** and mood, structure, images, lessons and observations about life and humanity—there are many paths to forming an interpretation of a poem. That's what AP° Readers are looking for in your essay. What paths did you take in the poem to arrive at your interpretation? What moves did the poet make that you noticed and considered? If you can express this journey effectively in writing, then you are on your way to AP° Exam success. And the good news is that the more poetry you read, the better you will get at understanding and appreciating it. It's like any other skill. How do you get better at shooting free throws? Practice shooting fifty free throws a day. Not that you have to read fifty poems a day, but you get the point. The more you read, the more experienced your brain will be with forming insights about poetry. This chapter will help you to know what to practice in order to be successful.

EXCAVATING THE PROMPT

When you read a prompt and go about understanding the task it is asking you to perform, think of it as an excavation—digging into the prompt for its important words, for clues into the meaning of the poem, and for directions to possibly guide your writing.

WORKSHEET 6

Important words	
Clues	
Direction	

- Important words provide the context and subject of the poem (who is the author, when it was written, and what it's about).
- Clues provide hints into understanding the complexities of the poem and its overall thematic message.
- Directions provide possible guidelines for writing.

Let's excavate free-response question 1 from the 2009 exam:

In the following speech from Shakespeare's play *Henry VIII*, Cardinal Wolsey considers his sudden downfall from his position as advisor to the king. Spokesmen for the king have just left Wolsey alone on stage. Read the speech carefully. Then write a well-organized essay in which you analyze how Shakespeare uses elements such as **allusion**, figurative language, and tone to convey Wolsey's complex response to his dismissal from court.

So farewell—to the little good you bear me.
Farewell? a long farewell to all my greatness!
This is the state of man: to-day he puts forth
The tender leaves of hopes, to-morrow blossoms,
5 And bears his blushing honors thick upon him;
The third day comes a frost, a killing frost,
And when he thinks, good easy man, full surely
His greatness is a-ripening, nips his root,
And then he falls as I do. I have ventur'd,
10 Like little wanton boys that swim on bladders,
This many summers in a sea of glory,
But far beyond my depth. My high-blown pride
At length broke under me, and now has left me,
Weary and old with service, to the mercy
15 Of a rude stream that must for ever hide me.
Vain pomp and glory of this world, I hate ye!
I feel my heart new open'd. O how wretched
Is that poor man that hangs on princes' favors!
There is, betwixt that smile we would aspire to,
20 That sweet aspect of princes, and their ruin,
More pangs and fears than wars or women have;
And when he falls, he falls like Lucifer,
Never to hope again.

Your chart may include different words and phrases, and may place them in different boxes, and that is okay. What is important is discovering the key components of the prompt and what it's asking you to do.

WORKSHEET 6 SAMPLE

Important words	speech, Shakespeare, *Henry VIII*, downfall from his position as advisor to the king, dismissal from court
Clues	considers, sudden, alone on stage, complex response
Direction	well-organized essay, analyze, allusion, figurative language, tone

Your Turn

Try your hand at excavating this prompt by replicating Worksheet 6 on a blank piece of paper or downloading it from the digital landing page.

In "We Real Cool" by Gwendolyn Brooks, the speaker observes a group of youth hanging out at the pool hall during school hours. Read the poem carefully. Then, in a well-written essay, analyze how Brooks uses literary elements to portray her complex observations and feelings about the young men's actions.

The Pool Players.
Seven at the Golden Shovel.

We real cool. We
Left school. We

5   Lurk late. We
Strike straight. We

Sing sin. We
Thin gin. We

Jazz June. We
10 Die soon.

The most important word you will see time and time again in free-response question prompts is *complex*, or *complexity*. If something is *complex* it is multifaceted and complicated, involving many different parts that are connected or related to each other. Complexity in poetry grows from the intricate ways the poem's parts work together and relate to each other to create meaning. The parts include all aspects of the poem: its individual words, lines, style, point of view, structure, etc. As mentioned in the introduction to this chapter, there is a whole universe of possibilities for you to explore when considering how a poem's parts work together to create meaning. Given the same poem, one student might link a striking **image** to a **metaphor** and discuss line breaks, while another student explores how **personification** works with figurative language and the poem's **shifts**—and both arrive at different, valid interpretations.

The prompt for free-response question 1 presents a passage of poetry and assesses your ability:

- to write a thesis statement that answers the prompt with a defensible claim and that presents an interpretation,
- to choose evidence from the poem and include it in your essay to support your ideas,
- to explicitly explain how the evidence supports the thesis with commentary,
- to use appropriate spelling, grammar, and mechanics in your writing.

Stable Prompt Wording

With the unveiling of the new Course and Exam Description came a fill-in-the-blank template for all of the free-response question prompts.

The text in italics will vary by question, while the remainder of the prompt will be consistently used in all Poetry Analysis essay questions.

In the following poem [*or excerpt from poem*] by [*author, date of publication*], the speaker [*comment on what is being addressed in the poem*]. Read the poem carefully. Then, in a well-written essay, analyze how [*author*] uses [*poetic or literary*] elements and techniques to [*convey/portray/develop a thematic, topical, or structural aspect of the poem that is complex and specific to the passage of the poem provided*]. (CED 138)

So that when all the blanks are filled in, a prompt looks like this:

> In the following poem "Greening" by Kevin Young (published in 2014), the speaker considers his role as a parent. Read the poem carefully. Then, in a well-written essay, analyze how Young uses poetic elements and techniques to portray the complex experience of raising a child.

It is important to note that with the new stable wording of the prompt, you will no longer see a suggested list of literary techniques. When referring to previously released exams or some older test prep books, you might notice that they included three techniques in the prompt that students *may* wish to analyze in their essay. They have since been removed because almost every student wrote about those same three techniques. Furthermore, we would argue that when provided with a list, it results in limitations in analysis, whether consciously or subconsciously, and discourages students from trusting their unique perspective on the poem. We encourage you to embrace what *you* notice as a reader. Finally, keep in mind that while literary techniques are no longer listed in the prompt, you certainly still need to be able to identify and analyze them to earn the maximum number of points on the Poetry Analysis essay rubric.

Techniques for Poetry Analysis

While this is not a definitive list, these are some of the terms that come up more frequently when reading and exploring poetry. As we walk through annotating a poem together, we will see some of these techniques in action.

alliteration the repetition of usually initial consonant sounds through a sequence of words—for example, "cease, my song, till fair Aurora rise" (Phillis Wheatley, "An Hymn to the Evening")

allusion brief, often implicit and indirect reference within a literary text to something outside the text, whether another text (e.g., the Bible, a myth, another literary work, a painting or a piece of music) or any imaginary or historical person, place, or thing

anaphora figure of speech involving the repetition of the same word or phrase in (and especially at the beginning of) successive lines, clauses, or sentences, as in "*We passed* the Fields of Gazing Grain— / *We passed* the Setting Sun—" (Emily Dickinson, "Because I could not stop for Death—")

assonance repetition of vowel sounds in a sequence of words with different endings—for example, "The d*e*ath of the p*oe*t was k*e*pt from his p*oe*ms" in W. H. Auden's "In Memory of W. B. Yeats"

caesura short pause within a line of poetry

connotation what is suggested by a word, apart from what it literally means or how it is defined in the dictionary

consonance the repetition of certain consonant sounds in close proximity, as in *mishmash*

end-stopped line line of verse that contains or concludes a complete clause and usually ends with a punctuation mark

enjambment in poetry, the technique of running over from one line to the next without stop, as in the following lines by Pat Mora: "I live in a doorway / between two rooms." The lines themselves would be described as *enjambed*.

imagery broadly defined, any sensory detail or evocation in a work; more narrowly, the use of figurative language to evoke a feeling, to call to mind an idea, or to describe an object. Imagery may be described as *auditory*, *tactile*, *visual*, or *olfactory* depending on which sense it primarily appeals to—hearing, touch, vision, or smell.

juxtaposition placing two or more things next to each other, side by side, to highlight their differences to create contrast, tension, or emphasis

metaphor figure of speech in which two unlike things are compared implicitly—that is, without the use of a signal such as the word *like* or *as*—as in "Love is a rose, but you better not pick it"

personification figure of speech that involves treating something nonhuman, such as an abstraction, as if it were a person by endowing it with humanlike qualities, as in "Death entered the room"

shift/volta/turn a turn of thought or argument in a poem

sibilance repetition of *s* or *sh* sounds, as in *sash*

simile figure of speech involving a direct, explicit comparison of one thing to another, usually using the word *like* or *as* to draw the connection, as in "My love is like a red, red rose." An *analogy* is an extended simile.

speaker the person who is the voice of a poem

stanza section of a poem, marked by extra line spacing before and after, that often has a single pattern of meter and/or rhyme

tone attitude a literary work takes toward its subject or that a character in the work or speaker of a poem conveys, especially as revealed through diction

ANNOTATING A POEM

Imagine spending a day in a new city. You visit some landmarks and go to a couple of popular stores or restaurants, but there's no way you could see *all* of the city in one day. While you did some exploring on your short visit, you certainly do not know the city as well as someone who lives there. Then you go back again for a second time and scout out some different spots to visit. And then the third time, even more new experiences and adventures. By the fourth time, you feel like you're getting to know the city quite well. Still not as well as an inhabitant, but you could probably show a first-time visitor around to some pretty cool places. The same idea can be applied to reading a poem. You aren't going to notice everything about a poem upon a first reading. It takes several readings to get to the heart of a poem, especially in the way that the AP* Exam wants you to.

> **Pro tip:** We suggest you read it through (at least) four times. With this close reading strategy, you build your understanding with each step.

Before reading the poem, read and excavate the prompt. What are they asking you to look for in the poem? Are there any hints or information that help you enter into your reading of the poem? You may consider taking these steps each time you read the poem:

1st read	Just read it. Slowly. Out loud if you can. Try to get a feel for what it is about.
2nd read	Underline words or lines that stand out to you.
3rd read	Annotate in the margins when you notice moves the poet is making in the poem and questions that arise while reading. Label literary devices that stand out to you.
4th read	Take in the whole poem one last time along with your annotations. Consider connections or patterns throughout the poem, as well as its tensions. In other words, its *complexity.*
After reading	Re-read the prompt. Make some notes at the bottom of the page to organize your thoughts. This step is often what leads to discovering a big idea, or a thematic message, to use as a basis for your line of reasoning.

Let's go through these steps with Aimee Nezhukumatathil's poem "On Listening to Your Teacher Take Attendance." Given that the first objective is simply reading the poem, go ahead and read it slowly and with intention and focus. This is not speed-reading; read each word deliberately and slowly.

On Listening to Your Teacher Take Attendance
AIMEE NEZHUKUMATATHIL

Breathe deep even if it means you wrinkle
your nose from the fake-lemon antiseptic

of the mopped floors and wiped-down
doorknobs. The freshly soaped necks

5   and armpits. Your teacher means well,
even if he butchers your name like

he has a bloody sausage casing stuck
between his teeth, handprints

on his white, sloppy apron. And when
10   everyone turns around to check out

your face, no need to flush red and warm.
Just picture all the eyes as if your classroom

is one big scallop with its dozens of icy blues
and you will remember that winter your family

15   took you to the China Sea and you sank
your face in it to gaze at baby clams and sea stars

the size of your outstretched hand. And when
all those necks start to crane, try not to forget

someone once lathered their bodies, once patted them
20   dry with a fluffy towel after a bath, set out their clothes

for the first day of school. Think of their pencil cases
from third grade, full of sharp pencils, a pink pearl eraser.

Think of their handheld pencil sharpener and its tiny blade.

After you've read it through once, move on to your second reading and identify words or lines that stand out to you. During the second reading of the poem,
underline anything that looks or sounds important to you. You don't have to
know *why* yet.

It is important to remember that not every reader will notice or underline the
same parts of a poem. Maybe you think we went underline-happy on the poem.
The approach we take with underlining is that if it seems like it *might* be important, then we underline it.

On Listening to Your Teacher Take Attendance
AIMEE NEZHUKUMATATHIL

Breathe deep even if it means you wrinkle
your nose from the fake-lemon antiseptic

of the mopped floors and wiped-down
doorknobs. The freshly soaped necks

5   and armpits. Your teacher means well,
even if he butchers your name like

he has a bloody sausage casing stuck
between his teeth, handprints

on his white, sloppy apron. And when
10   everyone turns around to check out

your face, no need to flush red and warm.
Just picture all the eyes as if your classroom

is one big scallop with its dozens of icy blues
and you will remember that winter your family

15   took you to the China Sea and you sank
your face in it to gaze at baby clams and sea stars

the size of your outstretched hand. And when
all those necks start to crane, try not to forget

someone once lathered their bodies, once patted them
20   dry with a fluffy towel after a bath, set out their clothes

for the first day of school. Think of their pencil cases
from third grade, full of sharp pencils, a pink pearl eraser.

Think of their handheld pencil sharpener and its tiny blade.

Upon underlining this poem, one of the first things we notice is that it's full of colors, concrete details, and imagery. We also notice emotions the **speaker** is feeling, even if we haven't yet figured out what those emotions are exactly. Let's read it a third time and make annotations for literary devices we notice, questions that arise, and other observations.

On Listening to Your Teacher Take Attendance

AIMEE NEZHUKUMATATHIL

Breathe deep even if it means you wrinkle　　　　　　who is "you"?
your nose from the fake-lemon antiseptic

of the mopped floors and wiped-down
doorknobs. The freshly soaped necks　　　　clean, sterile environment

5　　and armpits. Your teacher means well,
even if he butchers your name like　　　　this is a common saying

he has a bloody sausage casing stuck　　　　taking the idiom and making it
between his teeth, handprints　　　　into an image of a butcher;
　　　　　　　　　　　　　　　　　　bloody, gross imagery, body parts

on his white, sloppy apron. And when
10　　everyone turns around to check out

your face, no need to flush red and warm.　　blood, warm, red, blushing
Just picture all the eyes as if your classroom　　speaker is embarrassed

is one big scallop with its dozens of icy blues　　now icy and blue
and you will remember that winter your family　　shift to a family memory

15　　took you to the China Sea and you sank
your face in it to gaze at baby clams and sea stars　　ocean imagery, peaceful

the size of your outstretched hand. And when　　body words continue
all those necks start to crane, try not to forget　　Who is speaker saying this to?

someone once lathered their bodies, once patted them　　childhood innocence
20　　dry with a fluffy towel after a bath, set out their clothes

for the first day of school. Think of their pencil cases
from third grade, full of sharp pencils, a pink pearl eraser.　　*P* alliteration

Think of their handheld pencil sharpener and its tiny blade.　　seems
　　　　　　　　　　　　　　　　　　　　　　　foreboding?

After annotating the poem, consider its title again. When we look back to the title of this poem, the answer to our first question/annotation is provided. The "you" in the poem is the speaker herself. She is a student listening to her teacher, who is also the "butcher," take attendance; and if we look at the poet's last name (Nezhukumatathil), we can start to form some inferences. What we are doing now is moving into the fourth step.

Upon a fourth reading, we take in the poem again along with our annotations and questions, and ultimately look for patterns and connections to formulate some insights to form an interpretation. We encourage you to make notes in the blank space of the page below the poem in your exam booklet or on a separate sheet of paper; this will help you to organize the hive of thoughts you may have swarming around your brain. Notes don't need to be complete sentences; a simple bullet-style list can be very effective in helping to process a poem. Looking back at Nezhukumatathil's poem and our annotations, our notes might look like this;

- **Speaker** is talking to herself
- Clean, sterile environment (setting)
- Butchering her name & violent **imagery**
- Red/hot/blood/butcher **juxtaposed** with blue/icy/memory/family
- **Shift** in setting—goes from classroom to memory back to classroom
- Line indents start at the shift—like waves—calming breaths—like a coping technique
- Ends on an **image** of a pencil sharpener blade

The last bullet is important to note because it looks at the end of the poem.

Pro tip: As AP* Exam Readers, we've read more essays that leave out the end of the poem than those that don't. Perhaps students run out of time, or don't realize that essays that do not take into account, or even mention, the end of the poem feel incomplete. One easy way to have your essay stand out from the bunch is to discuss the last few lines of the poem. To help you achieve this, when you make your notes, write them in *chronological order* as you go through the poem, making sure you have at least one note about *each* part of the poem: the beginning, middle, and end. Later in this chapter, we will discuss the different ways you might organize your essay, and, by recording your notes in chronological order with the poem, you will be setting yourself up for success in writing a well-organized essay.

For Nezhukumatathil's "On Listening to Your Teacher Take Attendance," the last line is where much of the poem's meaning lies. Several structural moves Nezhukumatathil makes leading up to the end of the poem signal the importance of this last line:

1. She uses **anaphora** with "Think of their" repeated twice at the beginning of the final two sentences.
2. She uses **alliteration** of the letter P in the second to last line: "shar*p* pencils, a *p*ink *p*earl eraser."
3. The last **stanza** is the only singular line.

In regards to its structure, we see that the entire poem is in unrhymed couplets except for the last line, which is singular. Why might that be? It seems like the stanza is incomplete, doesn't it? Let's consider this train of thought. The subject of the final line is the third-grade students holding their little pencil sharpener with its "tiny blade." Tiny kids—tiny blade—tiny stanza? Maybe the kids aren't just tiny, but they, like the stanza, are also incomplete. As third graders, they certainly have a lot of living and learning ahead of them. When we consider the action the teacher, the butcher, is performing in the poem, which is an act of violence upon the speaker's identity (her name), we must also consider his audience. Who is learning from this teacher/butcher? The students. Students who are still innocent children patted "dry with a fluffy towel after a bath." Their biases and the ability to "butcher" names and perform other microaggressions are not yet fully realized—but they are watching. And learning. Look at them there in the last line with their "tiny blades." Will these same third-grade children grow up to be future butchers? Will their "freshly soaped necks" turn to "bloody" "handprints"? It is Nezhukumatathil's final line's singular structure and use of an image (the tiny blade) that conjure these questions from the reader. Without examining the last line, a reader would miss out on an essential argument of the poem.

Before we move on from this poem, let's look at one specific technique that you will see *a lot* in poetry. **Anaphora** is the repetition of the same word or phrase at the beginning of successive lines, clauses, or sentences. We see Nezhuku-matathil use anaphora in the last three lines:

<u>Think</u> of their pencil cases
from third grade, full of sharp pencils, a pink pearl eraser.

<u>Think</u> of their handheld pencil sharpener and its tiny blade.

There's many reasons a poet might choose to use anaphora. Poet Jon Sands, winner of the 2018 National Poetry Series, explains that anaphora can be especially useful:

- "to view a central image from a lot of different perspectives;
- to give the poem a kind of home base, or unified throughline, that allows the **similes** and metaphors that sprawl out from that image to be really adventurous;
- to create momentum and escalate the tension in the poem, propelling it forward."

While this list isn't definitive, it offers options to consider when we see anaphora in a poem. Techniques are typically pretty easy to *identify* in poems, but not always easy to *analyze*. When we notice an easy-to-spot technique like anaphora, or *any* technique for that matter, we must ask ourselves: *Why? What is it doing for the poem?* Of the options Sands gives for anaphora, perhaps the third one fits Nezhukumatathil's use the best. She is escalating the poem, propelling us along with the speaker's internal monologue to herself, her coping mechanism when dealing with microaggressions, to the "tiny blade," leaving us with a foreboding final image.

Let's try annotating a different poem. This time we will look at "Solitude" by Lord Byron, which represents two sections from his longer work *Childe Harold's Pilgrimage*. Later in this chapter, you will find student sample essays written about this poem. Please read the poem four times, following our process for each step. Compare your thoughts and annotations with ours afterward, keeping in mind that they may be different due to the open nature of poetry interpretation. Before you even start reading the poem, glance at how it looks structurally on the page. What is the first thing that you notice?

Solitude
Lord Byron

To sit on rocks, to muse o'er flood and fell,
To slowly trace the forest's shady scene,
Where things that own not man's dominion dwell,
And mortal foot hath ne'er or rarely been;
5 To climb the trackless mountain all unseen,
With the wild flock that never needs a fold;
Alone o'er steeps and foaming falls to lean;
This is not solitude, 'tis but to hold
Converse with Nature's charms, and view her stores unrolled.

10 But midst the crowd, the hurry, the shock of men,
To hear, to see, to feel and to possess,
And roam alone, the world's tired denizen,[1]
With none who bless us, none whom we can bless;
Minions of splendor shrinking from distress!
15 None that, with kindred consciousness endued,
If we were not, would seem to smile the less
Of all the flattered, followed, sought and sued;
This is to be alone; this, this is solitude!

Hopefully, you noticed that it is separated into two big stanzas. When a poet lays a poem out on the page, or in other words, crafts its structure, it is intentional, like we just saw with Nezhukumatathil's poem. A poem's structure can clue us into its meaning. Among our other noticings, let's see what we can derive from the structure of "Solitude."

Solitude
Lord Byron

To sit on rocks, to muse o'er flood and fell,   nature imagery / F alliteration

To slowly trace the forest's shady scene, "slowly," sibilance / also art words: *muse, trace*

---

1. An inhabitant, resident.

Where things that own not man's **d**ominion **d**well,   *D* alliteration

And mortal foot hath ne'er or rarely been;   unexplored territory

5   To climb the trackless mountain all unseen,   more nature

With the wild **f**lock that **n**ever **n**eeds a fold;   *F & N* alliteration, nature imagery

Alone o'er steeps and **f**oaming **f**alls to lean;   "alone" / *F*, nature imagery

This is not solitude, 'tis but to hold   important line—declarative statement

Converse with Nature's charms, and view her stores unrolled.   he talks to Nature?

10   **But** midst the **crowd**, the hurry, the shock of men,   But = shift / lots of commas

To hear, to see, to feel and to possess,   short phrases, caesuras

And roam alone, the world's tired denizen,   "roam" means they're lost / "tired"

With none who bless us, none whom   "none" & "alone" are repeated words
we can bless;

Minions of **s**plendor **s**hrinking from di**s**tre**ss!**   "minions" = negative connotation / sibilance / first exclamation mark

15   **None** that, with kindred consciousness endued,   another "none"

If we were not, would seem to smile the less

Of all the **f**lattered, **f**ollowed, sought and sued;   *F* alliteration, sibilance, commas

This is to be alone; this, this is solitude!   another "alone" / important line—THIS is solitude

Some notes we have on "Solitude" after going through the four-step reading process are as follows:

- 1st stanza = details of setting, nature imagery & appreciation → NOT solitude
- Punctuation increases in 2nd stanza—commas create short, quick phrases—rushed **syntax** like the rushed city—creates a frantic, distressed tone
- 2nd stanza = details of setting in a crowded city, chaotic → solitude
- **Ironic** that speaker feels alone in a crowd, but not when he is by himself in nature

Looking at our notes all together, we have started to form insights about the relationship between the speaker and the setting. How the speaker describes each setting (nature and a city) reveals his attitude about his surroundings, allowing us an opportunity to analyze **tone** based on the individual **connotative** details he includes for each. We also take into consideration the syntax of the poem, its use of punctuation and pacing, to create tone and meaning. Structurally, we notice a huge difference between the two stanzas, so the poem's shift is clear, signaled by the stanza break and the transitional word "but." We will return to Byron's "Solitude" in the next section on writing thesis statements, and in subsequent sections, to continue the process of working through a poem with the ultimate goal of writing an analytical essay.

Your Turn

Practice annotating with this poem by Joshua Bennett. What do you notice? What do you wonder? What literary devices stand out to you?

Ode to the Equipment Manager
JOSHUA BENNETT

In a sense, you are the valve
through which the game's hard
beauty finds its most fitting
point of egress. You who turn fist
5   swing & broken limbs into box scores,
boost a benchwarmer's prayer
with every figure you sketch
in that green book you keep, always,
flush to your chest, as if a secret
10 weakness or tale of a simpler time
long since gone rogue. Let popular culture
have its jokes, its jockstraps & sweaty socks
thrown like gossip across the locker room, the business
end landing squarely on your face each time.
15 What do they know of the math you bend
to make scholarships materialize, the scores
of glistening boys you daily break free?
It is a kind of love, I think, your tireless glare
trailing every shot, the waltz of iron
20 & wood you give back to the page, all those
small, black gifts exploding into song.

WRITING A THESIS STATEMENT

When writing a thesis statement for a Question 1 Poetry Analysis essay, there are elements that you *must* include and some that you *may* include.

Must	May
• Convey a defensible claim • Express an interpretation of literature • Respond to the prompt	• Establish a line of reasoning • Preview development of an interpretation

It is important to note that you are *not* required to list points of interpretation, literary techniques, or any specific evidence in your thesis. In fact, we encourage you to avoid writing a formulaic three-pronged, or chicken foot, thesis (see "General Writing Strategies" for more on crafting thesis statements). If an essay does not include everything from the *Must* criteria, it will not receive any points for the rubric's Row A, Thesis. For this part of the rubric, you either earn one point by meeting the required criteria for your thesis or you get zero points.

> **Pro tip:** Your thesis statement is allowed to be located anywhere in your essay. As AP® Readers, we have awarded many essays the thesis point that do not position it in the introduction paragraph. *However*, you would be setting yourself up for success *if you did* put your thesis in your introduction. We really can't stress enough that the best place for your thesis statement is most definitely in the introduction.

When stating your claim and interpretation early in your essay as your controlling argument, you are more likely to earn more points in the other rows of the rubric (Row B, Textual Evidence and Commentary, which is worth up to four points, and Row C, Sophistication, which is worth one point). The same idea applies to establishing a line of reasoning, which technically falls under the *May*, not *Must* category. Again, we strongly advise you to provide a baseline understanding—some overall big idea or insight into the poem in your thesis. The highest scoring essays' thesis statements establish a clear line of reasoning from an overall insight (consider this like a theme for the poem) about the poem that the student then works through and explains throughout the essay, always circling back to that baseline idea provided in the thesis.

If AP® Exam essay prompts focus on a work's complexity, then so should your thesis statement that answers said prompts. To achieve this, consider how a poem's intricate parts work together to formulate your interpretation. One way to think of complexity is as a *this* and a *that*. Take the *this* and the *that* and ask: *Why is the poet placing these two things together? What might this show about life or humanity? What big idea can I see connected to these two things?*

Let's look at some examples for Lord Byron's "Solitude" that would *not* earn the thesis point.

Thesis statement	Commentary
The speaker presents a complex attitude toward solitude in Lord Byron's "Solitude."	This thesis only restates the prompt.
In Lord Byron's poem, "Solitude," the poet uses diction, syntax, and imagery to convey his complex attitude toward solitude.	This thesis does not offer a defensible claim about the poem. It lists literary devices which describe features of the poem, but does not provide an interpretation.
In Lord Byron's "Solitude," the author goes through different emotions of how he feels about nature and solitude.	This thesis gets a little bit closer to earning the point but still does not offer a defensible interpretation of the poem.

Here are some examples written by students that earn the thesis point because they all provide a defensible claim and present an interpretation of the poem.

In Lord Byron's poem, "Solitude," he emphasizes that the true meaning of solitude is emotional disconnect, not being physically alone. He demonstrates this through contrasting his feelings in nature and in a crowd of people.

Lord Byron's poem, "Solitude," is about the different ways humanity experiences loneliness. Byron explores the experiences of being in the company of nature and how even in a crowd, one can feel lost and alone.

In "Solitude" by Lord Byron, the speaker is contemplating the true meaning of solitude and the difference between being alone in nature and being alone in society. The speaker displays complex thoughts of the differences in physical and mental solitude to display how the modern age has caused people to feel alone even when surrounded by others.

Let's look at a new poem. Read the following poem by Matthew Olzmann, considering its complexity. There's also a great audio of this poem read by national best-selling author John Green on the OursPoetica YouTube page, easily found with a quick internet search.

Mountain Dew Commercial Disguised as a Love Poem
Matthew Olzmann

Here's what I've got, the reasons why our marriage
might work: Because you wear pink but write poems
about bullets and gravestones. Because you yell
at your keys when you lose them, and laugh,
5 loudly, at your own jokes. Because you can hold a pistol,
gut a pig. Because you memorize songs, even commercials
from thirty years back and sing them when vacuuming.
You have soft hands. Because when we moved, the contents
of what you packed were written *inside* the boxes.
10 Because you think swans are overrated.
Because you drove me to the train station. You drove me
to Minneapolis. You drove me to Providence.
Because you underline everything you read, and circle
the things you think are important, and put stars next
15 to the things you think I should think are important,
and write notes in the margins about all the people
you're mad at and my name almost never appears there.
Because you make that pork recipe you found
in the Frida Kahlo Cookbook. Because when you read
20 that essay about Rilke, you underlined the whole thing
except the part where Rilke says love means to deny the self
and to be consumed in flames. Because when the lights
are off, the curtains drawn, and an additional sheet is nailed
over the windows, you still believe someone outside

25   can see you. And one day five summers ago,
when you couldn't put gas in your car, when your fridge
was so empty—not even leftovers or condiments—
there was a single twenty-ounce bottle of Mountain Dew,
which you paid for with your last damn dime
30   because you once overheard me say that I liked it.

What do you notice? What do you wonder? What literary devices stand out to you? Make some notes about the poem on paper.

Here are a few insightful things our students noticed about Olzmann's poem:

- I noticed the anaphora of the word *because* in the poem. Using the same word over and over again almost makes it feel like there are an infinite amount of reasons for the poet to love his significant other.
- The speaker **juxtaposes** many of the subject's actions throughout the poem (such as "you wear pink but write poems about bullets and gravestones").
- Nearly every sentence of the poem begins with *because* or is an addition to a list starting with *because* except for the last one. As a reader this adds emphasis to the final line.
- I noticed that all of the reasons why the marriage works are little things that are appreciated and that most of the lines are enjambed because the list keeps going.
- The emphasis on the last "damn dime" makes the love feel stronger.
- There are no spaces or breaks between the lines.
- The speaker uses italics to emphasize certain words and to mimic the way a person speaking would emphasize a word. They also include a lot of specific allusions to things like the Frida Kahlo cookbook and Rilke and Mountain Dew.

Here are some thesis statements written by students that would *not* earn the thesis point.

Thesis statement	Commentary
In Matthew Olzmann's "Mountain Dew Commercial Disguised as a Love Poem," Olzmann reveals his feelings towards his lover by describing all of their habits with different poetic devices.	This thesis describes features of the poem, but does not provide a defensible claim. To improve this thesis, we would suggest to specify what the feelings are exactly.
In the poem "Mountain Dew Commercial Disguised as a Love Poem" by Matthew Olzmann, there is complexity given by the speaker that is shown by the use of descriptive imagery, structure, and alliteration.	This thesis includes literary devices, but does not make a claim that requires defense. We would encourage this student to be more explicit about the speaker's complexity—to say what it is.

Here are some thesis statements written by students that would earn the thesis point because they all provide a defensible claim and present an interpretation of the poem.

In the poem "Mountain Dew Commercial Disguised as a Love Poem" by Matthew Olzmann, the speaker exemplifies how the little things in a relationship matter the most and small gestures can be more meaningful than people think.

Matthew Olzmann's "Mountain Dew Commercial Disguised as a Love Poem" highlights all of the attributes that characterize his loved one. Olzmann shows the complexity of love by noting all of the little habits that people usually feel are insignificant to demonstrate that loving someone means everything about them is unforgettable.

In Matthew Olzmann's poem "Mountain Dew Commercial Disguised as a Love Poem," Olzmann lists the major and minor reasons of why he believes his significant other and him are meant for one another. He reveals that people can admire even what may seem like small parts or qualities of a person, and this admiration for the little things can result in unconditional love for someone.

Your Turn

Please refer back to Gwendolyn Brooks's poem "We Real Cool" from earlier in the chapter, on page 60. Write a thesis statement that responds to the prompt below. Remember a thesis must be defensible and provide an interpretation of the poem.

In "We Real Cool" by Gwendolyn Brooks, the speaker observes a group of youth hanging out at the pool hall during school hours. Read the poem carefully. Then, in a well-written essay, analyze how Brooks uses literary elements to portray her complex observations and feelings about the young men's actions.

SELECTING EVIDENCE AND WRITING COMMENTARY

Selecting Evidence

Finding textual evidence to include in your essay will be easy if you follow the four-step reading process. By underlining, making annotations, and taking notes, you have already signaled to yourself important elements of the poem and have begun the process of connecting them. To select appropriate evidence, find *short* phrases from the poem to work into your body paragraphs. Pick out phrases that illustrate the literary techniques you notice, as well as specific words or details that carry a lot of weight in the poem. From the notes you wrote on the page underneath the prompt, try to find a specific phrase in the poem that you could point to and say, "I see that happening here."

For example, the first note we made about the poem "Solitude" by Lord Byron reads:

- 1st stanza = details of setting, nature imagery & appreciation → NOT solitude

Find a phrase in the poem that you could put your finger on where you see each of these elements happening. You might point to "forest's shady scene," "wild flock," and "foaming falls" for details of setting and nature imagery, and particularly connotative words like "muse," "Nature's charms," and "stores" as evidence for the speaker's appreciation of nature. Finally, to check off all items in the note, you could point to "This is not solitude" and "converse with" to illustrate that when we are in nature, we are not in solitude. Notice how we pointed to *multiple* phrases for each of our points, as the goal is to provide sufficient evidence, in terms of both quantity and quality.

Repeating this process for each of your notes will organically produce the controlling ideas, or line of reasoning, for your essay. If you think of each bulleted note as a body paragraph (or maybe a couple of bullets could be combined into one body paragraph), selecting a phrase in the poem for each note ensures that you will have specific textual evidence throughout your essay for all of your points. Remember when we encouraged you to write your notes about the poem in chronological order? Here is where we really see the benefits of that strategy paying off. If each chronological bullet of notes turns into a more fully developed body paragraph including specific phrases from the poem as textual evidence, your essay will be logically organized. We will go into more depth later in this chapter on the various ways to organize a Poetry Analysis essay.

Integrating Evidence

In chapter 2, we introduced the concept of using *quote sprinkles*, or short phrases of quoted evidence integrated smoothly into the body of your essay. The student whose work appears below effectively uses quote sprinkles (which we have underlined) in this first body paragraph addressing Byron's first stanza of "Solitude." Notice how his embedded quotes read seamlessly with his own syntax and how he includes several quote sprinkles spread out fairly evenly throughout the paragraph.

> **Pro tip:** It is important that you have multiple examples when it comes to textual evidence—quantity matters!

> In the first stanza, Lord Byron shows how the beauty and mechanisms of mother nature do not let us feel alone when we are in the wild. Lord Byron uses imagery to reveal mother nature's caring hands like we are a child in untouched territory. We are with the "wild flock" in nature to guide against the "trackless mountain" and "forest's shady scene." The imagery in the first stanza reveals that when we are camping

or taking a stroll in mother nature's realm, we are truly not
alone in the unsearched lands. We are to "<u>converse with
nature's charms</u>" and not feel alone. There is always something with us, like a "<u>wild flock</u>" when climbing up a mountain.
Every step we take is another step in which we are in awe of
"<u>nature's charms</u>."

In this one body paragraph, this student manages to include six quote sprinkles, all smoothly integrated into the interpretation and analysis. Furthermore, they all support the claim stated in the paragraph's topic sentence, which is that "Lord Byron shows how the beauty and mechanisms of mother nature do not let us feel alone." This topic sentence was derived from the first bulleted note we made as part of our four-step reading process. The student took the note and transformed it into a complete sentence. We know that the quotations are effectively integrated because if you closed your eyes and had someone read the paragraph out loud to you, you would not be able to tell where the quoted excerpts fall. Notice there are no introductory phrases to each quote, such as "when Byron says" or "the author writes." Moreover, this student does not use the dreaded phrase "this quote shows that . . ." Rather, by successfully embedding sufficient textual evidence smoothly and cohesively throughout the paragraph, the student avoids clumps and allows the syntax to read seamlessly. The next body paragraph would follow the same process for the next note about the poem.

Writing Commentary

Commentary is where you do your explaining. Any time you *identify* something in a poem, whether it be a literary device, a potent word, or striking image, you need to *explain* what it is doing in the poem. Some questions to consider when writing commentary are:

1. How does this piece of evidence or literary element help to illustrate meaning in the poem?
2. How does this piece of evidence or literary element affect the tone or mood of the poem?
3. How does this piece of evidence or literary element connect back to the paragraph's topic sentence claim?
4. How does all of the evidence provided in this paragraph work together to support the thesis statement?

Each body paragraph discusses a claim that supports your thesis, and the commentary in each paragraph should justify the selected textual evidence by explaining why it is included and connect back to the claim made in the paragraph's topic sentence. Ideally, at the end of each paragraph, once all of the evidence is provided and explained through your commentary, there should be a clear connection back to the overall argument made in the thesis statement.

In addition to what we've already covered about supporting claims, there are a couple more things you will need to do to get the maximum number of points for the Evidence and Commentary row (Row B) on the essay rubric. The Evidence and Commentary section is the only one worth more than one point; you can actually earn a total of *four* points. Therefore, you want to spend maximum time and effort in finding apt and specific evidence, and explaining its significance to the poem and your interpretation.

- You must explain how *multiple* literary elements or techniques contribute to the poem's meaning. This means that you will need to identify and discuss more than one literary device, including textual evidence, and explicitly explain how the technique helps to create meaning in the poem.
- You also need to analyze the importance of specific words and details, meaning that you have to go beyond a generalized discussion of the poem or a simple paraphrase. Getting into the nitty-gritty of the poem—its *specific* details and connotative words—along with distinctly explaining how several literary techniques are working in the poem—will offer you the best chance at earning the maximum score for Evidence and Commentary.

To reiterate, you have to go beyond just identifying a literary technique and providing quotes from the poem that show the technique in use. *You must always follow identification with explanation.* Here is a body paragraph from an essay on Byron's "Solitude" that could be improved by adding more commentary to the underlined section:

> To reveal the stark difference between the old times and new times, Lord Byron uses specific stanza breaks. When reading stanza 1, it is a melodious, soothing stanza with "foaming walls to lean" and to be one with "nature's charm, and view her stores unrolled." However, stanza 2 is accelerated to a pace where the reader feels tension and anxiety. Much like the feelings one would feel if they were walking in the streets of New York, stanza 2's pace demonstrates the emotions of solitude in our own cities and suburban areas. We are filled with human friends, but we feel most alone when we are with them because we see no one "to smile" towards or "to hear, to see, to feel." We are ironically truly alone when we are amongst others.

First, we commend this essay for its use of smoothly embedded quote sprinkles. But notice where the writer identifies that the pacing of the second stanza is accelerated. Pacing is a literary technique, and the writer even offers an effect of the device, but does not explain *how* the pacing is produced. The essay goes from point A to point C without stopping at B to make the connection between A and C. What specifically about the stanza causes it to accelerate its pace? If this paragraph was scored in isolation, we would give it three out of four possible points for Evidence and Commentary. To earn the full four points, the essay would have to include more commentary about *how* the pacing is created. For example, the writer might explain how Byron's use of commas dramatically increases in the second stanza, resulting in a flood of short choppy phrases. Pair that with the poem's first use of exclamation marks, and heavily connotative words like "distress," "crowd," and "tired," and we can see how the increased pace mirrors the chaotic, stressful hubbub of a busy city.

The first body paragraph from the next student essay on Byron's "Solitude" successfully integrates specific evidence and explanatory commentary:

> The poem is split into 2 stanzas; the first is all about solitude in nature. The alliteration between pairs of words drives home the idea that the speaker is never truly alone. Like the pairs of words such as "flood and fell," "shady scene," and "dominion dwell," the speaker's metaphorical partner in this scene is nature. The speaker says so in the last 2 lines of the poem: "This is not solitude, 'tis but to hold / Converse with Nature's charms." The experience of being one with nature is common for many people. The relaxed pace of the first stanza shows that the speaker themself is at ease. Most of the lines in the first stanza are end-stopped, which gives the reader a pause between each line. This brings about a feeling of thoughtfulness in both the reader and the speaker, which is directly contrasted in the second stanza.

This student identifies multiple literary techniques, provides textual evidence, addresses *how* each technique is produced, and how they operate in the poem to create meaning. The essay even includes a transition in the last sentence to the next body paragraph (which discusses the second stanza). Advice we would give to improve this body paragraph would be to develop the topic sentence to be more analytical, and to break up the long quote chunk in the middle. But even with these minor issues, if this paragraph were to be graded in isolation (assuming the rest of the essay is of similar caliber), it has hit all of the criteria for Evidence and Commentary to earn the full four points.

HOW TO ORGANIZE A POETRY ANALYSIS ESSAY

How you organize your essay, and the body paragraphs within your essay, are key elements in creating a *line of reasoning*. As discussed in chapter 2, a line of reasoning is the collection of major points you make to support your thesis; these points often become body paragraph topic sentences. Earlier, we advised you to read a poem at least four times, then to jot down some notes, ideally in chronological order. Maybe your teacher has shared another effective strategy for reading and analyzing a poem in preparation for writing an essay. When it comes time for exam day, understanding that you are under the pressure of time, however you can best manage to get your thoughts down about the poem is really up to you. The notes might look like a chaotic mess of arrows and carets (^), but all that matters is that *you* understand them. The more times you practice going through this process, the faster and more efficient you will get at it. The notes you take provide you with both an outline for your essay and a foundation for a line of reasoning. There are three ways to effectively organize a Poetry Analysis essay, although some are more effective than others:

1. By a chronological walk-through of the poem
2. By insights about the poem
3. By literary techniques

The student writers excerpted earlier in the chapter all organized their essays with chronological excerpts. After their introduction, which included their thesis, their first body paragraph tackled the first stanza, the second body paragraph analyzed the second stanza, and the rest of the essay dealt with the tension and complexity of both stanzas together. Each body paragraph included a topic sentence with a claim, textual evidence, and commentary. Chronological order essays are logical, and as long as each body paragraph ties back to the controlling claim in the thesis, they are typically successful in establishing a line of reasoning.

Another successful way to organize a Poetry Analysis essay is by insights, or ideas. Let's review the notes we made for "Solitude":

- 1st stanza = details of setting, nature imagery & appreciation → NOT solitude
- Punctuation increases in 2nd stanza—commas creates short, quick phrases— rushed syntax like the rushed city—creates a frantic, distressed tone
- 2nd stanza = details of setting in a crowded city, chaotic → solitude
- Ironic that speaker feels alone in a crowd, but not when he is by himself in nature

This thesis statement (shared previously in the thesis statement section) reads:

> In "Solitude" by Lord Byron, the speaker is contemplating the true meaning of solitude and the difference between being alone in nature and being alone in society. The speaker displays complex thoughts of the differences in physical and mental solitude to display how the modern age has caused people to feel alone even when surrounded by others.

Body paragraph topic sentences can stem from the different insights we have about the poem, which we derive from our annotations, notes, and interpretations. If we use this student's thesis, topic sentences based on insights might look like this:

1. Lord Byron emphasizes the true meaning of connection by describing the peace he feels in nature.

2. While the speaker is physically alone in nature, he only feels emotionally alone in a crowded city, showing that solitude can be felt differently in contrasting settings.

3. The chaos of modern life has only served to drive us apart as a society, and the only place the speaker feels companionship anymore is in nature.

The most sophisticated essays combine both of these organizational techniques in that their topic sentences include an insight *and* they are presented in chronological order. Ideally, topic sentences should say something analytical about the poem—an insight—and present these in a logical manner, from the beginning of the poem to the end. Here are topic sentences from an essay combining insights and chronological organization. You can read the full essay later in the Student Sample Essays section of this chapter.

Thesis statement	In Lord Byron's poem, "Solitude," he emphasizes that the true meaning of solitude is emotional disconnect, not being physically alone. He demonstrates this through contrasting his feelings in nature and in a crowd of people.
Topic sentence 1	Lord Byron emphasizes the true meaning of connection by describing the peace he feels in nature. *(This topic sentence provides an insight and the paragraph goes on to analyze the first stanza of the poem.)*
Topic sentence 2	Lord Byron continues to delve into the concept of solitude by contrasting the peace he feels in nature with being surrounded by people. *(This topic sentence includes a transition and an insight, and the paragraph is focused on the second stanza.)*
Topic sentence 3	After explaining his experiences in nature and in a crowd of people, Lord Byron finally unearths what he believes to be the true meaning of solitude at the end of the poem. *(This topic sentence includes a transition and introduces the final insight; the paragraph specifically explores the end of the poem.)*

Organizing an essay by chronological insights that explore the poem from beginning to end proves to AP® Readers that you understand the poem as a whole text and how its complex parts work together to shape your interpretation of it.

The final way to organize an essay is by literary technique, and we would argue that this way is usually the least effective of the three options. Think of this option as a last resort only. Remember that AP® Readers are looking for your interpretation—your thoughts and analysis—of the poem and explanation of how literary elements support your thoughts. *Your thoughts* are what should drive your essay (and therefore your paragraphs), *not* your ability to find literary techniques. In other words, the devices should support your thoughts, not the other way around.

Using the same notes and the same student's thesis, technique-driven topic sentences might look like this:

1. Byron uses imagery to describe the beauty of nature.
2. Byron uses increased punctuation, such as commas and exclamation marks, to quicken the pace of the poem.
3. The stanza break Byron employs separates the ideas of the two stanzas.
4. The tone in the second stanza is distressed and chaotic, which is created by connotative words and short phrasing.

There's nothing *wrong* with these topic sentences, but they do not share the same level of sophistication when they are grounded in a technique versus an insight. Technique-based topic sentences sound more formulaic, and we find that there is less cohesiveness to the essays as a whole. This is not to say that techniques don't belong in your essay. They do! Just don't make them the star focus of each paragraph.

> **Pro tip:** We suggest you organize each body paragraph with the following in mind:
>
> 1. Start each body paragraph with a chronologically ordered topic sentence that includes an analytical insight about the poem (derived from your notes).
> 2. The following sentences within the paragraph should introduce a literary technique (or multiple ones if they work together, as seen in the student's sample body paragraph) that functions to illustrate the insight being discussed, along with sprinkles of textual evidence and commentary connecting back to the insight.
> 3. Toward the end of the paragraph, circle back to your thesis statement by tying all of the evidence and commentary together. Finally, if it comes naturally, include a transition to your next paragraph.

SOPHISTICATION

In order to earn the final point on the AP® Exam essay rubric, the one awarded for sophistication, you should be aware of the following techniques. As stated in the previous section, one strategy to bump you toward earning the point is to consistently tie back to the thematic idea identified in your thesis statement, or in other words, an overall message or meaning of the poem. When doing so, be sure to use echo words, or synonyms, to avoid repetitive phrasing. Repeating the same theme over and over will actually hinder your ability to earn the point for sophistication, so synonyms are important. Also something that we've already discussed in this chapter is *complexity*. By structuring your thesis as a *this* and *that* involving the intricacies of the poem, which add together to equal an overall meaning in the poem, you are well on your way to earning this point, provided that you successfully support all parts of your thesis in your essay.

Another way to earn this point is to explain the relevance of an interpretation within a broader context—however, this must be a substantial part of your argument, not just a one-sentence reference tied on at the end. A broader context might be situating the poem in its historical or cultural context, or discussing how the poem specifically connects to society today. This student essay exemplifies how to do this successfully, here at the end of the essay connecting "Solitude" to its historical context and genre of the Romantic period:

> This poem speaks to a larger motif in poetry, especially in the Romantic Era of literature. Nature was seen as higher than human civilization. Lord Byron himself was a Romantic, and it is clear that influenced his work. The experience of losing yourself in everyday life was common, especially during the Industrial Age when nature was becoming less and less important. This poem offers a different view on the concept of solitude, claiming that we are more isolated in a crowd than alone in nature.

This student essay also explains the poem's relevance within a broader context, but in this case by taking a connection-to-modern-day approach:

> Much like the feelings one would feel if they were walking in the streets of New York, stanza 2's pace demonstrates the emotions of solitude in our own cities and suburban areas. We are filled with human friends, but we feel most alone when we are with them because we see no one "to smile" towards or "to hear, to see, to feel." We are ironically truly alone when we are amongst others.
>
> We are driven through a range of emotions throughout this poem. We experience tranquil imagery of nature, but then we are shifted to the hurried, alone feelings of the cities we have created. The poem portrays how humans have created their own dystopia by creating cities. We have filled our cities with the most extravagant, awesome activities, but many of us do not know each other, neither ever talked to each other. We have lost our ways of connecting to mother nature and also the way of connecting to other souls.

Another small thing you can do to create a flow from one thought to the next is to use transitional words throughout your essay that connect your paragraphs. Also, use parallel structure whenever you include multiple items in a list-like form in a sentence. There is no one way to earn the point for sophistication, but these are some tips to help you get there.

One last note on what *not* to do before we move on. Something we see often as teachers and AP® Readers is students trying to sound smarter than they are. We do not doubt that you are an intelligent individual; you are in a college-level class. But when writing becomes distorted with forced formality, it no longer sounds natural. One way to avoid writing outside of your voice is to avoid using words you aren't really sure of. Unless you know—*really* know—what a word means and how to use it correctly in a sentence, it's best not to employ it in an essay. On the other hand, you don't want to write like you are talking to your best friend either. Slang, a steady stream of *like*, and other especially informal elements don't belong in your essay. Finding the balance—sounding like yourself while maintaining a degree of academic professionalism is the sweet spot. Allow your writer's voice to shine. AP® Readers honestly enjoy essays where we can hear a student's voice. We much prefer your natural voice over contrived propriety. Be bold. Take risks. Write that sarcastic comment about the speaker's melodramatic exaggeration of a first-world problem. You might just make your AP® Reader laugh or nod in agreement, and your risk will pay off.

TIPS FOR WRITING INTRODUCTIONS AND CONCLUSIONS

While the Poetry Analysis essay does not officially score you on introductions or conclusions, they can offer you a chance to impress. See chapter 2, "General Writing Strategies," for more information on writing these sections, as here we will only discuss how they pertain to this particular essay question.

Introductions

You do not have time to write a full-blown introduction paragraph. Nor do you have time to invent some catchy attention-grabber. Considering where the majority of your points come from on the rubric, you need to focus on your body paragraphs, which ought to be full of insights, evidence, and commentary. As AP® Readers, we will not take points off of your score for not having a typical introduction as might be seen in more revised papers. This is a *rough draft*. Taking all of this into mind, we suggest you write a two-sentence introduction that includes the following:

1. One sentence that includes the author, title of poem, and brief general statement of what the poem is literally about
2. Your thesis statement

That's it. If you tend to write long thesis statements that get convoluted, break it up into two sentences. A one- or two-sentence thesis statement is perfectly acceptable. If you find yours is a little long, to test it for clarity, read it out loud to yourself. Do you get out of breath and start to sound like you are rambling? If so, then it is too long and you should consider splitting it into two sentences. End your introduction with your thesis statement and hop right into your first body paragraph.

Conclusions

Because students have limited time to write their essay, AP* Readers do not expect a fully developed conclusion. One sentence will suffice if it serves to wrap up all of your ideas. An ineffective move we often see is repetition of the thesis statement as the conclusion. While this isn't going to lose you any points, it's not going to help you get the Sophistication point. Here are some options for writing a successful conclusion:

- Close your essay with the close of the poem. Is there something from the culminating lines in the poem that would also serve as a concluding thought to your essay?
- End with a question to consider. As you were annotating and making notes on the poem, did a question arise from the poem that you could include as a final thought in your conclusion?
- Close your essay with a connection to modern society. This one can be tricky because it runs the risk of sounding forced, and you don't want to get too personal either. Take this route only if you feel confident about it.
- If all else fails, end by restating your thesis, taking significant effort to use synonyms and different syntax (especially the order of your words).

THE BIG THREE

At the end of each of the three essay chapters, we are providing you with THE BIG THREE, a list of three literary elements that you can analyze 99.9 percent of the time for the specific type of literature you will tackle for the exam's essays: (1) poetry, (2) a short prose passage, and (3) a full-length work. When it comes to poetry, there are some literary devices that will occur more frequently than in other modes of writing. Chances are that no matter which poem the College Board includes for the Poetry Analysis essay, you will be able to analyze it with any of THE BIG THREE.

1. Line Structure: End-Stopped or Enjambed and the Caesura

When poets craft a poem, they must decide where to end each line. There are two choices. The line is either end-stopped or enjambed.

- **End-stopped** lines contain a complete sentence, clause, or thought, which creates a distinct pause at the end of the line. The line may or may not end with punctuation, but there is always a sense of finality, or a finished idea, at the end of the line.
- The term **enjambment** comes from the French word meaning *stride over* or *straddle*. An enjambed line contains incomplete syntax because the

sentence, clause, or idea flows over into the next line. There is no punctuation at the end of an enjambed line. So why might a poet choose to use enjambment? There are a few possibilities:

- Enjambment naturally creates an emphasis on the last word of the line and the first word of the next line. The poet is calling attention to these two words by forcing a pause with the line break. The first two lines of R. A. Villanueva's "Annus Mirabilis" exemplifies this effect, resulting in a suspenseful and surprising line break:

  > From the shallows our son watches me play
  > dead. He sits on river rocks chucking sand,

  Our immediate impression in the first line is of a parent and a son playing in shallow water; sounds like a nice father-son outing. Ending the first line on the word "play" allows a brief moment for the reader to fill in the blank with guesses of what he might be playing. Volleyball? Parcheesi? But then Villanueva hits us with "dead" in the next line, a jarring and unexpected word. This surprise, this tension, is something we keep in mind as we read the rest of the poem.

- Enjambment can also create a more relaxed, leisurely pace, as seen in these lines of Robert Frost's "Out, Out—":

  > And from there those that lifted eyes could count
  > Five mountain ranges one behind the other
  > Under the sunset far into Vermont.

  The sprawling mountain range of the poem's pastoral setting is highlighted by Frost's use of enjambment. The line breaks stretch ideas across lines, just as the mountains reach "far into" the distance. This expansive natural setting is soon to be rudely interrupted, however, with the entrance of a buzz saw and end-stopped lines.

- A **caesura** is a pause within a line of poetry, often produced by the use of punctuation. Caesuras are easy to spot, and it's often easy to come up with an idea of why the poet wants you to take a pause in that exact spot. Is there some imagined action that might be taking place in the pause? Is it a pause to provide a moment of response or contemplation from the reader? Does it serve as a shift or moment of finality? Percy Bysshe Shelley uses a caesura in the first line of "Adonais: An Elegy on the Death of John Keats":

  > I weep for Adonais—he is dead!

The speaker is weeping for the death of his dear friend. The caesura might be an imagined action of the speaker collecting himself, taking a moment to pause before he continues. He might be taking a heaving breath in between heavy sobs. He might be crying so uncontrollably he can only manage to sputter out short abrupt phrases. He might be pausing to brace himself for what comes after the pause—the proclamation of death. As you can see, a caesura provides us with a variety of interpretations, all of which are reasonable and, in this case, help to ultimately characterize the speaker and reflect the poem's elegiac nature.

We chose line structure as the first of THE BIG THREE because every line in every poem is going to be either end-stopped or enjambed. Can you find just *one* line break where you see the effect of ending or continuing the line? Or one profound pause? One is all it takes, and noticing a nuance like a line break or a well-placed caesura will impress your Readers.

2. Sound Devices

Sound is next, and there's a good reason why a popular poetry anthology is titled *Sound and Sense*. Sound is essential to poetry. Like linear construction, sound can be found in every poem. Poet Alexander Pope writes about how the sounds of a poem should be crafted with extreme care and purpose in his poem "Sound and Sense":

> The sound must seem an echo to the sense:
> Soft is the strain when Zephyr gently blows,
> And the smooth stream in smoother numbers flows;
> But when loud surges lash the sounding shore,
> The hoarse, rough verse should like the torrent roar;

- **Euphony** and **cacophony**
  Look for lines that are particularly euphonic (pleasant to the ear) or cacophonic (ugly sounding). Soft sounds created by letters like *M, L, W,* and *S* are euphonic and could very well be paired with a pleasing image or tone in the poem. In Pope's lines from "Sound and Sense" above, the soft *S, W,* and *M* sounds in lines 2 and 3 create euphony simulating a gentle breeze.

  Cacophony is created by harsh sounds of the letters *R, K, T, P,* and so on. Check to see if the use of cacophony is paired with a disgusted tone, foul image, or generally anything negative. In line 5 of Pope's poem, the *R, K,* and *T* sounds mirror the "hoarse, rough verse."

- Alliteration, **consonance, assonance,** and **sibilance**
  When we identify alliteration, consonance, and assonance, we have to ask why the poet is using it with those particular words. Does the sound of the repeated letters mimic a sound in the poem, such as in the first lines of Shakespeare's sonnet 12?

> When I do count the clock that tells the time,
> And see the brave day sunk in hideous night;
> When I behold the violet past prime,
> And sable curls all silver'd o'er with white;

As our students notice in their sample essays, which you will read in the next section, these lines use alliteration to mimic the sound of a clock ticking to reinforce a main idea in the poem: that time is running out and death is approaching. If the sound of the letters don't mimic a sound, then ask why would the poet want to call attention to those particular words? Why create emphasis on those words by using a sound device?

Sibilance is a specific form of consonance with the repeated use of *S* and/or *Sh* sounds. It can mimic the sound of a whisper, a strong wind, or even a serpent. In Pope's "Sound and Sense," the sibilance in the line "But when loud surges lash the sounding shore," mimics the sound of the waves crashing on the shore. The *S* and *Sh* sounds are prolonged, so they can slow down the pacing of a line, or offer an extra moment's pause for contemplation, as seen in Hamlet's famous and extremely contemplative "To be or not to be" soliloquy, which is full of sibilance.

3. Speaker

Every poem has a speaker, which is why it makes our BIG THREE. It's usually a human speaker, but not always. On a previous AP® Exam, students had to analyze a poem where the speaker is a hawk. Another—a dog. But most of the time, you will encounter a human voice as the speaker of the poem. It is important to remember that we can *never assume the speaker is the poet.* Think back to Aimee Nezhukumatathil's poem at the beginning of the chapter. There is an inclination to claim that Nezhukumatathil is the speaker of the poem because of her last name and the whole attendance debacle that happens in the poem. But the speaker in the poem is younger and a student herself, so Nezhukumatathil *the poet* is not actually the speaker. It might be a remembered version of her past self, but the adult poet Nezhukumatathil is not the speaker. Even when a poem sounds autobiographical, without knowing for sure whether it is or not, it is always safer to err on the side of caution and to separate the speaker from the poet.

Exploring the speaker is an entrance into analyzing characterization and tone. After reading a poem four times, ask yourself what you know of the speaker and how you know it. What specific textual details help show the speaker's perspective and relationship to the subject of the poem? For example, we learn that the speaker in Shakespeare's sonnet 12, who takes notice of the "violet past prime," his "sable curls all silver'd o'er with white," and all the things around him shriveling up and losing their vitality, is consumed with aging and mortality.

STUDENT SAMPLE ESSAYS

We have discussed Lord Byron's "Solitude" at length in this chapter. Here is the prompt our student writers were given and two scored sample essays with commentary.

AP® English Literature and Composition Free-Response Questions

Question 1

(Suggested time—40 minutes. This question counts as one-third of the total essay section score.)

In the following poem "Solitude" by Lord Byron (1812), the speaker considers contrasting settings. Read the poem carefully. Then, in a well-written essay, analyze how Byron uses poetic elements and techniques to portray the speaker's complex attitude toward solitude.

Solitude
Lord Byron

To sit on rocks, to muse o'er flood and fell,
To slowly trace the forest's shady scene,
Where things that own not man's dominion dwell,
And mortal foot hath ne'er or rarely been;
5 To climb the trackless mountain all unseen,
With the wild flock that never needs a fold;
Alone o'er steeps and foaming falls to lean;
This is not solitude, 'tis but to hold
Converse with Nature's charms, and view her stores unrolled.

10 But midst the crowd, the hurry, the shock of men,
To hear, to see, to feel and to possess,
And roam alone, the world's tired denizen,[1]
With none who bless us, none whom we can bless;
Minions of splendor shrinking from distress!
15 None that, with kindred consciousness endued,
If we were not, would seem to smile the less
Of all the flattered, followed, sought and sued;
This is to be alone; this, this is solitude!

---

1. An inhabitant, resident.

STUDENT SAMPLE ESSAY 1

In the poem, "Solitude," Lord Byron explains the conditions necessary for solitude and peacefulness. He reveals that there is a separation or difference between being physically isolated and mentally secluded, which can affect the nature of humanity.

Throughout the poem, Lord Byron discusses the differences between being in nature as opposed to being in the city. He does this by breaking up the poem into two stanzas so that the stanzas juxtapose one another. In the first stanza, the speed of the poem is quite slow. It uses longer phrases such as "climb the trackless mountain" and "to sit on rocks," which suggests that the speaker is very at peace, and perhaps admiring nature, in this setting. By structuring the poem in this manner, it mirrors the main idea of the stanza. In fact, Byron says that humanity is constantly in the company of nature, which means that nature "is not solitude." This seems misleading or contradicting to popular belief because most would think of themselves to be alone when physically by themselves and separated from others.

In the second stanza, Byron places emphasis on the hustle and bustle of city-life. He does this by shortening the phrases in this stanza, which supports the main idea of the stanza, but also reflects the urban setting. The crowds of people that are associated with urban areas highlight "the hurry" and fast-paced nature of cities. Byron claims that "this is solitude" because no one is focused on anyone other than themselves. Despite being "midst a crowd," people are only looking out for themselves, which eliminates the stress of caring or being concerned for others.

The poem "Solitude" highlights the ambiguity surrounding the selfishness of human nature. Being in solitude helps people to eliminate any anxiety they may have towards the burden that is having to constantly worry about others. By ridding themselves of this stress, people are able to feel calm and at peace with themselves alone, which may help them to increase their self-worth. However, by only focusing on themselves as individuals, they fail to connect with the larger world and may tend to only look out for their best interests.

Score: 1-2-0

The essay earns the thesis statement point because it provides a defensible claim and an interpretation of the poem in the two sentences of the introduction. It earns two out of four points for Evidence and Commentary because it needs more textual evidence and targeted analysis in the body paragraphs. The first body paragraph is the strongest, but the other two need more development. What other techniques could be discussed besides the stanza break and long/short phrases? We suggest including more specific techniques along with those. There is an attempt for a broader context connection in the last paragraph, but it is unsuccessful due to lacking any discussion of the poem.

STUDENT SAMPLE ESSAY 2

As an established Romantic poet, Lord Byron often preaches the profound beauty of nature. In Lord Byron's poem, "Solitude," he emphasizes that the true meaning of solitude is emotional disconnect, not being physically alone. He demonstrates this through contrasting his feelings in nature and in a crowd of people.

Lord Byron emphasizes the true meaning of connection by describing the peace he feels in nature. In the first stanza, he uses descriptive imagery to prompt the reader to imagine the peaceful images of the natural landscape, such as the "foaming falls" and "the forest's shady scene." By describing nature in a good light, the reader can vicariously feel the solace he experiences when he is alone in nature. The beauty of nature grounds him to the true meaning of connection with the Earth. Additionally, he personifies nature to even further explore the connection he feels in nature when he says, "Converse with Nature's charms, and view her stores unrolled." By making it seem as though he is talking with nature, he explains that although he may be physically alone, he feels such a deep relationship with the natural elements of the Earth that he does not feel emotionally alone and feels safe enough in this setting to "converse" with nature.

Lord Byron continues to delve into the concept of solitude by contrasting the peace he feels in nature with being surrounded by people. At the very beginning of the second stanza, he utilizes quick, list-like phrases such as "the hurry, the shock of men, to hear, to see, to feel and to possess." Quickening the pace of the poem, Lord Byron is attempting to mimic the chaos of being surrounded by other people. Further, it is such a fast-paced environment that there is no time to slow down and truly connect with one's higher self, as one can do in nature. Nor can he slow down to build relationships with others. This can explain his feelings of disconnect, which he expresses when he says he "roam[s] alone." This fast, chaotic pace in the second stanza, when contrasted with the slow and peaceful pace of the first stanza, also highlights his dislike of crowds. Further, by splitting his description of nature and crowds into two different stanzas, he prompts the reader to compare the two and see the benefits of finding peace in nature, away from the hustle of humanity.

After explaining his experiences in nature and in a crowd of people, Lord Byron finally unearths what he believes to be the true meaning of solitude at the end of the poem. In the last line, he confesses that being in a crowd "is to be alone; this, this is solitude!" The build-up of the fast, busy pace of the last stanza allows for this catharsis where he is finally able to express his feelings of isolation in a crowd after describing it. Simultaneously, this catharsis exposes an irony in his statement. Although he is surrounded by people and is not physically alone, he cannot seem to bridge connections with others or ground himself in this setting, making him feel both emotionally and spiritually alone. This is emphasized through his use of depressing diction, such as "tired," "distress," and "alone." These words create a heavy and depressing tone, further shedding light on the emotional depravity he feels. This, in contrast to his beautiful, peaceful imagery he utilizes when he describes his time in nature demonstrates his distaste for humanity and the fast-paced world they have created.

Lord Byron's depiction of humanity is timeless, and serves as a reminder even to this day. When one gets caught up in humanity's fabrications and constructions, one can feel disconnected, which Lord Byron believes can be aided when one spends time in nature and finds peace within oneself. By doing so, one can venture one step closer to finding the true purpose of life.

Score: 1-4-1

This essay earns the Thesis point because it has a defensible thesis statement that offers an interpretation of the poem. The essay successfully presents a logical and well-organized line of reasoning. It earns all four points for Evidence and Commentary because it includes specific textual evidence and robust, persuasive commentary that explains consistently how the evidence supports the line of reasoning, and analyzes how multiple literary devices, such as pacing, structure, and tone, contribute to the poem's meaning. The Sophistication point is awarded because the writer effectively describes the complexities and tensions within the poem, and uses prose that is vivid and persuasive throughout the essay. Overall, this response demonstrates sophisticated thought and presents a complex literary argument.

· · ·

On the following pages, you will find two brand-new poems to practice going through the entire process from first reading to essay writing as a seamless process, as you will be expected to do on the AP® Exam. The first poem includes student sample essays with scorer's commentary. The final poem will be a true measure of your skills in that all you have to work with is the text. No notes, no student samples. Just you and the poem.

AP® English Literature and Composition Free-Response Questions

Question 1

(Suggested time—40 minutes. This question counts as one-third of the total essay section score.)

Carefully read sonnet 12 by William Shakespeare (1609). Follow the steps recommended earlier in this chapter. Then, in a well-organized essay, analyze how Shakespeare uses poetic elements and techniques to portray the speaker's complex attitude toward time and mortality.

Sonnet 12
WILLIAM SHAKESPEARE

When I do count the clock that tells the time,
And see the brave day sunk in hideous night;
When I behold the violet past prime,
And sable curls all silver'd o'er with white;
5   When lofty trees I see barren of leaves
Which erst from heat did canopy the herd,
And summer's green all girded up in sheaves
Borne on the bier[1] with white and bristly beard,
Then of thy[2] beauty do I question make,
10   That thou among the wastes of time must go,
Since sweets and beauties do themselves forsake
And die as fast as they see others grow;
    And nothing 'gainst Time's scythe can make defence
    Save breed,[3] to brave him when he takes thee hence.

Before you read the following student sample essays on this poem, pause to go through the process to excavate the prompt, read the poem four times, take notes, and write an essay, applying what you have learned in this chapter.

---

1. At a funeral, the stand a corpse or coffin is placed on to lie in state or to be carried to the grave.
2. Sonnet 12 is included in the sonnets addressed to a "Fair Youth."
3. To have children.

STUDENT SAMPLE ESSAY 1

Shakespeare describes time as ever-changing and beautiful but also as a powerful figure as he reveals that time swallows all things in its path except for the teachings and memories we pass onto our children. He uses a multitude of techniques to show the reader how time is the dictator of everyone's life.

In the first line, he mimics a clock with his diction. "When I do count the clock that tells the time," the sound of the c's and the t's remind me of a clock ticking as time moves forward, changing the things around it. He explains the changing things around him from hair to the seasons to the days, in order to reveal to the reader how time is controlling everything. He specifically chooses the season's because winter symbolizes death, which is what time has in store for all of us. He adds complexity by giving an exception that can survive time, and that is the children that live on far longer than we.

Shakespeare compares time to the grim reaper by equipping it with a scythe. This is a worthy allusion because time will kill all things at some point. He has a complex relationship with time, first remarking its beauty in the changing seasons, then questioning time's motives. He comes to the conclusion that the only thing to survive time's wrath will be our children and the things we pass on to them, but I would challenge that conclusion because given enough time, it is believed the whole universe will end at some point, taking life with it no matter how many children we have.

Shakespeare shows us the power, beauty, and ruthlessness of time in order to convey the message that our ideas can only live on through our offspring. He successfully reveals the complexity time carries and the only defense we may have against it.

Score: 1-2-0

This student's thesis statement answers the prompt, presents a defensible claim, and includes an overall insight into the poem. The first body paragraph discusses alliteration but never actually identifies the technique. The writer also does not include more than one piece of textual evidence, and does not fully develop commentary for the moves in the poem. The second body paragraph does not contain any quote sprinkles as textual evidence. Adding in a third body paragraph or adding to the current paragraphs would help to develop the argument. The Sophistication point is not earned due to the essay's brevity, therefore not establishing a thorough line of reasoning or accomplishing any of the other criteria required to earn the point.

STUDENT SAMPLE ESSAY 2

William Shakespeare's "Sonnet 12" discusses how time changes the world and the things that begin to leave us with unstopping force of time. The speaker's complex attitude towards time is encapsulated in his reminiscing look at what time has taken and his hopeful idea about how passing on ideas gives them life in the later generations. In this, the author reveals that what is lost to time by the current generation will still be preserved by the next one.

In the earlier portion of the poem, the speaker reflects on the negative elements of the passage of time. He points out the imagery of the "hideous night" and the "violet past prime" which show his sadness about the things time has taken by describing them as worse than their former state. In his descriptions, the use of alliteration gives the reader a structural sense of time passing by mimicking the sound of the ticking clock, adding to the feeling of discontentment about time that the speaker discusses. The speaker feels unhappy in what time has done to these things, but also reminisces on their original beauty like that of the "brave day" or "sable curls." The speaker is able to show how his positive reflection shapes his disappointed present feelings. By pointing out the things these things are cyclical and die as fast as they are reborn, the narrator shows that as much as time takes away from the current generation, it will bring back for those who come after.

In the poem's final lines, the speaker shares with the reader his hopes for the passage of time. Although the speaker is deterred that almost nothing can survive time, he is content that what is passed to the next generation will continue to be taken forward. By choosing to indent the poem's last two lines, the author emphasizes a shift between the speaker's noticing all of the things lost to time and his focus on what can remain. Although he sees the killing effects of time, he acknowledges its role in creating new life to carry on. Here, the speaker shows that not only will physical cycles reoccur in the future, but that ideas also can survive time if we chose to share them.

The poem, though it may seem like a dreary reminder of things taken by time, is effective in reminding the reader that all can continue even after we're gone if we chose to share it. By showing the narrator's disappointment in time's passage as well as his hope for what can be carried forward, the reader can reflect on their own feelings on time and what can be preserved.

Score: 1-3-1

The thesis statement answers the prompt, presents a defensible claim, and includes an overall insight into the poem. The first body paragraph presents an insight in the topic sentence, supported by ample textual evidence and commentary. The second body paragraph needs quote sprinkles added in as textual evidence; therefore, the essay earns 3 out of 4 points for Evidence and Commentary. The paragraphs are ordered in a logical manner and each one ties back to the overall meaning in the thesis. A clear line of reasoning and control of writing throughout earns it the Sophistication point.

STUDENT SAMPLE ESSAY 3

"Sonnet 12" focuses on the passage of time and how things are ever changing due to time. In "Sonnet 12," the speaker has the complex attitude that time is unstoppable and one must have children to pass on one's legacy. Through this attitude, Shakespeare reveals that death is an inescapable fate and one must live one's life fully to defeat time.

Shakespeare uses alliteration in order to create a certain tone towards the passing of time. The first line includes a lot of sharp sounds in the form of "c" and "t." The line reads, "When I do count the clock that tells the time." The words imitate the sound of a ticking clock to really emphasize time and how it is a continuous cycle that never ends. Along with this, Shakespeare writes, "And sable curls all silver'd o'er with white" to showcase the relationship between "sable" and "silver'd." The transition from black hair to silver related to aging and how time is inevitably winding down until our deaths. Through this alliteration, Shakespeare sheds light on the speaker's complex attitude that time is essentially our enemy and we have nothing to defend ourselves against it. On the other hand, the speaker understands time and that one can beat death through creating a legacy. With children, one's memory and existence lives on through the children and their children.

"Sonnet 12" also uses specific diction in order to drive the speaker's negative attitude about time. For example, the speaker says, "Since sweets and beauties do themselves forsake / And die as fast as they see others grow; / And nothing 'gainst Time's scythe can make defence." The speaker uses euphonic words such as "sweets" and "beauties" then flows into very dark words such as "die" and "scythe." Through this diction, the reader understands the speaker believes that time is an unstoppable killer. Even though the world can be a wonderful place, eventually, time will always kill away the beauty. Therefore, the tone is despair and focuses on the idea that there is no way to avoid "Time's scythe" yourself. On the other hand, the speaker uses "Save breed to brave him" to suggest beating time with children. The speaker specifically chose "brave" in this instance to highlight how having children is a way to defend oneself against time.

The rhyme scheme is ABAB and the meter is in iambic pentameter. Similar to the alliteration, the scheme and meter replicate the ticking of a clock. "Ba-boom" paired with the rhyme scheme furthers the familiar sound that we relate to time: "tick-tock." The speaker creates a repetitive rhythm that drives the idea that time is a predictable being that always passes and will always be there. Through this, the reader understands that time will always be lurking around, cannot be avoided, and will always get them in the end. Along with this structure, the whole poem is enjambed until the very last line. This relates to the passing of time as continuous, until it is not through death. The end-stop creates a feeling of finality similar to death that time caused. Therefore, the reader sees that the rhyme scheme, meter, and single end-stop work together to highlight that time is predictable, but complex because it is continuous and also final.

Overall, "Sonnet 12" focuses on the speaker's complex attitude about time in order to reveal that aging and the passage of time are invincible, irreversible processes and one cannot defeat them without creating something that lives on after themselves.

Score: 1-4-1

This essay has a defensible thesis statement that offers an interpretation of the poem. It successfully presents a logical and well-organized line of reasoning. The essay earns all four points for Evidence and Commentary because it provides specific textual evidence and thoroughly developed commentary explaining how the evidence supports the line of reasoning, and analyzes how multiple literary devices contribute to the poem's meaning. The Sophistication point is awarded due to the consistent persuasive voice throughout the essay. Overall, this response demonstrates sophisticated thought and presents a complete literary argument.

AP® English Literature and Composition Free-Response Questions

Question 1

(Suggested time—40 minutes. This question counts as one-third of the total essay section score.)

In the following poem "Daystar" by Rita Dove (1986), the speaker portrays the relationship between a mother's duty and her desire to experience solitude, if only for an hour. Read the poem carefully. Then, in a well-written essay, analyze how Dove uses poetic elements and techniques to develop her complex view of motherhood.

Daystar
RITA DOVE

She wanted a little room for thinking:
but she saw diapers steaming on the line,
a doll slumped behind the door.
So she lugged a chair behind the garage
5   to sit out the children's naps.

Sometimes there were things to watch—
the pinched armor of a vanished cricket,
a floating maple leaf. Other days
she stared until she was assured
10   when she closed her eyes
she'd see only her own vivid blood.

She had an hour, at best, before Liza appeared
pouting from the top of the stairs.
And just *what* was mother doing
15   out back with the field mice? Why,
building a palace. Later
that night when Thomas rolled over and
lurched into her, she would open her eyes
and think of the place that was hers
20   for an hour—where
she was nothing,
pure nothing, in the middle of the day.

Go through the process to excavate the prompt, read the poem four times, take notes, and write an essay, applying what you have learned in this chapter.

CHAPTER REVIEW

Let's do a quick recap of the process you've learned in this chapter in order to be successful in writing a question 1 Poetry Analysis essay.

1. Excavate the prompt before you read the poem.

2. Read the poem four times: read, underline, annotate, take notes.

3. Spend time with your notes: Look for patterns and shifts; make connections; discover and explore complexity.

4. Draft a thesis statement that includes a defensible claim, an interpretation, and an overall thematic idea to serve as a foundation for your line of reasoning.

5. Write a brief introduction paragraph with the thesis statement as its last sentence.

6. Determine how you will organize your essay; write your first topic sentence addressing the beginning of the poem. The topic sentence should include an insight and support your thesis.

7. Select evidence sprinkles from the poem and embed them smoothly into your paragraph.

8. Identify literary elements, explain their significance and how they work to support your insight, and connect them back to the thematic idea in your thesis.

9. Repeat steps 7 and 8 as many times as needed to discuss all of your main insights, progressing chronologically through the poem.

10. Write a brief conclusion that ties up all your main points and how they relate to the thesis. If you have time, address a broader context for the poem.

11. Read back through your essay for grammar and spelling edits, improving transitions and using synonyms for repetitive words or phrases.

4

Question 2: Prose Analysis Essay

INTRODUCTION

The second question on the AP® Literature and Composition Exam is the Prose Analysis essay. Prose, unlike poetry which is written in verse and relies on its conciseness, is any text written in sentences and paragraphs and follows everyday language. The word *prose* literally translates as "straightforward." Prose texts most often include short stories, novels, and drama. You may feel most comfortable with this essay since you probably have more experience reading prose than poetry, but in order to do well on this essay, you will need to give attention to the nuances found in the passage which require far more than a casual reading. The prose passage will most likely be an excerpt from a novel or longer short story, and you will read it as a stand-alone piece. The prompt will offer some context of the work as a whole, but for the most part you will not know what happened before or after the excerpt you will be reading and writing on. Focusing on an excerpt like this allows you to zero in on it and analyze it thoroughly. You'll be surprised at how in-depth you can go in one small section. When we're reading long passages, we typically don't slow down long enough to read specific scenes deeply, but the prose essay provides an opportunity to refine and improve not only your analytical writing skills but also your reading and thinking skills.

The best way to learn how to write a literary analysis is to start reading and writing. Reading in a way that supports writing analytically is a skill that develops over time. The more you read and write, the better you get at reading and writing. Just like lifting weights to build muscles, close reading, deep thinking, and clear writing require time and practice. You may benefit, especially when you're first learning, from breaking these activities into smaller chunks: reading and annotating for meaning, writing a thesis and outlining your line of reasoning, writing a strong body paragraph, and then writing a full essay. Over time, you will be surprised at how much easier reading and writing become when you consistently practice.

Understanding the passage is simply the starting point in prose analysis. By examining the passage through the Big Ideas laid out in the course framework—characterization, setting, narration, structure, and figurative language—you should be able to arrive at an interpretation of the passage that shows its complexity. After thoroughly reading, you will then use your literary argument skills to communicate your interpretation of the passage. This is what will be expected in the prose essay:

> Free-response question 2 presents students with a passage of prose fiction of approximately 500 to 700 words. This question assesses students' ability to do the following:
> - Respond to the prompt with a thesis that presents an interpretation and may establish a line of reasoning.
> - Select and use evidence to develop and support the line of reasoning.
> - Explain the relationship between the evidence and the thesis.
> - Use appropriate grammar and punctuation in communicating your argument. (CED 138)

EXCAVATING THE PROMPT

The prose prompt will not only give directives for writing about the passage but will also contain useful information about the passage. AP® prose prompts will include three sections: information on the text including the author's name, publication date, and usually the title; contextual information on what is happening in the excerpt; and the specific writing task or tasks.

- The basic information—author, title, and date—can be useful as we place the work in a broader context of culture.
- The context can help us understand the plot, shed light on a character's perspective, reveal conflicts, and establish relationships all of which can be important as you develop an interpretation of the work.
- The specific writing task or tasks will provide a focus for your interpretation.

You should spend between two to four minutes reading and gathering as much information as you can from each of these sections before reading the passage. The information you gather from the prompt will not only aid in understanding what is happening in the passage but will also give you a lens through which to read and build your interpretation.

Consider the 2018 College Board prompt (revised to reflect the new exam format):

> The following excerpt is from an 1852 novel by Nathaniel Hawthorne. In this passage, two characters who have been living on the Blithedale

farm—a community designed to promote an ideal of equality achieved through communal rural living—are about to part ways. Read the passage carefully. Then, in a well-written essay, analyze how Hawthorne uses literary elements and techniques to portray the narrator's complex attitude towards Zenobia. (CED 138)

Breaking down the prompt:

Section	Information learned
Basic information	1852, pre-20th century, possibly difficult syntax/vocabulary
	Nathaniel Hawthorne wrote *The Scarlet Letter* (maybe you know this, maybe you don't) and had a lot to say about Puritanism and its strict moral code.
	No title of work given
Context	Two characters who have been living on the Blithedale farm are about to part ways.
	Why are the characters about to part ways? How does this contribute to the complex attitude?
	Blithedale farm—a community designed to promote an ideal of equality achieved through communal rural living
	What importance does the idea of equality and communal and rural living have?
Specific writing task	Analyze how Hawthorne uses literary elements and techniques to portray the narrator's complex attitude towards Zenobia.

Your Turn

Now try your hand at excavating the prompt on the next page by filling out Worksheet 7 (replicating it on a blank piece of paper or downloading it from the digital landing page).

WORKSHEET 7

Section	Information learned
Basic information	
Context	
Specific writing task	

The following excerpt is from Dalton Trumbo's novel *Johnny Got His Gun* (1939). In this passage, the main character, Joe, is remembering a camping trip that he took with his father when Joe was fifteen years old. Read the passage carefully. Then, in a well-written essay, analyze how Trumbo uses literary elements and techniques to convey the complex relationship between the young man and his father.

Stable Prompt Wording

With the unveiling of the new Course and Exam Description came a fill-in-the-blank template for all of the free-response question prompts. "The text in italics will vary by question, while the remainder of the prompt will be consistently used in all Prose Fiction Analysis essay questions":

The following excerpt is from [*text and author, date of publication*]. In this passage, [*comment on what is being addressed in the passage*]. Read the passage carefully. Then, in a well-written essay, analyze how [*author*] uses literary elements and techniques to [*convey/portray/develop a thematic, topical, or structural aspect of the passage that is complex and specific to the passage provided*]. (CED 139)

The prompts in this chapter have been rewritten with the stable wording, but if you are using older prompts in class, you may notice a list of devices at the end of the prompt. Be aware that these will no longer be included in prompts.

ANNOTATING A PROSE PASSAGE

Think about your favorite movies; you know, the ones you watch over and over and over. Something interesting happens each time we rewatch a movie: we notice new things. Sometimes the revelations are big, especially in the first few times we rewatch; sometimes they are small details. The same is true when we read a text. The more times we read it, the more we notice. The level at which we concentrate on a passage also plays a role in how much we notice.

Just like the poetry prompt, the prose prompt will focus on some type of *complexity*. The complexity could center around a relationship, a character's feelings, or an experience. Understanding what complexity is and knowing how to look for it in texts is critical for a well-written Prose Analysis essay. Exploring complexity means going beyond surface level observations to the tensions and nuances in a passage. This requires more than making a claim which addresses the complexity; rather take the time to unpack these tensions and nuances at the word and phrase level in order to be very specific in analysis. The Big Ideas of the course provide a means for us to think about areas of complexity. Characters acting in conflicting or inconsistent ways are opportunities to explore motivation which will not only help answer the prompt but also develop interpretation. The same is true for settings that mirror or distort a character's feelings, nonlinear structural plots that confuse readers, or figurative language that forces us to think about subjects in an entirely different way—all are opportunities for exploring and unpacking complexity in a text. Don't be concerned about having questions when reading the excerpt; think of questions as opportunities to explore complexities rather than obstacles that prevent you from understanding the text. Exploring these complexities are key to developing an interpretation of the text and connecting to central and controlling ideas.

In the poetry chapter, you were introduced to a strategy where you read a poem four times, noting something different each time through. Because the prose passage is lengthier, you will most likely not be able to read through the text four times but more realistically two or possibly three. One approach to the prose passage is reading it two to three times focusing on *what*, *how*, and *why*. Here's how the process works:

- Read the passage the first time through for a literal understanding of *what* you notice in relation to the prompt. Use the background information and brief summary on what is happening from the prompt to provide context for the scene. Focus on the specific questions that need to be answered in the prompt as you read and note any lines that may seem significant to that. Sometimes it may be helpful to write characters' initials beside descriptions of them or their **dialogue** for reference. Do not mark or be concerned about literary techniques and devices during this first read.
- Once you have a grasp on the plot, reread and mark the passage paying attention this time to *how* the author uses literary techniques and devices in the excerpt and *why* these are important. As you notice and mark techniques, be sure to go beyond simple identification but note how these devices add to the text and expand our understanding of the subject. The *why* connects back to the question that the prompt is addressing, the central ideas of the text, and your interpretation of the passage.

Making a chart in the form of a tic-tac-toe board or hashtag with the headings *what*, *how*, and *why* can be a good way to record your information (see table on page 112).

One thing to keep in mind is that when we read we will all notice different things. Each text becomes a living work in our own hands. We bring different experiences, ideas, and understandings to a text, so we will come away from the text with different interpretations. Lean into the ways you connect with the text and what you're noticing. When you talk to classmates and share ideas about a text, listen and learn from them but do not worry if your ideas are not the same. Instead embrace what you're noticing and go with that. A question students frequently have is what to do with not understanding the text. Let's practice this process with the opening of *The Poisonwood Bible* by Barbara Kingsolver. This passage is narrated by Orleanna,

Techniques for Prose Analysis

While this is not a definitive list, these are some of the terms that come up frequently when reading and exploring prose. As we walk through annotating a prose passage together, we will see some of these techniques in action.

allusion brief, often implicit and indirect reference within a literary text to something outside the text, whether another text (e.g., the Bible, a myth, another literary work, a painting, or a piece of music) or any imaginary or historical person, place, or thing

conflict struggle between opposing forces. A conflict is *external* when it pits a character against something or someone outside himself or herself—another character or characters or some impersonal force (e.g., nature or society). A conflict is *internal* when the opposing forces are two drives, impulses, or parts of a single character.

connotation what is suggested by a word, apart from what it literally means or how it is defined in the dictionary

denotation a word's direct and literal meaning, as opposed to its connotation

dialogue words spoken by characters in a literary work

diction choice of words

epiphany sudden revelation of truth, often inspired by a seemingly simple or commonplace event

imagery broadly defined, any sensory detail or evocation in a work; more narrowly, the use of figurative language to evoke a feeling, to call to mind an idea, or to describe an object. Imagery may be described as *auditory*, *tactile*, *visual*, or *olfactory* depending on which sense it primarily appeals to—hearing, touch, vision, or smell.

juxtaposition placing two or more things next to each other, side by side, to highlight their differences to create contrast, tension, or emphasis

metaphor figure of speech in which two unlike things are compared implicitly—that is, without the use of a signal such as the word *like* or *as*—as in "Love is a rose, but you better not pick it"

personification figure of speech that involves treating something non-human, such as an abstraction, as if it were a person by endowing it with humanlike qualities, as in "Death entered the room"

selection of detail the specific details the author chooses to include in a text

simile figure of speech involving a direct, explicit comparison of one thing to another, usually using the words *like* or *as* to draw the connection

symbol person, place, thing, or event that figuratively represents or stands for something else

syntax word order; the way words are put together to form phrases, clauses, and sentences

tone attitude a literary work takes toward its subject or that a character in the work conveys, especially as revealed through diction

the mother of four girls, who moves with her husband to the Congo in the 1960s as a missionary. Kingsolver uses this passage to introduce central ideas in the text and set the **tone** for the entire novel by providing context to the complex environment—physically, socially, and culturally—they are moving to. While this is shorter than a prose essay prompt, the passage provides an opportunity to practice our reading and thinking skills. For the first read through, read and think about *what* you notice. Then reread a second and third time (this passage is short enough for three readings) and note *how* the author is communicating her ideas (devices and techniques) and *why* they are important.

You may notice that this approach is different from the note-taking approach in the poetry section. There is no one correct way to take notes and analyze a passage. Experimenting with different tools allows you to find what's right for you. Use these strategies as is or adjust them if you find a way that works better for you. The important thing is to have a plan to read, interact with, and take notes on the text which will help when it's time to write.

> Imagine a ruin so strange it must never have happened.
>
> First, picture the forest. I want you to be its conscience, the eyes in the trees. The trees are columns of slick, brindled bark like muscular animals overgrown beyond all reason. Every space is filled with life: delicate, poisonous frogs war-painted like skeletons, clutched in copulation, secreting their precious eggs onto dripping leaves. Vines strangling their own kin in the everlasting wrestle for sunlight. The breathing of monkeys. A glide of snake belly on branch. A single-file army of ants biting a mammoth tree into uniform grains and hauling it down to the dark for their ravenous queen. And, in reply, a choir of seedlings arching their necks out of rotted tree stumps, sucking life out of death. This forest eats itself and lives forever.
>
> Away down below now, single file on the path, comes a woman with four girls in tow, all of them in shirtwaist dresses. Seen from above this way they are pale, doomed blossoms, bound to appeal to your sympathies. Be careful. Later on you'll have to decide what sympathy they deserve. [. . .] The mother waves a graceful hand in front of her as she leads the way, parting curtain after curtain of

spiders' webs. She appears to be conducting a symphony. Behind them the curtain closes. The spiders return to their killing ways.

What do you notice?	*How* does the author do this?	*Why* is it important?
The narrator directly addresses the reader.	Commands—"Imagine a ruin," "picture the forest" Assigns a job for the reader—"I want you to be its conscience, the eyes in the trees"	The narrator has an intimate bond with the reader, telling us what to do as we read.
Description of the forest	Simile—"The trees are . . . like muscular animals" Selection of detail—"overgrown beyond all reason." Simile—"delicate, poisonous frogs war-painted like skeletons" Strong active verbs—"Vines strangling their own kin in the everlasting wrestle for sunlight." "A single-file army of ants biting a mammoth tree into uniform grains." Fragments—"The breathing of monkeys. A glide of snake belly on branch."	The trees are more than a plant—they are likened to muscular animals that are overgrown beyond reason, showing they cannot be tamed. War paint—sign of aggressiveness Skeletons—death imagery Strangling—harsh aggressive verb choice—denotes choking life out of something. Wrestle—denotes struggle The two fragments pick up the pace which makes more of a frantic feeling for the reader.
Contrasts	"Muscular" trees and "delicate" frogs "Every space is filled with life" "clutched in copulation, secreting their precious eggs" "Vines strangling their own kin" "seedlings . . . sucking life out of death"	The contrasts of life and death and savageness and fragility show the balance of how tough one has to be to survive in this setting but also how vulnerable one really is there.
First paragraph ends with a dichotomy.	"The forest eats itself and lives forever."	There's a relationship between death and life.
Narrator refers to herself in third person.	"comes a woman with four girls in tow"	While the narrator is intimate with us as readers, she is detached from herself at this point of the story—definitely something to explore for complexity.

This time the narrator gives the reader a warning.	"Be careful. Later on you'll have to decide what sympathy they deserve."	The invitation from earlier about what to do in our reading now turns to a warning for us not to form opinions too quickly.
Metaphor of the mother being a conductor	"The mother waves a graceful hand . . . parting curtain after curtain" "appears to be conducting a symphony. Behind them the curtain closes."	The mother is "conducting" her girls but the jungle (curtain) closes on them. She does not have as much control as she thinks she does.
Ominous tone, foreshadowing	"The spiders return to their killing ways."	This definitely reinforces the negative diction in the first paragraph—and takes it a step further.

After we have read through the passage with the *what*, *how*, and *why* in mind, we can begin to draw some conclusions:

- The narrator has an intimate bond with the reader—addressing the reader in the first sentence. Very unusual to start a novel by breaking the fourth wall.
- The narrator has a task for the reader. We are not just bystanders in the story—we have an active role.
- There's a shift from addressing the reader to describing the setting.
- Lots of contrasts in the setting—the purpose is to juxtapose.
- The last sentence of the first paragraph is a dichotomy.
- The narrator refers to herself in third person.
- The narrator addresses the reader again, this time with a warning and gives another task.
- The second paragraph ends with an ominous tone.

This passage is interesting for a few different reasons. First, the narrator has a deeply intimate relationship with the reader and invites us into the story with commands, a warning, and a reference to a future judgment we will make about each of her daughters. Her directions provide purpose in our reading with words and phrases like *imagine*, *picture*, *be careful*, and *later on you'll have to decide*, specifically directing us as to what we need and will need to do as we hear her story. This is atypical in that narrators don't usually directly address readers, and in a way this is her exercising her power or control over us. Not only is she going to tell us the story, she is telling us how to think and respond to her story.

In addition, the shift from her inviting us into her story to the scene itself is significant. These are her observations of the forest, and she has already warned us to be careful. Contrasts play an important role here. She frames up images of the savageness of the forest, which is a necessity for survival, with fragile images indicating vulnerability. The images described with words such as *muscular, overgrown, war-painted, strangling, wrestle,* and *biting* are contrasted with descriptions that include words such as *delicate, skeletons,* and *precious*; these **juxtapositions** invite us to further explore the relationship in the forest between strength and weakness.

Now let's practice on a passage that will be approximately the length of a prose essay on the exam. We will use the 2007 College Board–released prompt with an excerpt from *Johnny Got His Gun.* Read the prompt, and then read the story three times. The first time, mark *what* you notice and in the second and third reading *how* the author communicates these ideas and *why* they're important in regard to the prompt. The *what, how,* and *why* graphic organizer (Worksheet 8) is available if that helps to organize your thoughts, but you may choose to make *what, how,* and *why* notes without using a formal graphic organizer. There is no right or wrong way to annotate, make notes, or gather thoughts, but having a predetermined way to approach the text will be useful.

The following excerpt is from Dalton Trumbo's novel *Johnny Got His Gun* (1939). In this passage, the main character, Joe, is remembering a camping trip that he took with his father when Joe was fifteen years old. Read the passage carefully. Then, in a well-written essay, analyze how Trumbo uses literary elements and techniques to convey the complex relationship between the young man and his father.

The campfire was built in front of a tent
and the tent was under an enormous pine. When you
slept inside the tent it seemed always that it was
raining outside because the needles from the pine kept
5   falling. Sitting across from him and staring into the
fire was his father. Each summer they came to this
place which was nine thousand feet high and covered
with pine trees and dotted with lakes. They fished in
the lakes and when they slept at night the roar of
10   water from the streams which connected the lakes
sounded in their ears all night long.
    They had been coming to this place ever
since he was seven. Now he was fifteen and Bill
Harper was going to come tomorrow. He sat in front
15   of the fire and looked across at his father and
wondered just how he was going to tell him. It was a
very serious thing. Tomorrow for the first time in all
their trips together he wanted to go fishing with
someone other than his father. On previous trips the
20   idea had never occurred to him. His father had always
preferred his company to that of men and he had

always preferred his father's company to that of the other guys. But now Bill Harper was coming up tomorrow and he wanted to go fishing with him. He
25 knew it was something that had to happen sometime. Yet he also knew that it was the end of something. It was an ending and a beginning and he wondered just how he should tell his father about it.

     So he told him very casually. He said Bill Harper's
30 coming up tomorrow and I thought maybe I'd go out with him. He said Bill Harper doesn't know very much about fishing and I do so I think if you don't mind I'll get up early in the morning and meet Harper and he and I will go fishing.

35 For a little while his father didn't say a thing. Then he said why sure go along Joe. And then a little later his father said has Bill Harper got a rod? He told his father no Bill hasn't got a rod. Well said his father why don't you take my rod and let Bill use yours? I
40 don't want to go fishing tomorrow anyhow. I'm tired and I think I'll rest all day. So you use my rod and let Bill use yours.

     It was as simple as that and yet he knew it was a great thing. His father's rod was a very valuable one.
45 It was perhaps the only extravagance his father had had in his whole life. It had amber leaders and beautiful silk windings. Each spring his father sent the rod away to a man in Colorado Springs who was an expert on rods. The man in Colorado Springs
50 carefully scraped the varnish off the rod and rewound it and revarnished it and it came back glistening new each year. There was nothing his father treasured more. He felt a little lump in his throat as he thought that even as he was deserting his father for Bill
55 Harper his father had volunteered the rod.

     They went to sleep that night in the bed which lay against a floor of pine needles. They had scooped the needles out to make a little hollow place for their hips. He lay awake quite a while thinking about tomorrow
60 and his father who slept beside him. Then he fell asleep. At six o'clock Bill Harper whispered to him through the tent flap. He got up and gave Bill his rod and took his father's for himself and they went off without awakening his father.

Your Turn

Try your hand at filling out Worksheet 8 on a blank piece of paper or downloading it from the digital landing page.

WORKSHEET 8

What	How	Why

Here are some of my notes on *Johnny Got His Gun* after reading through the passage twice and using the *what, how,* and *why* strategy:

What	How	Why
The first paragraph has a strong emphasis on the father and son tradition.	The setting remains the same through the years. "They" pronouns—they fished, they slept, they had been coming	Shows the history of their relationship and how this trip is so important to that
Shift to Joe's thoughts and inner turmoil over breaking tradition and telling his father. Conversation is not written out in dialogue but told narratively.	Emphasis on "he" pronoun No dialogue	Shows Joe's maturity
The father blesses the change even though it's difficult.	The fishing rod is a symbol.	Passing of the torch to another generation

Remember that our notes will look different because we bring different experiences and backgrounds to the text. I read as a mother of grown children, which makes me sympathetic to the father and how difficult this must have been for him; you are reading as an adolescent relating to Joe and his desire to be independent. Your unique notes will serve as the basis for your argument that will be laid out in your essay. Another thing I like to do in my notes that you will notice above is how I chunk the text into three sections in chronological order. I like chunking the text into a beginning, middle, and end (or sometimes just a beginning and end) based on shifts in the passage. This not only keeps my observations from being jumbled but also ensures that I have notes from the entire passage which will lead to a more comprehensive analysis of the text. Also, if you're taking notes by hand, it's easy to draw a tic-tac-toe board and start writing.

WRITING A THESIS STATEMENT

The thesis statement for the prose prompt will be very similar to the thesis for the poetry prompt, but we should take time to review the thesis since it is so important. Before looking at what a thesis should do, let's consider some common mistakes writers make when writing thesis statements. Row A of the prose rubric outlines what does and does not constitute a thesis. You will not be awarded the Thesis point if:

- There is no defensible thesis.
- The intended thesis only restates the prompt.
- The intended thesis provides a summary of the issue with no apparent or coherent claim.
- There is a thesis, but it does not respond to the prompt.

Here's a reminder of what a thesis must include and may include:

Must	May
• Convey a defensible claim • Express an interpretation of the literature • Respond to the prompt	• Establish a line of reasoning • Preview development of an interpretation

Read the following examples and think about how they can be corrected to constitute a strong thesis:

Thesis statement	Commentary
Joe has a very complex relationship with his father which is seen through their annual camping trip.	This is a restating of the prompt and does not contain any insight which would make it defensible.
From an excerpt of his *Johnny Got His Gun*, Trumbo writes about Joe and his father going on a fishing trip by describing the setting, explaining his inner turmoil, and having his friend take his father's rod.	This statement outlines what happens in the passage but offers no defensible claim nor even addresses the prompt (why is the relationship complex?).
In Trumbo's *Johnny Got His Gun* (1939), the complex relationship of the father and son can be seen through the point of view, selection of detail, and symbolism.	While this statement brings in devices and techniques that Trumbo uses in the excerpt, the writer does not respond to the specific writing task of conveying the complex relationship between the young man and his father.

The most important part of the thesis is that it answers the prompt with a defensible claim based on what your reading has revealed at a deeper level. A literary analysis is an argument of your position or your thoughts regarding the passage. Your answer to the prompt is an opportunity to let the AP® Reader know the conclusions you have drawn, and the thesis is the place to clearly state your position. While you can be awarded the point on Row A of the rubric no matter where you place your thesis, the best place for it is at the beginning. Think about using the GPS on your phone. When you put in your destination, you have a clear idea of where you're going, and the GPS routes out a map to get there. The same is true for your paper. Starting your essay with a thesis that answers the prompt with a defensible claim lets the Reader assigned to your essay know the direction of your argument. This will not only heighten their interest in the subject but will also allow them to more easily follow your argument. Your job as a writer becomes more straightforward now because everything you include in the essay should point back to the thesis. If you cannot link your evidence or commentary to the thesis, there's no need for it to be in the paper.

There is no one template for a good thesis statement. Many students have learned that a thesis statement needs to have three points where each point is developed into a paragraph. As long as the three-pronged thesis statement answers the prompt with a defensible claim, this type of thesis statement will be awarded the point. However, writing a thesis which is awarded the point on Row A and writing a thesis that sets up a solid essay are often two different things. The three-pronged thesis, especially when organized by literary device alone, often limits the scope of the paragraph. Your thesis should open your essay to explore complexity rather than box in paragraphs to only discuss a particular device. Experiment with writing thesis statements that answer the prompt with a defensible claim but don't list three devices. Some thesis statements include a line of reasoning; while this is not necessary, these thesis statements typically set writers up for a successful essay. Finally, remember that a thesis can be more than one sentence, which is often necessary if you are establishing a line of reasoning or previewing an interpretation.

Here are some examples that earn the point for Row A because they all provide a defensible claim and present an interpretation of the poem.

In *Johnny Got His Gun* by Dalton Trumbo, the author characterizes the relationship between the boy and his father as maturing and less dependent in order to demonstrate that growing apart from your parent is a part of life that is necessary for becoming your own person.

Throughout the passage, Trumbo creates a serene environment which surrounds the father and son as they experience what the son views as a major conflict. The relationship between the son and the father is developed as a mutually giving relationship where both the son and the father care deeply for each other despite growing apart.

In Trumbo's passage he uses very specific details to describe the importance of the campsite and his father's fishing pole, a third person point of view in order to express the young boy's feelings, and simple/informal diction. This use of these literary techniques portrays the distance growing between the young man and his father as the young man is growing older and becoming less dependent on his father.

Let's revisit the 2018 prompt, which we discussed when practicing how to unpack the prompt. Now you can practice the skills we have been learning about as you read closely, annotate or take notes, and write a thesis statement for this passage.

The following excerpt is from an 1852 novel by Nathaniel Hawthorne. In this passage, two characters who have been living on the Blithedale farm—a community designed to promote an ideal of equality achieved through communal rural living—are about to part ways. Read the passage carefully. Then, in a well-written essay, analyze how Hawthorne uses literary elements and techniques to portray the narrator's complex attitude towards Zenobia. (CED 138)

Her manner bewildered me. Literally,
moreover, I was dazzled by the brilliancy of the room.
A chandelier hung down in the centre, glowingwith I
know not how many lights; there were separate lamps,
5   also, on two or three tables, and on marble brackets,
adding their white radiance to that of the chandelier.
The furniture was exceedingly rich. Fresh from our
old farm-house, with its homely board and benches in
the dining-room, and a few wicker chairs in the best
10   parlor, it struck me that here was the fulfillment of
every fantasy of an imagination, revelling in various
methods of costly self-indulgence and splendid ease.
Pictures, marbles, vases; in brief, more shapes of
luxury than there could be any object in enumerating,
15   except for an auctioneer's advertisement—and the
whole repeated and doubled by the reflection of a
great mirror, which showed me Zenobia's proud
figure, likewise, and my own. It cost me, I
acknowledge, a bitter sense of shame, to perceive in
20   myself a positive effort to bear up against the effect
which Zenobia sought to impose on me. I reasoned
against her, in my secret mind, and strove so to keep

my footing. In the gorgeousness with which she had
surrounded herself—in the redundance of personal
25   ornament, which the largeness of her physical nature
and the rich type of her beauty caused to seem so
suitable—I malevolently beheld the true character of
the woman, passionate, luxurious, lacking simplicity,
not deeply refined, incapable of pure and perfect taste.
30   But, the next instant, she was too powerful for all
my opposing struggles. I saw how fit it was that she
should make herself as gorgeous as she pleased, and
should do a thousand things that would have been
ridiculous in the poor, thin, weakly characters of other
35   women. To this day, however, I hardly know whether
I then beheld Zenobia in her truest attitude, or
whether that were the truer one in which she had
presented herself at Blithedale. In both, there was
something like the illusion which a great actress flings
40   around her.
        "Have you given up Blithedale forever?" I
inquired.
        "Why should you think so?" asked she.
        "I cannot tell," answered I; "except that it appears
45   all like a dream that we were ever there together."
        "It is not so to me," said Zenobia. "I should think it
a poor and meagre nature, that is capable of but one
set of forms, and must convert all the past into a
dream, merely because the present happens to be
50   unlike it. Why should we be content with our homely
life of a few months past, to the exclusion of all other
modes? It was good; but there are other lives as good
or better. Not, you will understand, that I condemn
those who give themselves up to it more entirely than
55   I, for myself, should deem it wise to do."
        It irritated me, this self-complacent,
condescending, qualified approval and criticism of a
system to which many individuals—perhaps as highly
endowed as our gorgeous Zenobia—had contributed
60   their all of earthly endeavor, and their loftiest
aspirations. I determined to make proof if there were
any spell that would exorcise her out of the part which
she seemed to be acting. She should be compelled to
give me a glimpse of something true; some nature,
65   some passion, no matter whether right or wrong,
provided it were real.

"Your allusion to that class of circumscribed
characters, who can live in only one mode of life,"
remarked I, coolly, "reminds me of our poor friend
70 Hollingsworth.[1] Possibly, he was in your thoughts,
when you spoke thus. Poor fellow! It is a pity that, by
the fault of a narrow education, he should have so
completely immolated himself to that one idea of his;
especially as the slightest modicum of common-sense
75 would teach him its utter impracticability. Now that I
have returned into the world, and can look at his
project from a distance, it requires quite all my real
regard for this respectable and well-intentioned man
to prevent me laughing at him—as, I find, society at
80 large does!"
          Zenobia's eyes darted lightning; her cheeks
flushed; the vividness of her expression was like the
effect of a powerful light, flaming up suddenly within
her. My experiment had fully succeeded. She had
85 shown me the true flesh and blood of her heart, by
thus involuntarily resenting my slight, pitying, half-
kind, half-scornful mention of the man who was all in
all with her. She herself, probably, felt this; for it was
hardly a moment before she tranquillized her uneven
90 breath, and seemed as proud and self-possessed as ever.

What do you notice? *How* do you see the author communicating this? *Why*
do you think it's important?

Here are a few insightful observations our students noticed about the Zenobia passage:

- The setting is reflective of Zenobia's present circumstances
  and contains lots of imagery detailing the lavishness of
  where she's staying.
- The speaker is "dazzled" and feels "powerless" but is also
  "irritated." These contrasting feelings are the base of the
  complex feelings.
- The mirror and chandelier act as symbols.
- Her comparison to an actress where Zenobia has a true self
  and a role she is playing shows the duality of her personality.

Here are some thesis statements written by students that *would not* earn the
Thesis point:

1. A charismatic member of the Blithedale community who assumes a leadership position.

Thesis statement	Commentary
Hawthorne portrays the narrator's attitude towards Zenobia through the setting of Zenobia's house, the dialogue between the narrator and Zenobia, and the contrast of their friend, Hollingsworth.	This thesis lists the techniques that Hawthorne uses but doesn't provide a defensible claim or tell why the attitude is complex. If the thesis included what makes the narrator's attitude complex, it would earn the Thesis point.
In the passage from a Hawthorne novel, the narrator and Zenobia, who formerly lived together on Blithedale farm, are about to part ways leaving the narrator with an attitude toward Zenobia.	This thesis simply restates the prompt but doesn't provide any interpretation of the passage nor a defensible claim.

Here are some thesis statements written by students that would earn the Thesis point because they all provide a defensible claim and present an interpretation of the poem. (The narrator's gender is not specified in this passage, thus students are not penalized for referring to the narrator as "he," "she," or "they.")

Through his contrast of grandiose and simple living as well as ponderous dialogue we are able to see the narrator's attitude toward Zenobia shift from that of utter bewilderment to contempt. Paired with the use of evaluative diction throughout the prose, we are able to see a clear picture of the disdainful opinions of Zenobia that exist in the narrator's mind.

Hawthorne, through the use of personification of Zenobia's individual features and the dramatic irony from the dialogue, portrays the jealous and scornful attitude the narrator has toward Zenobia.

At first glance, the narrator perceives Zenobia as haughty and condescending, an observation only bolstered by the imagery of her exuberant surroundings, but a glaring contrast between what Zenobia says and her actions sway the narrator to believe that she is more sympathetic than initially believed.

SELECTING EVIDENCE AND WRITING COMMENTARY

Close reading and annotating, developing insights, writing a thesis, selecting evidence, and providing commentary is not necessarily a linear process even though each of these are definitive steps of equal importance. Close reading and annotating help form insights that can lead to writing a good thesis statement and can also lead to choosing evidence for your argument. The evidence you choose will drive your commentary, and sometimes as you write commentary, your insights and thesis will become clearer. Yes, outlining and having a plan to gather evidence and write is of vital importance, but allowing yourself the room to be open to what you notice as you write is also important. The most important part of writing evidence and commentary is to keep everything centered on the text and not on personal or historical experiences.

Selecting Evidence

Your thesis will become a filter for all evidence, and your evidence will drive your commentary. Because you are supporting a defensible claim in your essay, it's important to remember that evidence can be interpreted differently by other readers.

Two important points to consider for evidence are the relevancy and adequacy of your evidence.

Relevant: Is this evidence the best to support your insight and thesis?

Relevant information directly supports your position. Think of your thesis as a sieve shaking out sand; only you are sifting through the details and shaking out the evidence that best strengthens your argument. Some evidence may offer support for your ideas but may not necessarily be the most persuasive for your argument.

Adequate: Is there sufficient evidence to support your insight and thesis?

Adequate evidence means you have enough details to support your claim. The more evidence you have to support your claim, the stronger your argument will be. Having multiple pieces of evidence work together to support a claim makes for a far stronger argument than having only one piece of evidence. Consider the following claim:

> As the narrator speaks with and observes Zenobia, she struggles
> with the belief that Zenobia is falsely representing herself. . . .

Here's a passage with italicized portions that could be used for evidence.

But, the next instant, she was too powerful for all my opposing struggles. I saw how fit it was that *she should make herself as gorgeous as she pleased*, and should do a thousand things that would have been ridiculous in the poor, thin, weakly characters of other women. To this day, however, *I hardly know whether I then beheld Zenobia in her truest attitude*, or *whether that were the truer one in which she had presented herself at Blithedale*. In both, *there was something like the illusion which a great actress flings around her.*

You now have options of how to present this evidence. You can either paraphrase or summarize the portion of the text that you want to use for support, or you can use a direct quote. Using a direct quote is preferable as this shows your close reading and points the reader back to the exact portion of the text.

> **Pro tip:** However, be cautious not to fill up your entire paper with quotes, leaving little or no room for analysis. The important part of this essay is your own thoughts, so limit quotes to the key words and phrases which can be integrated into your analysis.

Look at the following example:

> As the narrator speaks with and observes Zenobia, she struggles with the belief that Zenobia is falsely representing herself, calling her an "illusion" believing Zenobia wants her to feel ashamed and small, fighting "against the effect which Zenobia sought to impose" upon her. Comparing her to a "great actress" further implies that the role she is presenting is not her true self. The narrator also thinks however that Zenobia had the right to "make herself as gorgeous as she pleased." The narrator wars with which thought rings true, and settles upon asking Zenobia where the last traces of the familiar, more humble, woman she knew had gone, wishing to witness a sincere response.

Note in the example how the author uses words and phrases to explain, rather than inserting a whole sentence and then offering explanation. There's no perfect ratio of evidence to analysis, but your analysis should outweigh your evidence; this will better guarantee that you have done the heavy lifting of explaining the quotes rather than having them stand alone or explained too shallowly.

Writing Commentary

Selecting the right evidence is just one step in developing good body paragraphs. Once you have chosen the evidence that best supports your thesis, the next step is to fully explain it. Since you are arguing a defensible claim, your commentary will be the meat of the essay as it explains the importance of your evidence and relates it to your argument. Let's look at the definition of analysis from the Course and Exam Description:

> *Analyze:* Examine methodically and in detail the structure of the topic of the question for purposes of interpretation and explanation. (CED 140)

Let's look at some of the key components in this definition. First, we need to "examine." Think about the last time you went to the doctor for a specific reason. The doctor will begin by asking you some questions to gather information. What are your symptoms? How long have you been experiencing symptoms? Was the onset sudden or gradual? Are there any particular patterns to your symptoms? Do you have any family history connected to what you're experiencing? When we are choosing evidence and writing commentary, we always approach it with a mindset of finding answers to questions. The definition continues telling how to examine: "methodically and in detail." Methodically means having a systemized way to think about the text. We have already talked about the *what, how,* and *why* method of working through the text. Another systematic way to analyze is to chunk the text and work through each section. The idea is not to haphazardly or frantically look all over the passage but to have a plan of how to work through the passage and explain it. The next phrase "in detail" is a crucial part of this definition. Considering small details can make a big difference in commentary. When commentary is given on several lines of the text at once, analysis tends to be more general and not as in-depth. Connotations, nuances, and meanings of specific words and phrases are the building blocks for analyzing patterns, juxtapositions, and other complexities in texts. Finally, you need to consider all of these things "for the purposes of interpretation," or the meaning you contrive from the text. Whew—that's a lot, but understanding the different components of analysis is useful as we are continuously adjusting our reading pace depending on the difficulty of the passage, how easily we make connections with the text, and our overall understanding of it.

Good commentary as referenced in Row B notes patterns, contrasts, and meanings within the text and explains why they are important. The Big Ideas (characterization, setting, structure, narration, and figurative language) are not the only ways to think systematically about a text. Here are some other avenues to explore ideas that can lead to good commentary:

- Shifts: Shifts can occur in perspective, tone, time, and tense, just to name a few. A shift signifies a change, and the reason for the shift provides an opportunity for analysis. For example, in the Zenobia excerpt there is a shift from description of the setting to the description of the speaker's feelings. Why the emphasis on setting? What do we learn about the setting? Why switch to the feelings of the speaker? Are there parallels between the two? If so, what exactly are they? Shifts often draw emphasis to contrasts within a text.
- Contrasts: Contrasting characters and ideas or other inconsistencies invite us to consider values or perspectives which affect our interpretation of the passage. Consider the narrator committed to rural living and Zenobia living in a lavish setting or the narrator and his own conflicting feelings of bewilderment and irritation. These contrasts serve as opportunities for us to dive deeper and consider what these differences show us and why they're important.

- Patterns: If you notice certain words, phrases, images, or ideas that continue to reappear throughout a passage, they are not there by accident but rather serve as avenues to think more deeply on their significance and explore further. Sometimes a word or image is repeated exactly while other times there may be a slight variance but the same idea. These patterns are most often noticed when rereading a passage. The first paragraph of the Zenobia excerpt shows a pattern of bright light with words and images such as "brilliancy," a glowing chandelier, and "white radiance." The recurring idea of a bright light invites us to question its importance.

These are just a few of the common elements to look for that provide a way into the text for you to gather insights and develop an interpretation. No matter how you choose to enter and make meaning from a text, always ask *why* to every piece of evidence you provide to see if you can push it further. Look at the following example:

The narrator describes their view on Zenobia's current situation as being "self indulgent," "brillant", & "costly." The diction used creates a sense that **the narrator is in awe** of what Zenobia has surrounded herself with. However, **they also see these furnishings as a reflection on Zenobia being "proud," "imposing" and "incapable of pure and perfect taste."** Through the diction used to describe Zenobia's ornate ornamentations, it is clear that **the narrator sees them as too beautiful and impressive.** They stated that the narrator saw through the "gorgeousness with which she [Zenobia] had surrounded herself" to her true nature, of **which she was using the beauty as a mask to hide**.

> *Why* is the narrator in awe?

> *Why* might the narrator view the furnishings this way?

> *Why* is this important?

> *Why* is this important, or *so what?*

Asking *why* after every piece of evidence and commentary is a built-in check for you to see if you have pushed your analysis as far as possible. Of course, you do not want to force something in the text or your interpretation that is not there, but this happens far less than leaving missed opportunities to fully explain your evidence.

Pro tip: A final word of caution when writing commentary: Avoid falling into the trap of plot summary. Plot summary merely retells or recounts the events of the story which is far different from analysis.

Consider the following excerpt from the passage, then the difference between a summary of this section versus an analysis of it:

But, the next instant, she was too powerful for all my opposing struggles. I saw how fit it was that she should make herself as gorgeous as she pleased, and should do a thousand things that would have been ridiculous in the poor, thin, weakly characters of other women. To this day, however, I hardly know whether I then beheld Zenobia in her truest attitude, or whether that were the truer one in which she had presented herself at Blithedale. In both, there was something like the illusion which a great actress flings around her.

> **Summary:** The narrator feels powerless when confronted with Zenobia which causes an internal struggle. She compares Zenobia to an illusion and implies she is an actress.
>
> **Analysis:** As the narrator speaks with and observes Zenobia, she struggles with the belief that Zenobia is falsely representing herself, calling her an "illusion" believing Zenobia wants her to feel ashamed and small, fighting "against the effect which Zenobia sought to impose" upon her.

Analysis answers *why* questions and considers what is not said more than rephrasing what is said. The short quotes are incorporated for support but do not dominate or overpower the writing.

This student writer does a good job of balancing evidence and commentary and asking *why* often in order to take analysis as far as possible. Let's read the paragraph:

> To understand the changed nature of his friend, the narrator must compare his different perceptions of her over time. There is the shamelessly extravagant woman of the present, the calmly self-assured woman of the Blithedale era, and somewhere in between, an intoxicating woman of "rich . . . beauty" that threatens to defeat the narrator's discipline. These contrasting images of Zenobia confuse and frustrate the narrator, but he doesn't give up hope that his friend of the past is the *real* Zenobia. To do so, he engages in a battle of the mind, strategically framing questions to manipulate Zenobia's answers. The series of dialogue, beginning in the middle of the passage, shifts the story because Zenobia speaks for the first time. When she suggests that the narrator's ideology is "poor and meagre" and part of a "dream," she provides fuel for the narrator to grow "irritated." He becomes determined to prove that Zenobia is only "acting" and crafts the climax of his battle, comparing their mutual friend to a "poor fellow" by Zenobia's new

standards. This comparison, which painfully forces Zenobia
to see her own reflection in her gilded mirror, wins her
heart, and she settles back into her "proud and self-
possessed" self.

Notice how the student's topic sentence is a claim based on *what* the student noticed after reading the passage and thinking about the prompt: "the narrator must compare his different perceptions of her over time." The student writer then moves to *how* the author communicates this by incorporating techniques such as characterization of Zenobia, dialogue and questions, and comparison for evidence, and follows it by answering *why* this evidence is important through the analysis.

HOW TO ORGANIZE A PROSE ANALYSIS ESSAY

There is no one right way to organize an essay: This can be both a blessing and a curse. Establishing a line of reasoning, however, is essential. A line of reasoning is simply a logical order to your argument and will be demonstrated through three things:

1. A progression of ideas that moves the argument forward
2. Connecting the ideas not only to each other but also back to the thesis
3. A logical order to the argument. Think of it as a thread that runs throughout the essay that sews all of the ideas together. This thread begins with the thesis and weaves together every claim in each topic sentence, pieces of evidence used for support, and commentary which explicitly shows the connection to the thesis.

Sometimes paragraphs may contain information that addresses the prompt but do not establish a line of reasoning. One common error is referred to as helicopter writing. This is when the writer makes one point really well but either fails to make multiple supporting claims or to adequately support more than one claim. In other words, the writer hovers over the same idea throughout the essay just like a helicopter hovers over one area. Another common error is disjointed writing. This writer could have two or more claims that address the prompt, but the ideas are not connected to other claims or back to the thesis. Instead, they are on their own without any common thread tying the ideas together.

The following chart is a reference for three common ways to organize an essay, with advantages and cautions to consider about each method. Keep in mind that these methods of organization can be used simultaneously, and using a combination of them may be helpful.

Organizational method	Explanation	Advantages	Caution
Insight	Organization with paragraphs centered on an observation which is further unpacked with textual evidence or devices and commentary linking back to the meaning.	Builds off of *what* you notice and addresses the prompt; commentary comes more easily when it's tied to an insight you have (*why*), flows easily to establish a line of reasoning, and can use several different devices for support.	Be sure to include *how* the author develops the passage through devices or elements.
Order	Organization by paragraphs centered on chunks of the passage divided by shifts or clear segments.	The text as a whole is considered; the progression of character development or passage is easy to notice.	Be careful not to fall into plot summary; be sure to address the central or controlling idea.
Device	Organization built around paragraphs centered on a particular device with examples of the device from the text.	Devices are identified; they are easy to organize if the student is having difficulty understanding the passage.	Be sure to include the *what* and *why* of insights and commentary to explain the function of the devices and establish a line of reasoning.

Examples

Order of the Passage and Insight

The line of reasoning in this essay is strong as the writer uses a combination of chronological order and insight through the passage.

> **Thesis:** In this excerpt from Nathaniel Hawthorne, the author shows the internal struggle of the narrator as she tries to reconcile the Zenobia she is currently interacting with, against her memories of the old one. This struggle results in inner discord, and Hawthorne ultimately portrays the narrator's attitude toward Zenobia as one full of wariness and contempt, condemning the woman's selfishness.

If we use this thesis, topic sentences based on insights might look like this:

1. The excerpt opens with the narrator regarding the evidence of Zenobia's love of opulence and "self-indulgence," in what at first seems to be awe and appreciation, but later turns into disgust and disapproval.

2. As the narrator speaks with and observes Zenobia, she struggles with the belief that Zenobia is falsely representing herself, calling her an "illusion," believing Zenobia wants her to feel ashamed and small, fighting "against the effect which Zenobia sought to impose" upon her.

3. Zenobia's reply, however, is not what the narrator had been hoping for, and solidifies her belief that the woman is selfish and untrustworthy, leaving the narrator with a contemptuous attitude toward her.

4. The narrator longs for Zenobia to remain as she always had, and when it is revealed that Zenobia has changed, the narrator discards any positive feelings for her.

The four insights, or what the writer noticed about the complex relationship between the narrator and Zenobia, appear in the order that the reader encounters them in the passage. This makes for a logical reading of the essay and covers the entire passage.

Devices and Insight

Another common method of organization is by device. While organizing by device is not wrong, this method can often limit the scope of each paragraph since it will feature only one device. If organizing by device, include an insight with the device to guarantee that you move beyond identification of the device.

> **Thesis statement:** Hawthorne portrays the narrator's surprise and irritation towards Zenobia through descriptive imagery, first-person point of view, and dialogue between the two characters.

If we use this thesis, topic sentences based on insights might look like this:

1. After having lived in a rural setting, the narrator is initially dazzled by the setting that she finds Zenobia in.

2. Just as vivid imagery helps to portray the narrator's attitude towards Zenobia, so does the use of the first-person point of view as it shows her inner thoughts of amazement and bewilderment.

3. Finally, the use of dialogue between the two displays the narrator's shocked and irritated attitude towards Zenobia.

Again, these topic sentences work in that they establish a logical order to the essay but this limits how in-depth the analysis of the insight can go since only one device is explored in each paragraph.

SOPHISTICATION

There are four basic paths to earning the Sophistication point, but not all four are equal. The first path—exploring complexities—is most likely the best because you will already be doing this work in your analysis. The second path—placing the work in a broader context—is also manageable if you have a clear understanding of the time period and its cultural implications. Paths three and four are more difficult. Let's look at them one by one.

1. Identifying and exploring complexities or tensions within the passage

Complexity cannot be described with a one-word adjective or even unpacked in one well-written sentence. Characters' feelings or attitudes often appear to be contradictory, yet they all remain true to the character. In other words, it's complicated. Think of a labyrinth and its design. The labyrinth is all one thing; however, many different paths make it up. The same is true when exploring complexities in a text. Tension can be shown through mental or emotional strain. Think of a rubber band fully stretched. When characters are placed in strenuous circumstances or have difficult relationships, the tension shown there provides an opportunity to explore the causes and effects which lead to good analysis. Look at this body paragraph from an essay and how deeply the student explores complexities and tensions and uses transition words and signal verbs to notify the reader of the contrasts.

> The passage opens with the narrator observing, in awe, the luxuries of Zenobia's home. It is beautiful, "the fulfillment of every fantasy of the imagination," but although the narrator is "dazzled," he is uneasy and feels a "bitter sense of shame." Hawthorne magnifies this feeling of shame through terms such as "costly self-indulgence" and "redundance of personal ornament," the narrator expresses his disapproval of Zenobia's overly-indulgent lifestyle, which is fundamentally different from the values of his own community. He further states his dislike of Zenobia when he says he "malevolently [beholds] her true character," implying Zenobia has been hiding her true personality. By claiming she is a "passionate, luxurious" woman "lacking simplicity, not deeply refined, incapable of pure and perfect taste," the narrator harshly criticizes her debauchery and makes evident his disapproval.

This is true	Transition/ signal verb	And this is also true
Narrator is in awe; "dazzled"	although; magnifies	Narrator is uneasy and feels a "bitter sense of shame"
The narrator disapproves of Zenobia's overly indulgent lifestyle	fundamentally different from; further	The values of the narrator's own community
"[M]alevolently [beholds] her true character"	implying	Zenobia has been hiding her true personality
"passionate, luxurious"	then harshly criticizes	"[L]acking simplicity, not deeply refined, incapable of pure and perfect taste"

2. Illuminating the student's interpretation by situating it within a broader context

While this path is doable, students tend to have more success with it on question 3 when dealing with an entire novel that has been read and thought through ahead of time as opposed to an unfamiliar prose excerpt in a timed setting. However, if you would like to explore this option, there are a few things to remember. First, a broad general time period referenced in the essay is not enough to gain this point. A brief reference to a historical event or even a paragraph detailing a related historical event is not enough to place a work within a broader context. The references of the broader context must be developed and sustained throughout the entire essay to gain the Sophistication point through this path. Finally, remember that the time period when the work was published is not necessarily the time period of the story. Do not be so concerned about exploring a broader context for the Sophistication point that you sacrifice time providing solid evidence and commentary.

3. Accounting for alternative interpretations of the work

In order to gain a point through this path, the writer would need to defend more than one interpretation with multiple supporting examples and analysis of each interpretation. A solid interpretation cannot be built on a word, phrase, or even a feeling but on thoughtful and sustained evidence throughout the text. Constructing and supporting one interpretation of a passage in a timed setting is challenging enough; more than one is almost impossible.

4. Employing a style that is consistently vivid and persuasive

Writers who earn the Sophistication point through vivid and persuasive writing are those who are naturally talented or have spent a lot of hours practicing writing. Earning this point requires more than using advanced vocabulary or varying sentences. Students must display a strong command of language consistently throughout the essay to earn this point. Experiment with different techniques as you practice in class, then show up on exam day and write as strongly as possible.

> **Pro tip:** In a timed setting such as the AP® Exam, your time is best spent focusing on Row B—Evidence and Commentary—fully exploring the tensions and complexities which could also earn the Sophistication point through the first path.

TIPS FOR WRITING INTRODUCTIONS AND CONCLUSIONS

The AP® prose rubric does not award points specifically for introductions and conclusions; however, you cannot simply jump into an argument without an introduction or end an argument abruptly. While these points are far less important than the evidence and commentary, let's talk briefly about introductions and conclusions.

Introductions

Since the timed essay is a rough draft, the standard introduction is not required or even necessary. Your introduction can be as short as two sentences; really anything longer is just taking time from providing evidence and commentary in your body paragraphs. The introduction is an opportunity for you to answer the prompt and establish your voice as a writer. The introduction should most definitely include your thesis, which will allow the Reader to clearly know your position and what to expect in the remainder of the essay.

If you save your thesis with your position for the end of the paper as a big ta-dah moment, the evidence and commentary throughout the essay loses its purpose. Avoid plot summary in the introduction as a way of giving the Reader a summary of the passage; write with the assumption that the reader knows the work. Having said this, you should reference the title and author just as good practice in writing. The introduction is also not a time to give lengthy historical context. If this is going to be part of your essay in establishing the work in a broader context, save those explanations for the body paragraphs. Finally, introductions should not have generalizations, rhetorical questions, or other types of hooks you may have used in prior essays.

Conclusions

Conclusions may be even more difficult than introductions. They should not simply sum up the essay but rather offer an insight as to why this piece of literature is still important and significant. Here are a few methods that work for an organic conclusion.

Circle back—The circle back method is a reference back to a key word or phrase in your intro or possibly the beginning of the passage and a way to bookend your ideas. You do not need to fully repeat ideas or arguments, but a brief reference or reframing of the idea in light of the end of the passage will give the essay a sense of closure.

Extend the idea—Another way to conclude an essay is to connect the essay to a universal theme. This includes big picture ideas which expand and extend the essay forward to push the reader to consider broad implications about humanity. When forming this type of conclusion, students should consider what universal truth they want the reader to be thinking about at the end of the essay and then explain how the essay relates to this universal truth. These conclusions answer the *so what?* and the *larger why* of the analysis.

Reference the last sentence—This may be the easiest way to draw the essay to a close without restating your argument. Prose excerpts are specifically cut off where they are for a specific reason, and they always provide a logical end to this particular portion of the larger worker.

> **Pro tip:** Commenting on the last line will allow you to once again revisit your interpretation through that lens and also provide commentary that extends throughout the entire work.

Whatever you do, avoid saying "In conclusion" to end your essay, restate your thesis verbatim, or summarize your points.

THE BIG THREE

At the end of each of the three essay chapters, we are providing you with THE BIG THREE, which is a list of three literary elements that you can analyze 99.9 percent of the time for the specific type of literature you will have to tackle. When it comes to prose, there are some literary devices that will occur more frequently than in other modes of writing. Chances are that no matter which work College Board includes for the Prose Analysis Essay, you will be able to analyze it with any of THE BIG THREE.

1. Tone

This small word packs a big punch in a text. Tone opens the door to so many avenues of thinking and analysis. Tone is the attitude a literary work takes toward its subject or that a character in the work conveys, especially as it is revealed through diction, but tone allows us to consider so much more. For example, the narrator's background experiences have a direct impact on the tone they convey about what is happening in the text, and this in turn will affect our interpretation of the events. The narrator's perspective will also shape tone and thus allows us an opportunity to question why they feel a certain way about the events, other characters, or subject.

Several techniques and devices can contribute to tone, but the most common three are **diction, syntax,** and **selection of detail**. Let's examine each of those in more detail.

- *Diction* in its most basic definition is word choice. Diction is often described as either *informal* or *colloquial* if it resembles everyday speech or as *formal* if it is instead lofty, impersonal, and dignified. Here are some common words that can be used to describe diction; as you read, create your own list of words that can be used to describe diction.

formal	*informal*	*emotional*
didactic	*colloquial*	*detached*
elevated	*poetic*	*passionate*
pretentious	*trite*	*judgmental*
verbose	*convoluted*	*frantic*

- *Syntax* is the word order or the way words are put together to form phrases, clauses, and sentences. Like diction, syntax helps create tone as it slows down or speeds up the pace of the narration. Here are some common words used to describe syntax, but think of your own descriptions as you read and consider tone.

complicated	*choppy*	*plain*
frantic	*simple*	*interrogative*
flowing	*jumbled*	*commanding*

- *Selection of detail* refers to the information the narrator is choosing to give us, whether it be a description of an event or the order in which the details are presented, and it can also affect the tone. These details are largely connected to a narrator's past or present circumstances but have a direct effect on how we construct our interpretation of a text.

Exploring tone is one of the easiest ways to get into the small details of the text, which we have emphasized are so important in writing good commentary. You should have a few key tone words memorized going into the exam but use these only as a starting point and continue to learn new words and add to your list. Here are a few words to get you started: *optimistic, threatening, disturbed, sarcastic, nostalgic, critical,* and *candid*.

2. Conflict

Conflict is one of the least examined devices in literary analysis yet opens up so many opportunities for analyzing characters, structure, and perspective. Every story has a conflict, so we should be prepared to think about the role it plays in the text. A conflict in its most basic definition is a struggle between opposing forces. Let's review the components of conflict, then talk about how they can be used in analysis.

Conflict is the tension that results between competing values either within a character, known as internal or psychological conflict, or with outside forces that obstruct a character in some way, known as external conflict.

- A conflict is *internal* when the opposing forces are two drives, impulses, or parts of a single character. Some examples of internal conflict include struggles around identity, change, fear, or overcoming the past.
- A conflict is *external* when it pits a character against something or someone outside him- or herself—another character or characters or some impersonal force. Some common external conflicts include those with other characters, society as a whole, nature, or possibly even technology.

Conflict can serve several purposes in a text, but the one thing that conflict always does is highlight values, beliefs, and ideas that the author is communicating. Let's begin by looking at the relationship between conflict and characters. When characters wrestle—either within themselves, with others, or with society as a whole—with a conflict, they are pointing us to the central and controlling ideas in a text. Joe in *Johnny Got His Gun* has an internal conflict of wanting to have his independence but struggles with how to tell his father that he no longer wants to go fishing with him, but his friend Bill Harper instead. This conflict addresses ideas that independence from parents also comes with making difficult decisions and having hard conversations. Conflicts can also be seen through contrasting characters with each character valuing different things. Joe values growing up, new experiences, and independence while his father values the father-son tradition shown in their yearly trip together. We learn about character motivation through conflict, and motivation will shape the perspective of the text. The son is eager to grow up; the father is eager for his son not to grow up. Since *Johnny Got His Gun* is told through a third-person limited point of view, we are more sympathetic to the son's desire for independence. This can—and most likely should—affect our interpretation of the story.

Inconsistencies in what characters do are ways for us to consider complexities in the characters and relationships. When Joe tells his father that he is going fishing with Bill Harper the next day, "[f]or a little while the father doesn't say anything." This signals to us that the father is processing and thinking through being replaced in their annual trip with a friend. The father then says, "[W]hy sure go along Joe" and "does Bill have a rod?" and claims he's really too tired to go and Bill should use his rod. These actions are inconsistent with the father's planning this trip for him and his son and shows us that he is having an **epiphany**, realizing that Joe is maturing.

Finally, the way characters respond to a conflict shows what they value. Characters can either yield to the conflict or rebel against it; either response helps us learn more about the character. Joe responds to his internal conflict of what to do by moving forward with the plan even though he feels "a little lump in his throat" as he "was deserting his father for Bill Harper." This shows us that Joe is willing to step closer to independence even if it means hurting his father; he values independence. Joe could have stuffed all of these feelings deep down and gone fishing with his father in spite of his feelings, but his choosing to yield to that internal conflict shows us how important his desire to grow up is. Joe's father also has a choice about how he will respond to the conflict presented to him. He can tell Joe that this is their trip, and he doesn't want him to go with Bill Harper. Or he can tell him to go ahead and give up his fishing rod for the boys, showing that he values how his son is feeling even though it may hurt him. We can learn a lot about a character's personality by the way they respond to conflict.

Conflict also provides ways to analyze the structure of a text. As noted above, the way characters respond to conflict will have a direct result on the plot and what happens next. Conflict drives action. Significant scenes often show competing value systems which are present in the conflict. In the prose essay, we can assume the chosen excerpts feature some type of significant conflict being acted upon. The buildup of the conflict—whether quick or slow—also has an impact on the structure and our interpretation. A slow rise in the conflict builds suspense which allows us more time to build sympathy or hatred for a character and also provides more time for us to draw our own conclusions about the subject. A quick escalation of events that push to a resolution in conflict can disorient readers and leave us confused on how we feel toward a subject. Sometimes conflicts are left unresolved. All of these factors affect our interpretation of the text, and the smart reader will be aware of them.

3. Figurative Language

Poets rely on figurative language because of the conciseness of its nature; the figurative language can communicate what they literally do not otherwise have room for in a poem. Fiction writers also rely on figurative language because of the way it extends our thinking on a subject or idea. If we read over these devices, we will miss the layers of meaning they add, which can have a direct impact on our interpretation of the text. The Course and Exam Description divides figurative language into two categories: figurative language centered on word choice, **imagery**, and **symbols**; and figurative language centered on comparisons. The important thing to remember with either of the skill sets is that the "comparisons, representations, and associations shift meaning from the literal to the figurative and invite readers to interpret a text" (CED 26).

Figurative language centered on word choice, imagery, and symbols:

- *Denotation* is the literal definition of a word while **connotation** is feelings, other meanings, or implied associations from a word. Exploring connotations can expand our thinking about a subject and lead us to consider the complexities and nuances associated with the word. *Johnny Got His Gun* ends with the clause "they went off without awakening his father." The word *awakening* is significant here because it not only refers to letting the father continue with his sleep but also the word has a connotation of awakening to a new phase of life where his son is less reliant on him. This points us to the central idea in the text.

- *Imagery* is details that appeal specifically to the senses. Authors choose to use imagery in a text because these details allow us to connect with an aspect of the text in a very specific and personal way. Two scenes in the passage from *Johnny Got His Gun* contrast with each other through imagery; they occur at the beginning and end of the passage. When thinking back on prior trips, the imagery has a very positive connotation describing the father and son sleeping "at night with the roar of water from the streams [. . .] in their ears all night long" in a way that makes the water seem a calming force to soothe them to sleep. However, after the conversation, "[t]hey went to sleep that night in a bed which lay against the floor of pine needles," reinforcing a hard sleeping surface pointing back to the difficult conversation that had occurred and pointing forward to the hard transition ahead.

- *Symbols* are objects that represent an abstract idea; understanding the abstract idea the symbol represents opens a new way for us to think about a central idea in the text. The father's fishing rod is a symbol in this excerpt for the passing of a blessing from a father to his son. By volunteering something "very valuable" and "perhaps the only extravagant thing his father ever had in his whole life," the father is showing that he values his son's independence.

Figurative language centered on comparison:

- **Simile**   direct explicit comparison from one thing to another usually using the words *like* or *as* to draw the connection
- **Metaphor**   comparison between two unlike things without the use of a signal word
- **Personification**   comparison made by giving human characteristics to an inanimate object
- **Allusion**   reference to another text, piece of art, song, etc., or a historical person or event for the sake of comparison

These figures of speech reframe the way we think about certain words to expand the literal meaning of the word or comparison subject and add layers to central ideas in the text.

STUDENT SAMPLE ESSAYS

We have discussed the 2018 Zenobia passage by Hawthorne at length in this chapter. Here is the prompt our student writers were given and three scored sample essays with commentary.

AP® English Literature and Composition Free-Response Questions

Question 2

(Suggested time—40 minutes. This question counts as one-third of the total essay section score.)

The following excerpt is from an 1852 novel by Nathaniel Hawthorne. In this passage, two characters who have been living on the Blithedale farm—a community designed to promote an ideal of equality achieved through communal rural living—are about to part ways. Read the passage carefully. Then, in a well-written essay, analyze how Hawthorne uses literary elements and techniques to portray the narrator's complex attitude towards Zenobia.

Her manner bewildered me. Literally,
moreover, I was dazzled by the brilliancy of the room.
A chandelier hung down in the centre, glowing with I
know not how many lights; there were separate lamps,
5   also, on two or three tables, and on marble brackets,
adding their white radiance to that of the chandelier.
The furniture was exceedingly rich. Fresh from our
old farm-house, with its homely board and benches in
the dining-room, and a few wicker chairs in the best
10 parlor, it struck me that here was the fulfillment of
every fantasy of an imagination, revelling in various
methods of costly self-indulgence and splendid ease.
Pictures, marbles, vases; in brief, more shapes of
luxury than there could be any object in enumerating,
15 except for an auctioneer's advertisement—and the
whole repeated and doubled by the reflection of a
great mirror, which showed me Zenobia's proud
figure, likewise, and my own. It cost me, I
acknowledge, a bitter sense of shame, to perceive in
20 myself a positive effort to bear up against the effect
which Zenobia sought to impose on me. I reasoned
against her, in my secret mind, and strove so to keep

my footing. In the gorgeousness with which she had
surrounded herself—in the redundance of personal

25   ornament, which the largeness of her physical nature
and the rich type of her beauty caused to seem so
suitable—I malevolently beheld the true character of
the woman, passionate, luxurious, lacking simplicity,
not deeply refined, incapable of pure and perfect taste.

30   But, the next instant, she was too powerful for all
my opposing struggles. I saw how fit it was that she
should make herself as gorgeous as she pleased, and
should do a thousand things that would have been
ridiculous in the poor, thin, weakly characters of other

35   women. To this day, however, I hardly know whether
I then beheld Zenobia in her truest attitude, or
whether that were the truer one in which she had
presented herself at Blithedale. In both, there was
something like the illusion which a great actress flings

40   around her.
       "Have you given up Blithedale forever?" I
inquired.
       "Why should you think so?" asked she.
       "I cannot tell," answered I; "except that it appears

45   all like a dream that we were ever there together."
       "It is not so to me," said Zenobia. "I should think it
a poor and meagre nature, that is capable of but one
set of forms, and must convert all the past into a
dream, merely because the present happens to be

50   unlike it. Why should we be content with our homely
life of a few months past, to the exclusion of all other
modes? It was good; but there are other lives as good
or better. Not, you will understand, that I condemn
those who give themselves up to it more entirely than

55   I, for myself, should deem it wise to do."
       It irritated me, this self-complacent,
condescending, qualified approval and criticism of a
system to which many individuals—perhaps as highly
endowed as our gorgeous Zenobia—had contributed

60   their all of earthly endeavor, and their loftiest
aspirations. I determined to make proof if there were
any spell that would exorcise her out of the part which
she seemed to be acting. She should be compelled to
give me a glimpse of something true; some nature,

65   some passion, no matter whether right or wrong,
provided it were real.

70

75

80

"Your allusion to that class of circumscribed characters, who can live in only one mode of life," remarked I, coolly, "reminds me of our poor friend Hollingsworth.[1] Possibly, he was in your thoughts, when you spoke thus. Poor fellow! It is a pity that, by the fault of a narrow education, he should have so completely immolated himself to that one idea of his; especially as the slightest modicum of common-sense would teach him its utter impracticability. Now that I have returned into the world, and can look at his project from a distance, it requires quite all my real regard for this respectable and well-intentioned man to prevent me laughing at him—as, I find, society at large does!"

85

90

Zenobia's eyes darted lightning; her cheeks flushed; the vividness of her expression was like the effect of a powerful light, flaming up suddenly within her. My experiment had fully succeeded. She had shown me the true flesh and blood of her heart, by thus involuntarily resenting my slight, pitying, half-kind, half-scornful mention of the man who was all in all with her. She herself, probably, felt this; for it was hardly a moment before she tranquillized her uneven breath, and seemed as proud and self-possessed as ever.

1. A charismatic member of the Blithedale community who assumes a leadership position.

STUDENT SAMPLE ESSAY 1

The excerpt from Nathaniel Hawthorne's 1852 novel, centers around the narrator's initial curiosity in Zenobia and later disapproval. Hawthorne includes many specific details and imagery to describe Zenobia herself and her reactions. The first person perspective allows us to experience the speaker's thoughts and the shift in his attitude towards Zenobia, and the select use of dialogue helps to reveal this shift. Hawthorne's use of descriptive imagery, first-person narration, and dialogue portrays the narrator's initial interest in Zenobia and later disdain for her.

The excerpt opens with a vivid description of the extravagance of Zenobia's manner, comparing it to that of Blithedale where they were previously living. Whereas Blithedale had "homely board and benches in the dining-room, and a few wicker chairs in the best parlor," Zenobia's manner has a chandelier in the center which dazzles the narrator. The narrator compares the greatness and beauty of the manner to Zenobia herself which demonstrates the high regard they have for her initially. Later in the excerpt, after the narrator has lectured Zenobia about criticizing those who choose to stay at Blithedale, Zenobia is described with "her cheeks flushed; the vividness of her expression was like the effect of a powerful light, flaming up suddenly within her." This expression of real emotion delights the narrator though Zenobia quickly neutralizes her demeanor, and this contributes to the narrator's feeling that Zenobia is acting and not truly being real.

Hawthorne's decision to tell the story from the first-person perspective of the narrator is greatly beneficial to the reader's understanding of how the narrator perceives Zenobia. At the beginning of the excerpt, the narrator's interest in Zenobia and wish to know her true demeanor is demonstrated. A bit later in the excerpt, the narrator states that they feel Zenobia is acting and wishes that Zenobia "should be compelled to give me a glimpse of something true; some nature, some passion," which shows that despite their growing disapproval of Zenobia, they still yearn to know her real thoughts. And finally, in the last paragraph, the reader gets to experience the narrator's delight in their successful experiment and withdrawal of true emotion from Zenobia.

The use of dialogue is very important and helps further along with the narrator's shift in attitude toward Zenobia. The dialogue starts when the narrator asks if Zenobia has given up Blithedale forever. Zenobia's critical response to the narrator's comparison of Blithedale to a dream-like state irritates the narrator. The narrator perceives her attitude as almost arrogant and full of self-importance, and this is when their shift in attitude begins. The narrator begins to believe that Zenobia is acting and not showing her true thoughts or self so the narrator speaks to Zenobia in a way that will provoke some real emotion from her. Though we do not see Zenobia's response to this, the narrator is satisfied with the small amount of emotion she shows. The dialogue in the passage guides the shift in the narrator's attitude toward Zenobia. In the last line of the excerpt, the narrator acknowledges that Zenobia probably felt she was reacting in a way that would expose her true feelings and nature which is why she tranquilizes her expression. This just furthers the narrator's feeling that she is acting.

Score: 1-3-0

This essay begins with a short introduction addressing the prompt by making the defensible claim that the narrator is initially interested in Zenobia but later has disdain for her. In Row B the student earns three points for having solid body paragraphs. The essay is organized by device but could be strengthened if there were stronger insights linked to the device. For example, the first topic sentence does link the imagery to the contrast between the mansion and Blithedale farm, but the second topic sentence—while identifying the point of view—could go even further and tell specifically how it benefits the reader. While the essay contains three literary elements and evidence to support the claims, the commentary is not specific enough to support all the claims consistently. This essay, however, is a solid example of literary analysis. This essay would not earn the Sophistication point because it does not show enough complexity in the body paragraphs. This is a good example of an essay organized by device and insight, and while the essay is solid in its analysis of devices, this limits the writer's ability to explore complexities of the insight since the focus of each paragraph is on only one device.

STUDENT SAMPLE ESSAY 2

In this excerpt, Nathaniel Hawthorne uses imagery and metaphor to express that the narrator sees Zenobia as an Enigma: a code that must be cracked, and a dangerous con artist hiding behind a facade. The narrator's way of viewing Zenobia is similar to that of the way society portrays Eve as Adam's seductress and compromiser or Femme Fatale.

In the first paragraph of the passage, the narrator begins by saying that Zenobia's manner bewildered him but "literally, moreover," he was "dazzled by the brilliancy of the room." He describes the room as having a chandelier with an unknown amount of lights, multiple tables, marble fixtures, and "rich" furniture. The narrator equates Zenobia's manner to the room and juxtaposes them by saying that her manner is more literally the room that he is bewildered by. As a result, the intense imagery that Hawthorne uses to describe that decadent room is transferred onto Zenobia as well. This paints our initial picture of her as luxurious and lavish. The narrator continues to describe the room, Zenobia, as "the fulfillment of every fantasy of an imagination," and says that she represents "costly self-indulgence and splendid ease." From this selection, we can see how the narrator believes that Zenobia is excessive and that much of her exterior and appearance is unnecessary. We can also learn that he disapproves of self-indulgence and luxury.

More imagery is used when the narrator places Zenobia's reflection in a "great mirror" where he also sees himself next to her beauty and opulence but then scolds himself for being weak and indulging himself even if it were for just a second. He says "I reasoned against her in my secret mind, and strove so to keep my footing." Not only does this imagery of him seeing his and Zenobia's reflection in the mirror portray his distaste for her indulgent appearance and attitude, but also his fear that she will compromise him by seducing him with her luxury. This is similar to the literary archetype, the Femme Fatale, where a female is portrayed as a dangerous weapon against men and oftentimes society because of her seductive powers.

The narrator's suspicion of Zenobia is perpetuated with metaphors that he uses to describe her and the situation. He compares her to an actress with an allusion that she "flings around her," and uses words such as "opposing" and "struggle" to compare his conversation with her to a battle where he is trying to keep his purity from being destroyed. He interrogates her and asks if she has "given up Blithedale forever," implying that she has cast it aside in search of something newer and shinier. He continues to compare her to an actress by saying he "determined to make proof if there were any spell that would exorcise her out of the part which she seemed to be acting," implying not only that she is a liar but also that he would be the one to defeat her evil.

Finally, he is able to phase and disrupt her perfect facade by bringing up her old friend Hollingsworth. He describes her as her "eyes darted lightning; her cheeks were flushed," which was exactly his goal to see her at a vulnerable state where she was not manufacturing her appearance or mood. She immediately snapped back into her role, but the narrator took pride in finally defeating the Femme Fatale by causing her appearance and confidence to falter even for a second.

Score: 1-3-1

This student writer receives the Thesis point by identifying the narrator's attitude as viewing Zenobia as a "code to be cracked" and that she is a "con artist hiding behind a facade." The writer then places the work in a broader context by identifying Zenobia as an archetype of the femme fatale. The line of reasoning, though not established in the thesis, is centered on chronological order of the passage and unpacking devices as they appear in the passage. Each body paragraph identifies a device, builds a claim around the device (e.g., "the intense imagery that Hawthorne uses to describe that decadent room is transferred onto Zenobia as well"), then comments on how Zenobia displays the femme fatale archetype. The archetype analysis in each paragraph does place this excerpt in a broader context earning the Sophistication point on Row C. However, there is not enough evidence and commentary to consistently support all claims in the paragraphs, thus earning three points on Row B.

STUDENT SAMPLE ESSAY 3

The excerpt from the 1852 novel by Nathaniel Hawthorne describes two characters, Zenobia and a narrator, who have lived on Blithedale farm and are about to part ways. Hawthorne portrays the narrator as having a critical but caring attitude towards Zenobia through her questioning of Zenobia's new life and way of thinking, coupled with her actions to try and bring back some of the Zenobia that she knew before.

From the first paragraph, it is evident that Zenobia is living a lavish life compared to her old life at Blithedale, which causes the narrator to question Zenobia's morals and new life in general. The narrator describes the rich furnishings in the room in a bewildering tone. She says, "...I know not how many lights; there were separate lamps, also on two or three tables, and on marble brackets..." (3-5). By listing all of the different extravagant sources of light, it is almost like the narrator is questioning why there needs to be so many different lamps or chandeliers. She doesn't understand why all of it is necessary, which causes the readers to infer that the narrator and Zenobia's life at Blithedale was not rich or luxurious. This is further proven when the narrator says, "Fresh from our old farm-house, with its homely board and benches in the dining room... it struck me that here was the fulfilment of every fantasy..." (7-11). This sentence directly contrasts the narrator's life at Blithedale to what she is seeing before her eyes, but the bewildered tone in which she reveals her surroundings shows that she doesn't find the luxurious items or Zenobia's new morals pleasing.

This disapproving attitude towards Zenobia is accelerated when the narrator directly criticizes Zenobia, either in her thoughts or out loud. The narrator says, "I malevolently beheld the true character of the woman, passionate, luxurious, lacking simplicity, not deeply refined, incapable of pure and perfect taste" (27-29). The narrator "malevolently" examined the "true character" of Zenobia. The negative connotation of malevolent paired so closely with Zenobia's true character portrays that the narrator is not fond of what Zenobia is displaying. The descriptions of Zenobia's character also get progressively worse, showing the narrator's disapproving attitude. Then, Zenobia outwardly criticizes her life at Blithedale, something the narrator holds close to her heart (by the way that she describes the furniture in Blithedale as "homely" as her apparent disgust with the luxurious life Zenobia is living). The narrator in return thinks, "It irritated me, this self-complacent, condescending, qualified approval and criticism of a system [life at Blithedale]..." (56-58). The narrator directly states that she is "irritated" with Zenobia's new outlook on life and almost attacks it in her mind, cementing the idea that she has a critical attitude towards Zenobia.

At the end of the passage, it seems that the narrator does not want to accept that Zenobia has changed. It is evident that she disagrees with her way of life but cannot fully believe that this is the way Zenobia feels. She says, "She should be compelled to give me a glimpse of something true; some nature, some passion..." (63-65). This attempt to bring part of the "old" Zenobia back shows that the narrator may be critical, but she still loves and cares about Zenobia. The narrator goes on to describe Hollingsworth, a man that does not fit with Zenobia's new standards. It is clear that Zenobia likes this boy, because "her cheeks flushed; the vividness in her expressions was like the effect of a powerful light..." (81-83). This reaction seems to comfort the narrator because the last paragraph has a happier, lighter tone. This change in tone and the mention of Hollingsworth in general proves that the narrator may disagree with Zenobia but still cares about her.

Score: 1-4-1

This essay begins with a thesis answering the prompt with a defensible claim (the narrator has a critical but caring attitude) then continues to establish a line of reasoning by noting that Hawthorne does this through her questioning Zenobia's new way of life and trying to bring her back to her old self. This essay is organized by insights that occur at the beginning, middle, and end of the passage and pulls multiple devices and techniques into each paragraph for support. This student earns four points in Row B as the evidence and commentary consistently support the claims. For example, the first body paragraph centers on the claim that the new lavish lifestyle of Zenobia causes the narrator to question her morals; she then supports this with examples of a "bewildering tone" and repetition of light before contrasting that with the setting of Blithedale farm. Each body paragraph provides relevant and adequate evidence and consistent analysis of literary techniques. The writer ends with commentary on the last paragraph and circles back to the critical and caring attitude. This essay earns the Sophistication point through fully exploring the complexities and tensions.

We have discussed the following passage by Dalton Trumbo at length in this chapter. Here is the prompt our student writers were given and two scored sample essays with commentary.

AP® English Literature and Composition Free-Response Questions

Question 2

(Suggested time—40 minutes. This question counts as one-third of the total essay section score.)

The following excerpt is from Dalton Trumbo's novel *Johnny Got His Gun* (1939). In this passage, the main character, Joe, is remembering a camping trip that he took with his father when Joe was fifteen years old. Read the passage carefully. Then, in a well-written essay, analyze how Trumbo uses literary elements and techniques to convey the complex relationship between the young man and his father.

In your response you should do the following:

- Respond to the prompt with a thesis that presents a defensible interpretation.
- Select and use evidence to support your line of reasoning.
- Explain how the evidence supports your line of reasoning.
- Use appropriate grammar and punctuation in communicating your argument.

The campfire was built in front of a tent
and the tent was under an enormous pine. When you
slept inside the tent it seemed always that it was
raining outside because the needles from the pine kept
5   falling. Sitting across from him and staring into the
fire was his father. Each summer they came to this
place which was nine thousand feet high and covered
with pine trees and dotted with lakes. They fished in
the lakes and when they slept at night the roar of
10   water from the streams which connected the lakes
sounded in their ears all night long.
    They had been coming to this place ever
since he was seven. Now he was fifteen and Bill
Harper was going to come tomorrow. He sat in front
15   of the fire and looked across at his father and
wondered just how he was going to tell him. It was a

very serious thing. Tomorrow for the first time in all
their trips together he wanted to go fishing with
someone other than his father. On previous trips the
20 idea had never occurred to him. His father had always
preferred his company to that of men and he had
always preferred his father's company to that of the
other guys. But now Bill Harper was coming up
tomorrow and he wanted to go fishing with him. He
25 knew it was something that had to happen sometime.
Yet he also knew that it was the end of something. It
was an ending and a beginning and he wondered just
how he should tell his father about it.

  So he told him very casually. He said Bill Harper's
30 coming up tomorrow and I thought maybe I'd go out
with him. He said Bill Harper doesn't know very
much about fishing and I do so I think if you don't
mind I'll get up early in the morning and meet Harper
and he and I will go fishing.

35 For a little while his father didn't say a thing. Then
he said why sure go along Joe. And then a little later
his father said has Bill Harper got a rod? He told his
father no Bill hasn't got a rod. Well said his father
why don't you take my rod and let Bill use yours? I
40 don't want to go fishing tomorrow anyhow. I'm tired
and I think I'll rest all day. So you use my rod and let
Bill use yours.

  It was as simple as that and yet he knew it was a
great thing. His father's rod was a very valuable one.
45 It was perhaps the only extravagance his father had
had in his whole life. It had amber leaders and
beautiful silk windings. Each spring his father sent the
rod away to a man in Colorado Springs who was an
expert on rods. The man in Colorado Springs
50 carefully scraped the varnish off the rod and rewound
it and revarnished it and it came back glistening new
each year. There was nothing his father treasured
more. He felt a little lump in his throat as he thought
that even as he was deserting his father for Bill
55 Harper his father had volunteered the rod.

  They went to sleep that night in the bed which lay
against a floor of pine needles. They had scooped the
needles out to make a little hollow place for their hips.
He lay awake quite a while thinking about tomorrow

60   and his father who slept beside him. Then he fell
       asleep. At six o'clock Bill Harper whispered to him
       through the tent flap. He got up and gave Bill his rod
       and took his father's for himself and they went off
       without awakening his father.

STUDENT SAMPLE ESSAY 1

In the passage, Johnny Got His Gun, by Dalton Trumbo, a boy and his
father go on their annual camping trip to fish during the summer. However, this time the boy does not want to go fishing with his father anymore, he wants to bring his friend instead. In Trumbo's passage he uses
very specific details to describe the importance of the campsite and his
father's fishing pole, a third person point of view in order to express the
young boy's feelings, and simple/informal diction. This use of these literary techniques portrays the distance growing between the young man
and his father as the young man is growing older and becoming less
dependent on his father.

The attention to detail is very important when it comes to describing the location of the campsite and especially his father's fishing rod. In
the first paragraph, the author states, "When you slept inside the tent it
always seemed that it was raining outside because the needles from the
pine kept falling." This vivid sensory imagery lets the reader know that
there is a connection between this campsite and the boy and his father.
If it was your first time camping you would not notice these specific
details and you would not be able to describe it as well as compared to
someone who has camped multiple times. It establishes the connec-
tion/memories they have to the campsite, which are about to be broken when the author states, "Tomorrow for the first time in all their
trips together he wanted to go fishing with someone other than his
father." The boy wants to make memories at this campsite with someone other than his father. Now the boy's friend does not own a fishing
pole, so his father allows his son to take his, as if he is being replaced.

The point of view of this passage is 3rd person. The 3rd person
point of view allows the reader to view and understand each character's
feelings and thoughts. While the young boy's feelings/thoughts are more
thoroughly described throughout the passage, the reader is left to interpret the father's emotions. The passage states, "He felt a little lump in his
throat as he thought that even as he was deserting his father for Bill
Harper his father had volunteered the rod." From this third person point

of view, the reader is able to see/feel the guilt that is being expressed by the young man. This guilt shows how much the young boy cares for the father. Even though he is choosing not to take his father fishing, he still feels guilty about it because of how tight their relationship was.

In the passage, the father and the young man share simpler diction in the way they talk to each other. The father states, "has Bill Harper got a rod?" and the son replies with "no Bill hasn't got a rod". When you meet someone for the first time and they either have an accent or use different diction, it is normally because they got it from one of their parents. The young boy is around his father a lot and has a strong relationship with him that he talks just like his dad.

Score: 1-3-0

The thesis in this essay is straightforward, makes a defensible claim, and answers the prompt by addressing the complexity as a result of "the distance growing between the young man and his father as the young man is growing older and becoming less dependent on his father." The essay is organized by device which establishes a line of reasoning. Each paragraph has sufficient support, but because the quotes are in long chunks instead of small words and phrases sprinkled throughout, the writer misses opportunities to push analysis further. For example, in the first body paragraph, the writer claims that the imagery lets the reader know there's a connection between the son and his father but never specifies what that connection is. The second body paragraph only brings in one example of third-person point of view and how that is relevant; other examples with commentary would strengthen this paragraph.

SAMPLE STUDENT ESSAY 2

This passage is about a camping trip that a boy and his father take each year. However, this year is different because the boy wants to fish with his friend instead of his father. The boy struggles to tell his father this, but his father's response is very thoughtful. In *Johnny Got His Gun* by Dalton Trumbo, the author characterizes the relationship between the boy and his father as maturing and less dependent in order to demonstrate that growing apart from your parent is a part of life that is necessary for becoming your own person.

Trumbo uses point of view to highlight the importance of developing oneself away from one's parents. The point of view is third person limited because the narrator only knows the boy's thoughts and feelings. Trumbo's choice of perspective prevents the reader from knowing the father's inner thoughts and forces the reader to wonder how the father will react to the boy wanting to fish with his friend. Therefore, the readers are just as clue-less about the father's emotions as the boy. For example, when the boy is trying to tell his father the news, "he sat in front of the fire and looked across at his father and wondered how he was going to tell him. It was a very serious thing." Through the point of view, Trumbo highlights the inner conflict the boy is feeling and conceals how the father may be feeling about everything. The boy could think it is a "very serious thing" while the father could think it is nothing. The third person limited point of view focuses on the boy, not his father. This sheds light on the idea that the boy is his own individual person who must make decisions and grow for him-self. His father's thoughts should not hinder what the boy feels or wants. Therefore, the perspective is important because it shows how the boy is breaking free from his father and maturing into an adult.

Along with point of view, Trumbo uses selection of detail to highlight how some traditions need to be broken to develop as a human being. Trumbo emphasizes specific aspects of the story to drive his point across. For example, he explains how the boy grew up going on this camping trip each year because, "they had been coming to this place ever since he was seven. Now he was fifteen and Bill Harper was going to come tomorrow." Trumbo specifically chose this detail because the reader will better understand the boy's reluctance to telling his father that his friend is coming. With year after year, the routine gets stronger, and one becomes more and more attached to the specific ways of doing things. However, the boy is a very different person at fifteen than he was at seven. So, the routine must change in response to the boy's development. Therefore, Trumbo's detail about how long the boy and his father have been going on this trip shows the reader that the boy needs to tweak his actions in order to develop as an individual. Along with this, Trumbo emphasizes how the fishing rod is loved by the father by explaining that the, "rod was a very valuable one. It was perhaps the only extravagance his father had in his whole life . . . There was nothing his father treasured more." This spe-cific detail about the value of the rod highlights how the father letting the son use it is like a right of passage. The father recognizes that the boy is growing up when he chooses to fish with his friend. Therefore, the father entrusts the boy with his prized possession to show the boy that the father sees how he is growing up and is mature enough to take care of valuable things. Trumbo highlights this detail because it emphasizes the importance of the father allowing his son to use the rod because if it was a cheap rod, the act would not be so powerful.

Furthermore, Trumbo utilizes syntax to shed light on how the relationship between the boy and his father is blossoming into a mature stage as the boy learns to be more independent. The syntax is very straightforward and explains each detail clearly. It is a series of events that is simply organized. Trumbo flows the idea of one sentence into the next by writing, "he knew it was something that had to happen sometime. Yet he also knew that it was the end of something. It was an ending and a beginning." The arrangement of words in the sentences work together to add onto a previous idea. The boy "knew" flows from the first sentence to the second, then the idea that an era was "ending" flows from the second to the third. The syntax demonstrates how the boy understands that he is transitioning from a child to a less dependent adolescent. Therefore, the reader sees how the boy and his father's relationship is just morphing into a different shape where the boy is no longer an attachment of his father. This is a critical stage in life because everyone must take a step back from the people who raised them in order to find out which characteristics best represent them.

In the novel Johnny Got His Gun by Dalton Trumbo, Trumbo uses point of view, specific details, and syntax to describe the relationship between the boy and the father as maturing in order to demonstrate how it is imperative for children to become less dependent on their parents to find who they truly are as a person.

Score: 1-4-1

This essay does so many things well, starting with the thesis which addresses the prompt but also extends the idea by claiming that "growing apart from your parent is a part of life that is necessary for becoming your own person." The body paragraphs that follow are both insightful and full of evidence. The writer organizes mostly by device and insights in the topic sentences. There are enough quotes sprinkled throughout, but note the amount of commentary provided on the evidence. This writer shows the complexity by using words like "however" and "therefore" to contrast ideas and seemingly conflicting feelings. This attention to juxtaposition and contrasts earns the Sophistication point through the first pathway.

The following question about Kate Chopin's "The Story of an Hour" is completely new. We recommend that you go through the process on your own. Excavate the prompt; read the excerpt multiple times to think through the *what, how,* and *why*; take notes; and apply what you have learned in this chapter to write your answer.

AP® English Literature and Composition Free-Response Questions

Question 2

(Suggested time—40 minutes. This question counts as one-third of the total essay section score.)

In "The Story of an Hour" by Kate Chopin (1894), Louise Mallard is confronted with the news that her husband has been killed in a train wreck. Read the passage from this short story carefully. Then, in a well-written essay, analyze how Chopin uses literary elements and techniques to portray Mrs. Mallard's complex feelings about her marriage to Mr. Mallard.

In your response you should do the following:

- Respond to the prompt with a thesis that presents a defensible interpretation.
- Select and use evidence to support your line of reasoning.
- Explain how the evidence supports your line of reasoning.
- Use appropriate grammar and punctuation in communicating your argument.

> She did not hear the story as many women have
> heard the same, with a paralyzed inability to
> accept its significance. She wept at once, with sudden,
> wild abandonment, in her sister's arms. When the
> 5   storm of grief had spent itself she went away to her
> room alone. She would have no one follow her.
>   There stood, facing the open window, a
> comfortable, roomy armchair. Into this she sank,
> pressed down by a physical exhaustion that
> 10   haunted her body and seemed to reach into her soul.
>   She could see in the open square before her
> house the tops of trees that were all aquiver with the
> new spring life. The delicious breath of rain was in the
> air. In the street below a peddler was crying his wares.
> 15   The notes of a distant song which someone was singing

reached her faintly, and countless sparrows were
twittering in the eaves.

    There were patches of blue sky showing here and
there through the clouds that had met and piled one
20   above the other in the west facing her window.

    She sat with her head thrown back upon the
cushion of the chair, quite motionless, except when a
sob came up into her throat and shook her, as a child
who has cried itself to sleep continues to sob in its
25   dreams.

    She was young, with a fair, calm face, whose lines
bespoke repression and even a certain strength.
But now there was a dull stare in her eyes, whose gaze
was fixed away off yonder on one of those patches of
30   blue sky. It was not a glance of reflection, but rather
indicated a suspension of intelligent thought.

    There was something coming to her and she was
waiting for it, fearfully. What was it? She did not
know; it was too subtle and elusive to name. But she
35   felt it, creeping out of the sky, reaching toward her
through the sounds, the scents, the color that filled
the air.

    Now her bosom rose and fell tumultuously. She was
beginning to recognize this thing that was
40   approaching to possess her, and she was striving
to beat it back with her will—as powerless as her
two white slender hands would have been.

    When she abandoned herself a little whispered word
escaped her slightly parted lips. She said it over and
45   over under her breath: "free, free, free!" The vacant
stare and the look of terror that had followed it went
from her eyes. They stayed keen and bright. Her pulses
beat fast, and the coursing blood warmed and relaxed
every inch of her body.

50   She did not stop to ask if it were or were not a
monstrous joy that held her. A clear and exalted
perception enabled her to dismiss the suggestion as
trivial.

    She knew that she would weep again when she
55   saw the kind, tender hands folded in death; the face that
had never looked save with love upon her, fixed and
gray and dead. But she saw beyond that bitter moment
a long procession of years to come that would belong
to her absolutely. And she opened and spread her arms

60   out to them in welcome.

There would be no one to live for her during those coming years; she would live for herself. There would be no powerful will bending hers in that blind persistence with which men and women believe they

65   have a right to impose a private will upon a fellow-creature. A kind intention or a cruel intention made the act seem no less a crime as she looked upon it in that brief moment of illumination.

And yet she had loved him—sometimes. Often

70   she had not. What did it matter! What could love, the unsolved mystery, count for in face of this possession of self-assertion which she suddenly recognized as the strongest impulse of her being!

"Free! Body and soul free!" she kept whispering.

CHAPTER REVIEW

Let's recap the process you've learned in this chapter in order to write a successful Prose Analysis essay.

1. Unpack the prompt before you read the prose excerpt.

2. Read the prose prompt two to three times, taking notes on *what* you notice, *how* you see it—literary devices—and *why* this is important as you read.

3. Write a thesis statement that answers the prompt, is defensible, and includes your interpretation of the text.

4. Organize your essay so there is a clear line of reasoning.

5. Select evidence that is both relevant and sufficient to support your insights.

6. Make sure the commentary on the evidence connects back to the thesis.

7. Conclude the essay by either circling back to the beginning, extending the idea, or referencing the last sentence of the excerpt.

8. If time allows, proofread for smooth transitions and clear communication of ideas.

5

Question 3: Literary Argument Essay

INTRODUCTION

In comparison to the first two essays, question 3, the Literary Argument essay, is a different beast. For the other essays, you are given a text to read, analyze, and write about. But for this third and final essay question, there is no text provided. Instead, you will need to select a full-length work of literary merit that you've read, know well, and can discuss at length to answer the prompt. You can think of it like a "reader's choice" essay. Hopefully, you will read some full-length works of fiction or drama in your AP® Literature class, as students are typically the most successful on this essay when they have read their chosen work recently and it's still fresh in their minds. Furthermore, the thoughtful discussions you have in class on the novels and plays you read, and the lessons provided by your teacher to guide your close reading and thorough understanding of each work's complexities and literary elements, are all going to benefit you when approaching this essay.

One thing you will quickly notice about this essay is the part of the prompt that says to *avoid plot summary*. Every prompt says this same thing; they *really* don't want you to just retell the story. Instead, aim for a nuanced analytical discussion of the work as it relates to the prompt and how an overall meaning of the work is illuminated by the author.

EXCAVATING THE PROMPT

Every question 3 essay prompt will center around a topic or idea commonly found in literary fiction and drama. The prompt might ask about a character who experiences injustice, a common **symbol** (like a house), how **setting** affects a character, or the quandary of moral ambiguity. Whatever topic the prompt is based on will be general enough that you could apply it to almost any book. The prompt will be followed by a list of about thirty titles, which are all works identified by College Board's test development committee that fit the prompt. Keep in mind that while these titles are provided, you are *not* required to use a book from the list. You can write on *any* work of literary merit you know well and that works with the prompt.

The Literary Argument essay assesses your ability to:

- write a thesis statement that responds to the prompt and provides a defensible interpretation,
- provide textual evidence to support your claim,
- explain *how* the evidence supports your claim, and
- use appropriate grammar, spelling, and punctuation.

All Literary Argument essay prompts will offer some sort of brief introduction to the prompt's main topic or idea, followed by directions to choose a work from your own reading that applies to the prompt or to select a work from the provided list. Then, every prompt will direct you to write an essay analyzing how the prompt's topic contributes to the meaning of the work as a whole. Finally, there will always be a reminder not to merely summarize the plot.

Here is a prompt from a previous exam:

> Many works of literature feature characters who have been given a literal or figurative gift. The gift may be an object, or it may be a quality such as uncommon beauty, significant social position, great mental or imaginative faculties, or extraordinary physical powers. Yet this gift is often also a burden or a handicap. Select a character from a novel, epic, or play who has been given a gift that is both an advantage and a problem. Then write a well-developed essay analyzing the complex nature of the gift and how the gift contributes to the meaning of the work as a whole.
>
> You may choose a work from the list below or another work of equal literary merit. Do not merely summarize the plot. (2018 AP® Free-Response Question 3)

Most prompts will be laid out this way—with the introduction to the topic provided in the first part of the prompt, followed by the instructions for executing your essay. We will continue to come back to this prompt throughout the chapter, culminating with student sample essays with teacher commentary at the end of the chapter.

As you read question 3 prompts, underline key words and the writing task they are asking you to do. We can see that this prompt has a few elements you need to cover in your essay:

- Identify a character and the gift
- The advantage of the gift
- The problem of the gift
- The gift's relation to the work as a whole (which is just another way of saying a theme)

Pro tip: Most prompts will have more than one task, so before deciding which work to write about and planning your essay, read the prompt several times to make sure you address each part. Also, as you near the end of your essay, go back and check the prompt for any potential missing elements you may still need to work into your essay.

Your Turn

Try your hand at excavating this prompt, also from a previous exam.

Select a novel, play, or epic poem that features a character whose origins are unusual or mysterious. Then write an essay in which you analyze how these origins shape the character and that character's relationships, and how the origins contribute to the meaning of the work as a whole.

You may choose a work from the list below or one of comparable literary merit. Do not merely summarize the plot. (2017 AP* Free-Response Question 3)

TECHNIQUES FOR LITERARY ARGUMENT

Due to the nature of this essay, you won't be explicitly analyzing literary techniques in your response as you do in the other two essays. But they still matter. They matter in the way that the author uses different stylistic elements to craft themes, or messages, throughout the story. And since **theme** is an essential part of your argument for a question 3 essay, we'll be looking at some of the techniques that help to construct it. When you read a full-length work of literature, whether it is on your own or with your class, you should be paying attention to the way the author is wielding the elements in the chart below to create that all-important overall meaning of the work.

Key Terms

antagonist a character or a nonhuman force that opposes or is in conflict with the protagonist

characterization the presentation of a fictional personage. A term like "a good character" can, then, be ambiguous—it may mean that the personage is virtuous or that he or she is well presented regardless of his or her characteristics or moral qualities.

climax the third part of plot, the point at which the action stops rising and begins falling or reversing

conflict struggle between opposing forces. A conflict is *external* when it pits a character against something or someone outside himself or herself. A conflict is *internal* when the opposing forces are two drives, impulses, or parts of a single character.

foil   character that serves as a contrast to another

motif   recurrent device, formula, or situation within a literary work

motive   animating impulse for an action, the reason why something is done or attempted

plot   arrangement of the action. The five main parts or phases of plot are exposition, rising action, climax or turning point, falling action, and conclusion or resolution.

protagonist   main character in a work

sequence   the ordering of action in a fictional plot

setting   time and place of the action in a work of fiction, poetry, or drama

symbol   person, place, thing, or event that figuratively represents or stands for something else

theme   the insight about a topic communicated in a work (e.g., "All living things are equally precious"). Most literary works have multiple themes. Usually, a theme is implicitly communicated by the work as a whole rather than explicitly stated in it.

CHOOSING A WORK

As we said in the chapter's introduction, it would behoove you to select a work that you have:

- read recently (within the past two years, preferably in your AP® Literature class),
- closely read and analyzed,
- studied in class or outside of school, and/or
- already written about for a practice essay or other writing assignment.

None of the criteria listed above are requirements, but we believe it will strongly benefit you to keep them in mind when deciding which book or play to write your essay about. There are very few limitations to your options so go with what you know.

> **Pro tip:** We suggest preparing two or three works as your go-to choices heading into the exam. Review each one—its main characters, themes, and **plot**—the week leading up to exam day.

Let's imagine a worst-case scenario—that *none* of the books you have read fit the essay prompt. This actually happened to our students when a question 3 essay asked for students to write about a coming-of-age book and we hadn't read one all year, or even the year prior. Don't panic if this happens to you. You'll just need to get creative. While none of the *books* we read were technically coming-of-age works, some of the characters within the stories could be considered as such. For example, we read *Beloved* by Toni Morrison, so some students wrote their essays on Denver, who has a beautiful coming-of-age moment when she finally gains the confidence and strength to step off the porch to seek help for her mother. Remember that even if an entire *book* doesn't seem to fit the prompt topic perfectly, you can probably think of an individual character, or a particular **conflict** or subplot storyline, that does. Once you identify one, roll with it and start writing. Chances are it will pay off since you'll likely be writing a unique and original essay that Readers will find refreshing.

Without fail, every year, students ask us the same three questions about selecting a work:

1. Can I write about *Harry Potter* (or any other popular children's book)?
   Answer: Sure. You can write about any work of literature if it relates to the prompt. But . . . Of course, there's a *but*, right? We have both been AP® Readers for several years, and we have *very* rarely seen these essays score highly. Students tend to focus too much on plot summary with perhaps some surface-level analysis, most likely because they haven't had the robust analytical discussions they have had with works studied in class. Essays on books like *Harry Potter* typically score in the low- to midrange on the rubric.

2. What if the Reader scoring my essay hasn't read the book I choose to write on?
   Answer: Don't worry about this. We promise you that if we haven't read it, our Table Leader has, or another Reader at our table has, or a Reader in the room of over 1,000 Readers has, or we have at least heard of it and know the basics to fairly evaluate your essay. And even if *none* of us has heard of the book, we will still read your essay with the care and attention it deserves. Along with this question, students have asked if they can make up a book to write on. We do not suggest doing this, because your Reader could very well look it up to see if the book is real, but more so because your essay will be lacking the specific textual evidence and quality commentary that comes from an actual book.

3. Can I write about a movie based on a book?
   Answer: You can, but we don't recommend it. We often see this happen with *The Great Gatsby*. Some students will accidently write, "In the movie *The Great Gatsby*," or will even go so far as to write about a movie that is only a movie, not adapted from a book. Here's the problem with writing about movies—oftentimes, they are different, and in some cases, much different than the book. Therefore, your evidence runs the risk of being inaccurate. As with essays on children's books, essays based on movies are

not as successful because the time spent studying movies in class comes nowhere near the amount paid to novels and plays.

Taking all of this advice into consideration, once you have a book in mind, go back to the parts of the prompt you underlined. Check to see if your selected work will cover all the elements the prompt is asking you to include. If not, you probably want to find another work that does.

PLANNING YOUR ESSAY

After you have chosen the work you want to focus on for your essay, you need to carefully plan what elements of it would best answer the prompt. This can be difficult since you have some three hundred (or more!) pages to consider and only forty minutes to write. There is no way you will be able to cover the whole story and we actually don't want you to. The prompt's directions explicitly say to avoid plot summary. Therefore, stick to what the prompt is asking. In the blank space underneath the prompt, jot down some notes on anything related to the prompt that comes to mind.

Returning to the prompt provided earlier and reprinted below, we have provided an example of what brainstorming notes might look like using *The Great Gatsby*:

> Many works of literature feature characters who have been given a literal or figurative gift. The gift may be an object, or it may be a quality such as uncommon beauty, significant social position, great mental or imaginative faculties, or extraordinary physical powers. Yet this gift is often also a burden or a handicap. Select a character from a novel, epic, or play who has been given a gift that is both an advantage and a problem. Then write a well-developed essay analyzing the complex nature of the gift and how the gift contributes to the meaning of the work as a whole.
>
> You may choose a work from the list below or another work of equal literary merit. Do not merely summarize the plot. (2018 AP® Free-Response Question 3)

Once you have gathered some ideas on paper, the next step is to identify two or three specific scenes from the work that you can use as textual evidence. Having these scenes in mind *before* you write will help your essay to maintain focus and the specificity and depth Readers are looking for. Consider scenes from different parts of the book, particularly the **climax** and perhaps a scene from both the beginning and the end of the work.

Normally, you would combine these steps into one fluid chart like the one we have provided for you, but we've split them into two parts (Worksheet 9) to demonstrate the thought process and steps to take when planning a successfully organized essay.

WORKSHEET 9 SAMPLE

Elements from prompt to cover in essay	Brainstorming notes
Identify a character and the gift	Jay Gatsby's gift for infinite hope
The advantage of the gift	• ambition to succeed • lavish lifestyle • legal protection • optimism • dream of reuniting with Daisy
The problem of the gift	• illegal behavior • disillusionment • results in multiple deaths, including his own
The gift's relation to the work as a whole	Gatsby's unbridled desire leads only to destruction, revealing that the American Dream is nothing but a façade created by unrealistic hope.

WORKSHEET 9 SAMPLE, *continued*

Brainstorming notes	Scenes
Jay Gatsby's gift for infinite hope	"Can't repeat the past? Of course you can." *(famous quote, could be used in introduction)*
• ambition to succeed • lavish lifestyle • legal protection • optimism • dream of reuniting with Daisy	• Gatsby party scene • reunion with Daisy scene
• illegal behavior • disillusionment • results in multiple deaths, including his own	• hotel room scene—Tom exposes Gatsby as a bootlegger, causing Gatsby to lose Daisy • car accident scene—Myrtle's death • Gatsby's death scene—Tom and Gatsby's death
Gatsby's unbridled desire leads only to destruction, revealing that the American Dream is nothing but a façade created by unrealistic hope.	Tie back to the theme, or parts of the theme. Along with each piece of evidence, explicitly explain its relevance to the prompt or your chosen theme to create a line of reasoning.

Your Turn

Refer back to the 2018 question 3 prompt on page 154, consider a novel, epic, or play that you have read, and try your hand at filling in Worksheet 9 on a blank piece of paper or by downloading it from the digital landing page.

WORKSHEET 9

Elements from prompt to cover in essay	Brainstorming notes	Scenes

WRITING A THESIS STATEMENT

While there is no one way to write a thesis statement, there are some general guidelines to follow to ensure you earn the point for the thesis statement. Further explained below, the three elements you should include in a Literary Argument thesis statement are:

- Author and title
- Defensible claim that answers the prompt
- Thematic idea

Author and Title

This part is easy enough, except for when the author's name escapes you at the worst possible moment—on exam day. Don't panic. As AP® Readers, we see this all the time. If you can't remember the author's name, don't guess or make up a fake name; simply say "the author" or completely leave out any reference to an author. Your score will not be affected.

Defensible Claim That Answers the Prompt

Your job in this part of the thesis is to *answer the prompt*. For example, who is the character and what is the injustice? Whose house is it and how is it symbolic? What is the setting and how does it affect a character? Who is morally ambiguous and how? Here, you should provide a specific character's name and a defensible claim about the character that speaks to the prompt idea.

Pro tip: Very rarely are question 3 essays *not* centered on a character, and very rarely do they ask about more than one character. Unless you encounter an anomaly of a prompt, force yourself to focus your analysis on *one* character.

We've read too many essays that will divide the essay in half with discussion of two characters, when the prompt only asks about one. *Frankenstein* essays are notorious for doing this—with equal attention paid to both Victor and the creature. What Readers have to do in these cases is to consider the half of your essay that more successfully answers the prompt and disregard the other half. You can imagine what this does to the essay's score. If you are going to include discussion of other characters, it should only be in relation to the main character of your essay—the relationship between them, or how another character affects the character of focus.

Thematic Idea

The final part of your thesis states a thematic idea, or overall meaning of the work, written as a complete statement. We aren't looking for one-word theme seeds, but full-fledged theme statements.

NO (theme seeds)	YES (theme statements)
Abandonment	Being abandoned at birth leaves a hole in one's character that must be replenished at the cost of the abandoner.
Motherhood	If one dedicates herself solely to motherhood, she risks being all-consumed by the lives of her children.
Difficulty of overcoming one's painful past	Remnants of the past can manifest in horrifying ways if one cannot learn how to cope with their trauma.

Notice how the theme statements are specific enough that they can be applied directly to whatever novel the student selected, but general enough that the idea works *outside* of the work as well.

Here is a student's thesis statement for the prompt on a character's gift seen earlier in the chapter:

Author and title

In **Jesmyn Ward's novel *Sing, Unburied, Sing,*** Jojo's **ability to see and talk to ghosts** allows him to **help lingering spirits find closure** and enables Jojo to **discover his family history.** However, this extraordinary power **takes a toll on his mental health and traumatizes him** through constantly reliving violent events. Jojo's gift is crucial in his personal journey of self-discovery, and reveals how **the generational effects of racism can both strengthen and limit a family's bond.**

Defensible claim that answers the prompt: what the gift is and how it is an advantage and a problem.

Thematic idea: presents an overall interpretation of the work that is relevant to the prompt.

If you find yourself struggling to craft a thesis statement, this template might provide you a good starting place:

In [author]'s [*title of work*], [character of focus's name] [defensible claim that answers the prompt], revealing that [thematic statement].

SELECTING EVIDENCE AND WRITING COMMENTARY

To score the maximum number of points for Row B: Evidence and Commentary on the exam rubric for question 3, you need to:

Evidence	Commentary
Provide specific evidence to support all claims in a line of reasoning.	Consistently explain how the evidence supports a line of reasoning.
Focus on the importance of specific details from the selected work to build an interpretation.	Organize and support an argument as a line of reasoning composed of multiple supporting claims, each with adequate evidence that is clearly explained.
Use appropriate grammar, mechanics, and spelling.	
Address the interpretation of the selected work as a whole (a theme).	

If you spend the time to take good brainstorming notes in planning your essay, your evidence will consist of the specific scenes you identify, some of which might stand alone as their own paragraphs, or that might be combined into the same paragraph if closely related. Notice in the Evidence column in the chart above that you are asked to include *specific* details. We really want you to dig into—analyze— the scenes you identify as evidence, which means that you need to be strategic in your selections. You won't have time to include every major scene of the plot, or even all of the scenes you have identified in your planning, which means some are not going to make it into your essay. Choose the scenes that you feel *best* support the parts of the prompt and your controlling thematic idea.

Commentary is derived from explicitly explaining *how* the scene serves as evidence. You can't just summarize the scene and call it a day, expecting AP® Readers to connect the dots on their own. You need to spell it out and take us through your thought process on making those connections. Ask yourself:

- How does this scene work to exemplify a part of the prompt I am supposed to address?
- How does this scene work in conjunction with my thematic idea?

Include your answers in your essay as your commentary. Each piece of evidence should be paired with an explanation of how it contributes to your line of reasoning. Here is an example from two different student essays on Toni Morrison's *Beloved*. Both students write a body paragraph on the positive qualities of the gift of Beloved's ghost taking physical form and returning to Sethe, her mother. Student 1 provides textual evidence, but lacks commentary and thematic connection, while Student 2 successfully intertwines evidence and thematically related commentary together. We have highlighted the commentary for you.

Student 1	Student 2
Beloved's return is a great gift in that Sethe never truly forgave herself for what she did. She did what was necessary in her mind, but it was something that haunted her to the present. Having Beloved come back was a dream come true, even though she didn't originally know it was her long lost daughter. Beloved appears one day by a tree stump in front of their house with no idea of where she came from. Sethe realizes it was her daughter when she hears Beloved humming the same tune Sethe made up and hummed to her children. During Beloved's time at 124, she gets to grow closer to Sethe and Denver and they have a great time bonding through ice skating and dancing.	Beloved's ability to resurface traumatic memories in the characters, although it is done harshly, creates the potential for healing among the characters. For example, when Beloved returns as an actual woman to 124, she and Paul D struggle for the position as head of the house. As an attempt to regain this role from Paul D after he forced her ghost out of the house, she slowly pushes him out—from the room, to the porch, to the outhouse, where she finally rapes him. This forces Paul D's tobacco tin heart to burst open and reveal a red heart. His tobacco tin heart is a metaphorical place where he stores all of his terrible memories from his years in slavery to never be revisited. Due to his closed and locked heart, he believes he should never love anything too much, otherwise he will end up disappointed. By Beloved psychologically and physically prying his tin heart open, she forces him to revisit these traumatic memories and heal himself so he can fully love again. Further, Beloved's being symbolizes the millions of unnamed slaves lost to slavery. Thus, her presence could symbolize the physical manifestation of the horrible memories of slavery come back to revisit him.

Pro tip: The most successful essays consistently tie back to the thematic portion of the thesis statement in the commentary of *each* body paragraph, while taking care to avoid sounding repetitive. When making connections back to the theme, use synonyms, or refer to different parts of the thematic statement each time.

HOW TO ORGANIZE A LITERARY ARGUMENT ESSAY

The most logical way to set up this essay is to go in chronological order with the book, with the scenes you are including as evidence in the same procession as they occur in the storyline. If you brainstorm and designate specific scenes *before* writing, as we advise, the order of your essay will be determined from these notes. Are you starting to see how important we think taking an extra few minutes to plan your essay is for question 3? While there are no hard rules on how many paragraphs you should have, we think this general outline will help guide you in organizing your essay. We will cover introductions and conclusions more specifically later in the chapter.

1. Introduction paragraph with thesis statement
2. Body paragraphs that start with strong topic sentences and provide evidence and commentary
3. A final body paragraph that focuses on the thematic idea in your thesis and possibly connects to a broader context
4. Conclusion paragraph

Topic Sentences

Each body paragraph should begin with a topic sentence that addresses a part of the prompt. In the student sample paragraphs above, each of their paragraphs is answering the positive qualities of the gift element of the prompt. In their next paragraph, they address the negative qualities, then discuss the gift's complexities, continuing to tie back to the work's overall meaning stated in their thesis in each paragraph. By stating this thematic idea early and in your thesis, you can create and maintain a successful line of reasoning throughout your essay, by continually linking the evidence back to your claim through your commentary.

Topic sentences should also introduce the paragraph's focus by saying something analytical like Student 2's paragraph above, not just stating a plot point from the book. The topic sentence should set up a frame for the evidence that you are about to include: What is the scene showing? What part of the prompt is it addressing? Try to answer both of these questions in your topic sentence.

Body Paragraphs

Once you have your topic sentence crafted, you can start providing evidence through describing details of a specific scene (refer back to your brainstorming notes). Which scenes stand out the most to you as illustrations of what the prompt is asking and what you are claiming in your thesis? These scenes should be highlighted and described using specific details in the body of your essay, ideally with one scene per paragraph serving as evidence in response to the prompt. Paired with the scene's details, as we mentioned in the previous section, is your commentary explaining why the scene is important and how it serves to support your argument.

Let's look at one of those prompt anomalies we mentioned earlier. The likelihood that you will encounter a prompt that is not character driven is slim, but we still want to address one on the off chance that you encounter one on your exam. There was a prompt from several years ago that asked about how a work deals with a social or political issue, and how the author uses literary elements to explore the issue. The student paragraph below on Colson Whitehead's *The Underground Railroad* is in response to this prompt and serves as a model for a well-crafted body paragraph.

Topic sentence

In between chapters organized by different states, Whitehead devotes a short chapter to a minor character to portray different roles in the institution of slavery. For example, there is a chapter on Martin's wife Ethel who despises having Cora in her house because **she thinks harboring a fugitive slave will get her killed.** However, Ethel's demeanor softens when **she can read the Bible to Cora when she is sick,** finally living out her goal to be a missionary. Her selective kindness shows that **she is only interested in helping Black people when it is convenient for her own Christian agenda.** This highlights a broader perspective that coexisted with the system of slavery known as the **white-savior complex,** or the feeling of responsibility some white people have to "save" people of color from their problems. So, Ethel's version of freedom, or the American Dream, is intertwined with superiority and denying the freedom of Black people because it is her "personal responsibility" to do so. **Ironically, white citizens in America at this time are depriving slaves of freedom and success while preaching the ideals of the American Dream.**

Textual evidence of a scene with specific details

Commentary explaining the significance of the scene

Connection back to thematic idea in the thesis statement

Theme-Focused Paragraphs

Finally, either as your last body paragraph or perhaps your conclusion, to boost your chances of earning the Row C: Sophistication point, devote an entire paragraph's worth of discussion into the thematic idea you present in your thesis statement. After going through the scenes serving as evidence and your commentary for them, this paragraph will offer a comprehensive look at the theme and really hit on that "overall meaning of the work" that we see pop up in every question 3 prompt. This paragraph is also an ideal place for a connection to a broader context, which is another potential way to earn the Row C point.

Here is an example of what a theme-based paragraph looks like, taken from the end of the same student essay on Whitehead's *The Underground Railroad*. The thematic idea presented in her thesis statement is that "the American Dream is distorted, since enslaved people are unable to take full advantage of America's opportunities."

> In *The Underground Railroad*, the distortions of the American Dream are presented in a myriad of ways. For slaves and free Black people, the systemic and individual racism reinforced by the institution of slavery prevents them from attaining the fundamental ideals of the American Dream, such as freedom, economic success, and simply being seen as human. For many white people, the American Dream involves oppression of others for their own success and omitting the horrors of slavery for personal convenience. While this book took place almost 200 years ago, the integration of the American Dream into American identity and the remnants of slavery persist to this day. *The Underground Railroad* should, therefore, be a reflection of past American history, but also used to analyze the systemic racism that manifests itself in present day America.

SOPHISTICATION

While there are many differences between the question 3 essay and the other two essays, one way in which they are all the same is the criteria for earning the point for Row C: Sophistication on the rubric. Probably your best two options for achieving this point for a Literary Argument essay are: (1) to situate the work into a broader context and (2) to employ a style of writing that is consistently vivid and persuasive.

Broader Context

Relating a work of literature with a broader context might be easier for question 3 than in the other two types of essays. There are a couple of different ways you can achieve this, and both should be done consistently throughout your essay, not just tagged on somewhere as a one-sentence addition.

1. Relate some idea in the work, whether it be a character's behavior or moral or the thematic idea you identify in your thesis, to our world today. How can you tie Othello's spiral of jealousy written centuries ago to our present

day? No matter when they were written, most full-length works will have commonalities with today's age and society because the author is writing about human experience. Human stories can connect us even across centuries; try to tap into that connection for this option.

2. Identify and discuss the genre or age from which the author is writing. For example, Mary Shelley is an author of the Romantic genre, which is clearly influential on her writing. What elements of Romanticism make her work representative of that genre? Another way to situate authors in a broader context is to explore if there's something in their personal biography that helps to inform their work and its meaning. Take Franz Kafka, for instance; his relationship with his abusive, overbearing father certainly influences his characters' stories. Connecting the work to its genre or its author's biography shows that you have considered it on a larger scale beyond its plot.

Style of Writing

As we discussed in chapter 3, be true to your individual writer's voice. Write appropriately for academic writing by using correct spelling, grammar, and mechanics, but *be yourself*. Don't overwrite by trying to sound like a gray-haired professor; that only results in you sounding like a pretentious phony. As you maintain a natural writer's voice, you can still pay attention to the way you write. Use varied sentence lengths and constructions; use transition words in between ideas; use synonyms to avoid being repetitive; and use a clear and specific diction.

TIPS FOR WRITING INTRODUCTIONS AND CONCLUSIONS

Introductions

For this essay, you are going to want a more developed introduction paragraph than a one-sentence thesis/introduction. Recall how the prompt for question 3 is set up—with an introduction of the prompt's topic, then directions on what to write. Your introduction should mirror this setup:

1. Begin by briefly introducing the topic situated in the specific work you have chosen.
2. Provide a one- to two-sentence overview of the selected work as a whole.
3. End with your thesis statement.

Note that items one and two in the above list may be swapped, but we always recommend the thesis statement coming as the last sentence of your introduction. Here is an example of a student's introduction paragraph for the gift prompt we've discussed throughout the chapter.

Gifts are usually received with gratitude and thanks, but what happens if a gift has harmful consequences? One character whose gift is both a benefit and a burden is Victor Frankenstein from Mary Shelley's novel *Frankenstein*. Victor is a skilled scientist who is determined to learn the secrets to create artificial life. Victor's gift of an unparalleled desire for knowledge seems to benefit him as it allows him to further research what no one else deemed possible, but with his completion of the research comes the burden of knowledge no one should have. The result of Victor's quest reveals that when man has no limits to desire and ambition, the result is inevitably catastrophic.

Conclusions

Sometimes an essay's thematic-based paragraph can successfully serve as its conclusion. If you feel like it caps off your line of reasoning and deals a final blow that settles your essay naturally, then we don't think you necessarily need to write a separate conclusion paragraph. There may be times, though, where you feel like you need that additional couple of sentences to tie up any loose ends or to make a final reminder of your overall claim. Either way works.

> **Pro tip:** If you are struggling to come up with something to finish off your essay and feel like you need further closure beyond your theme discussion, think of the end of the book. How can an element from the end of the story provide closure for your essay? Ending your writing with the end of the story provides your essay a sense of completion.

Following is the conclusion from the same student who wrote the introduction example above. The essay then ends with the end of the story.

Without the ruthless desire for knowledge that Victor maintained, he would never have taken the necessary steps and succeeded in his dangerous endeavor to create life. Victor's gift allowed him to complete his life's work while equally destroying every other aspect of his life and cursing him with knowledge that should be unobtainable by man. Victor's final warning to Walton urges him to not follow the same path and to realize that ambition must have limitations. By Walton heeding Victor's advice, he saves his own life and the lives of his crew, breaking the cycle of destructive desire created by Victor.

THE BIG THREE

Before we dive into literary elements of focus for the question 3 essay, it is necessary to reiterate that this essay is *not about techniques.* You most likely will not even mention them in an essay. Unless you get an extremely rare prompt, these techniques will only be a part of your *thinking,* not part of your *writing.* We offer THE BIG THREE here in terms of how they work to establish meaning in the work; in other words, how they inform a work's themes.

1. Characterization

As discussed in chapter 1, **characterization** is created by many different components. The **motives** that drive characters to act and think the way they do, the conflict between the **protagonist** and **antagonist**, pairing up opposite characters as **foils** to highlight the other's features more profoundly, what a character says— all these things, and more, help to develop characterization. Think about the choices the author makes in creating the character. What complexities do you see working in your character that might add depth of analysis to your argument?

2. Plot

Even though you should avoid pure plot summary, there is no way to *not* incorporate elements of the plot in a question 3 essay. The textual evidence comes from the plot so it's going to be in your essay; we just don't want your essay to be *only* about the plot. Consider the **sequence** of events in the story and how you can use it to present your evidence in the most logical way. Compare key scenes from the plot of the book and which ones offer the best support for your argument. You aren't going to be able to include them all, so weigh your options carefully.

3. Theme

We save the best for last. Theme is crucial to this essay, not as a technique per se, but as a message—an overall meaning of the work—to discuss *at length* in your essay if you want to do well. One of the ways you can identify a work's themes is looking for patterns, or **motifs**, throughout it. Repeated images, symbols, details, and so forth are placed purposefully by the author to call your attention to them. Reflect on motifs you notice, along with characterization and plot, to help you determine a work's major themes.

STUDENT SAMPLE ESSAYS

We have discussed the prompt about a character's gift at length in this chapter. Here is the prompt our student writers were given and two scored sample essays with commentary.

AP® English Literature and Composition Free-Response Questions

Question 3

(Suggested time—40 minutes. This question counts as one-third of the total essay section score.)

Many works of literature feature characters who have been given a literal or figurative gift. The gift may be an object, or it may be a quality such as uncommon beauty, significant social position, great mental or imaginative faculties, or extraordinary physical powers. Yet this gift is often also a burden or a handicap. Select a character from a novel, epic, or play who has been given a gift that is both an advantage and a problem. Then write a well-developed essay analyzing the complex nature of the gift and how the gift contributes to the meaning of the work as a whole.

You may choose a work from the list below or another work of comparable literary merit. Do not merely summarize the plot.

- *The Aeneid*
- *Alias Grace*
- *All the Light We Cannot See*
- *Beloved*
- *Beowulf*
- *Crime and Punishment*
- *Death in Venice*
- *Dracula*
- *Frankenstein*
- *The Goldfinch*
- *Great Expectations*
- *Heart of Darkness*
- *Homegoing*
- *The Iliad*
- *Kindred*

- *King Lear*
- *Madame Bovary*
- *Mama Day*
- *Man and Superman*
- *The Metamorphosis*
- *Midnight's Children*
- *A Passage to India*
- *The Picture of Dorian Gray*
- *The Portrait of a Lady*
- *The Power of One*
- *A Raisin in the Sun*
- *The Return of the Native*
- *The Tempest*
- *Things Fall Apart*
- *To the Lighthouse*

STUDENT SAMPLE ESSAY 1

In *The Metamorphosis* by Franz Kafka, the main character, Gregor Samsa, wakes up one morning in the body of a beetle. This transformation was a gift both metaphorically and physically. Although this transition allowed Gregor to change into a happier and more independent person, it also left him feeling alienated and isolated from not only the outside world, but even his own family.

Gregor Samsa was a respectable travelling salesman who worked to support his family. However, all of this changed when one morning he woke up in the body of a beetle. This permanent physical transformation forced Gregor to adapt to his new body. While Gregor learned to accept this big change his family ignored him. His family locked him in his room. Grete Samsa, Gregor's sister, would barely open the door to slide food inside his room. Mrs. Samsa couldn't even walk into his room or look at him without fainting. When Gregor would creep out of his room, Mr. Samsa would chase him back in his room and throw objects at him, like apples. These events make Gregor feel isolated and alone. During a time when Gregor needed his family the most, they abandoned him. Since he can no longer support his family financially, they alienated him. In the beginning, Gregor felt guilty for not being able to work and support his family anymore. But, near the end of the novel, Gregor grows angry because he realized the love and support he deserves after taking care of his family for so many years. This anger leads to his metaphorical transformation where he finds his humanity and freedom.

This long period of loneliness actually gifts Gregor the time to grow on the inside. He accepted his physical transformation and realized his family was not going to help him during this time. When this realization came, Gregor found peace within himself and began to rebel against his family. He rebelled by walking out of his room to show that he didn't care that his family feared him. After years of working to help his family, he finally did something for himself. He felt freed from the guilt he was carrying for letting his family down. This makes the reader feel sad for Gregor because it took Gregor turning into a beetle to find his freedom and humanity. Gregor feels more "human" when he becomes a beetle than he did when he was physically human. With his transformation, Kafka illustrates that we can only discover our true humanity once we are free from guilt and duty.

The title "Metamorphosis" represents Gregor's both physical and internal transformation throughout the novel. The gift of a physical transformation into a beetle led to Gregor's internal transformation where he found freedom and happiness. The process of metamorphosis is mostly associated with a caterpillar turning into a butterfly. In this novel, Gregor turned into a beetle. This emphasizes the internal changes within Gregor rather than the physical. Although his family couldn't overcome his physical changes, Gregor was more focused on himself mentally. By the end of the novel, Gregor sees his physical state as a gift that finally gave him the time to find himself and be happy with who he is.

Score: 1-3-0

This essay earns the Thesis point as it identifies the gift of Gregor's transformation and offers the interpretation of how it affects his character. There is no thematic statement included in the thesis, which doesn't discount the Thesis point, but *does* impact the other two scores. Earning three points in the Evidence and Commentary row, this essay provides specific textual evidence for both the positive and negative qualities of the gift, but the thematic idea (that "we can only discover our true humanity once we are free from guilt and duty") is withheld until the penultimate paragraph. Had the student placed this idea in the introduction and continually tied back to it in the commentary, it would help to strengthen the line of reasoning. This essay does not earn the Sophistication point due to its choppy syntax and the need for more nuanced discussion of the work as a whole.

STUDENT SAMPLE ESSAY 2[1]

In the book *Beloved*, Toni Morrison tells a haunting story about the lives of ex-slaves. Sethe, an ex-slave, killed her baby daughter, Beloved, in hopes of saving her from a life in slavery. However, Beloved comes back to haunt Sethe and her family as both a ghost and later, as a physical person. Beloved's complex nature as a ghost and a physical representation of millions of slaves gives her the ability to prompt healing of traumatic memories amongst the people in the home 124, but also creates a disruptive power balance which psychologically harms those in 124. Thus, Beloved's capability to psychologically pry the minds of those in 124 demonstrates that traumatic

1. This is the full essay excerpted as Student 2 on page 163.

events such as slavery, although in the past, can come back to haunt oneself if the memories are repressed rather than accepted and healed.

At the beginning of the book, Sethe and her daughter Denver are living in their house, 124, which is haunted by Beloved. The supernatural events occurring in the house, unfortunately, isolate Sethe and Denver from their community because everyone is too afraid to enter into Sethe's house. Additionally, they are afraid since Sethe murdered her own child. Thus, Beloved's ghost acts like a constant reminder of Sethe's decision, which can be seen as psychological torture since she doesn't even have a community to escape to when Beloved's ghost becomes too much to mentally handle. It is only until Paul D forces Beloved's ghost out of 124 that Sethe and Denver can begin developing new relationships with others, such as Paul D. This demonstrates that Beloved's ghost has psychologically hindered Sethe from feeling like she deserves any form of love and meaningful relationship with anyone outside of her immediate family. Thus, Beloved's psychological presence, despite her death, is a burden on Sethe and Denver in finding acceptance of the past, moving on, and finding happiness in the present.

Beloved's ability to resurface traumatic memories in the characters, although it is done harshly, creates the potential for healing among the characters. For example, when Beloved returns as an actual woman to 124, she and Paul D struggle for the position as head of the house. As an attempt to regain this role from Paul D after he forced her ghost out of the house, she slowly pushes him out—from the room, to the porch, to the outhouse, where she finally rapes him. This forces Paul D's tobacco tin heart to burst open and reveal a red heart. His tobacco tin heart is a metaphorical place where he stores all of his terrible memories from his years in slavery to never be revisited. Due to his closed and locked heart, he believes he should never love anything too much, otherwise he will end up disappointed. By Beloved psychologically and physically prying his tin heart open, she forces him to revisit these traumatic memories and heal himself so he can fully love again. Further, Beloved's being symbolizes the millions of unnamed slaves lost to slavery. Thus, her presence could symbolize the physical manifestation of the horrible memories of slavery come back to revisit him.

Towards the end of the book, Beloved begins to use her manipulative psychological powers to suck the life out of Sethe. She does this because she believes Sethe abandoned her as a result of her murder. As a result, Sethe became, both physically and mentally, extremely frail, dependent, and skinny. Beloved, contrastingly, has become huge and fat because Sethe gives all of her food to her. As there is no food in the house, Beloved's manipulative behaviors force Denver to seek help in her community to feed her house. Eventually, the members of the community exorcise Beloved out of the house. This complex section of the book demonstrates both the burdens that Beloved's supernatural capabilities had on others, but also the potential for healing. She drained Sethe of her life force and motherly capabilities as an act of revenge, but it also prompted the community to save the members of 124, thus reuniting them with the community they were shunned from years ago as a result of Beloved's continued supernatural presence. This demonstrates that, although not always immediate nor easy, the revisiting of past memories and accepting them can bring healing and newfound community with others.

Aforementioned, Beloved represents the millions of unnamed and unrecognized people who lost their lives to the horrible institution of slavery. Beloved's being is difficult to fully process and accept, however, it is through fully loving others that Sethe and her community, as well as anyone, can heal through the unimaginable.

Score: 1-4-1

This essay is well-organized, specific, analytically sound, and beautifully written. The thesis provided in the introduction includes all necessary components. The interpretation of the work as a whole, or the thematic idea, is clearly established in the introduction's final sentence. Apt and specific evidence is logically presented for all parts of the prompt, paired with persuasive commentary that explains consistently how the evidence supports the line of reasoning. Focusing on the character of Beloved, this essay explores the complexities of her return, its effect on other characters, and argues for a symbolic interpretation of her character. This essay walks its reader through a fully developed line of reasoning, uses effective transitions and sophisticated diction and syntax, easily earning it the Sophistication point.

·   ·   ·

Next, you will find two brand-new prompts to practice going through the process on your own, as you will be expected to do on the AP® Exam. The first prompt includes student sample essays with scorer's commentary, and the second one does not.

We also encourage you to try writing all three of the essay types (Poetry Analysis, Prose Analysis, and Literary Argument) in a row, back-to-back, and to time yourself. Two hours is how long you will get to write all three essays on the exam, so practicing all three together will be an opportunity for challenging and realistic practice.

AP® English Literature and Composition Free-Response Questions

Question 3

(Suggested time—40 minutes. This question counts as one-third of the total essay section score.)

Select a novel, play, or epic poem that features a character whose origins are unusual or mysterious. Then write an essay in which you analyze how these origins shape the character and that character's relationships, and how the origins contribute to the meaning of the work as a whole.

You may choose a work from the list below or one of comparable literary merit. Do not merely summarize the plot.

- *Beloved*
- *Brave New World*
- *Dracula*
- *The English Patient*
- *Frankenstein*
- *Great Expectations*
- *Grendel*
- *The Iliad*
- *The Importance of Being Earnest*
- *Jane Eyre*
- *Light in August*
- *Macbeth*
- *The Mayor of Casterbridge*
- *The Metamorphosis*
- *Middlemarch*
- *No Country for Old Men*
- *The Odyssey*
- *Oedipus Rex*
- *Orlando*
- *Oryx and Crake*
- *The Playboy of the Western World*
- *A Prayer for Owen Meany*
- *Their Eyes Were Watching God*
- *Tom Jones*
- *Twelfth Night*
- *Waiting for Godot*
- *Wuthering Heights*

STUDENT SAMPLE ESSAY 1

In *The Metamorphosis* by Franz Kafka, Gregor unusually and mysteriously transforms into an oversized bug one morning. His transformation illuminates the true nature behind his character and his relationships. Through Gregor's experience, Kafka illustrates how sometimes people have irrational feelings that they are a burden to their loved ones, and it isn't until they free themselves from this guilt that they can achieve self-fulfillment.

His sudden transformation shapes Gregor as a character because we immediately see he is not concerned with the well-being of himself, but what his boss will do because he will be late. His boss comes to the door and, with the help of his parents, scolds him for not coming to work, which shows the absurdity of this novella and strengthens the characterization of Gregor. Gregor is overly selfless, thinking of everyone but himself. This irrational and tragic pyramid where Gregor resides at the bottom conveys how little he thinks of himself. He eventually comes to the conclusion his family will be better off without him which ultimately leads to his death.

The relationships between himself and his family deteriorate as they can no longer depend on him for money. He is a bug not capable of working, so his family must pick up the slack. They essentially swap places with Gregor—where his family becomes the host and he transforms into the parasite. They must care for him while simultaneously work, which makes his family despise him. Because he is a bug, they find him repulsive and result to inhumane tactics in order to care for him. One day, his sister and mother come to his bedroom to remove all of his furniture. Since he is no longer human, they see no need for him to own human possessions. As Gregor becomes more and more accustomed to his bug-life, he enjoys the open space in his room and can crawl around freely. But once he causes trouble for them financially and chases away the Boarders who are paying rent, his family finds it harder and harder to deal with him. This shows how he becomes a burden to his family and ruins the relationships they had because of his mysterious transformation. He sees himself as a blockade to his family's success which causes him to give up. By freeing himself from feelings of obligation to his family, Gregor is finally able to find peace with himself.

Gregor knows his transformation has put a gigantic burden on his family. They have to take care of a huge bug. When he realizes this, he cannot stand to put his family through more pain even though they treat him poorly. At the end of the novella, he lays down and dies in his last selfless act to lift the weight off his family's shoulders. Gregor's characterization as selfless and his deteriorating relationships with his family bring him to give up due to the immense burden he felt he put on his family. Since the whole novella is absurdist, the reader takes his situation as irrational. Therefore, the message that you are a parasite to your family comes as an irrational fear as well.

We get a close look inside Kafka's psyche to find he has an irrational fear of not living up to his family's expectations, and therefore becoming a burden. The novella is unrealistic and harsh like the ideas it presents which show how Gregor and simultaneously Kafka's mind was set around pleasing others before himself. Gregor is Kafka's way of portraying his own fears that he is a burden on his family. Like Gregor was locked inside his room, Kafka was trapped inside this misconception.

Score: 1-4-0

This essay earns the Thesis point because it offers an interpretation of the work and provides a defensible claim. The evidence provided is specific and paired with commentary connecting it back to the prompt or the thematic idea expressed in the thesis. We did not award this essay the Sophistication point because, while there is an attempt made at situating the work within a broader context in the final paragraph, it is not done recurrently throughout the essay. Inconsistencies in the style of writing also withhold the essay from earning the Row C point.

STUDENT SAMPLE ESSAY 2

In Mary Shelley's *Frankenstein*, Dr. Frankenstein mysteriously creates a living monster, which then attempts to seek revenge on Dr. Frankenstein throughout the book. The monster's mysterious origins make him question whether he really belongs in this world and make him resentful of Dr. Frankenstein for leaving him on the day of his creation. Through this development, the author reveals that being abandoned at one's birth leaves a hole in one's character that must be replaced at the cost of the abandoner.

The unnamed monster begins to question his place in the world when he is rejected by a family for his appearance. The creature spends several months observing a farming family so he can learn their language and behavior. One day, he attempts to use these skills by confronting the family for help and hospitality only to be thrown out of the house because of his monstrous appearance. His one chance to fill the void of loneliness originally caused by his creator is destroyed and the monster swears revenge on Victor.

The creature then isolates himself from human society and begins to kill members of Frankenstein's family. The creature's origins of being pieced together with animal and human remains and then abandoned by Frankenstein have led him to ostracize himself until he learns how to act like a human. He believes the problems stemming from his origin and the hole left by Frankenstein can be resolved through human interaction. Frankenstein's abandonment has left a hole that the creature is obviously trying to fill by speaking with this family.

Score: 1-2-0

This essay starts out strong with a solid thesis statement with an impressive thematic interpretation. However, the student fails to include multiple instances of specific evidence that support a line of reasoning. The evidence provided is mostly general and it appears as though the student may have run out of time as the essay ends abruptly. Without a complete line of reasoning, the Sophistication point cannot be awarded.

AP® English Literature and Composition Free-Response Questions

Question 3

(Suggested time—40 minutes. This question counts as one-third of the total essay section score.)

In literary works, storms often function symbolically or as a crucial turning point in the story for an individual character. A storm may be a literal weather phenomenon or a figurative storm within a character, like an internal conflict or struggle. Select a novel, play, or epic poem in which a literal or figurative storm is important. Then write a well-developed essay analyzing how the storm affects a character and how it functions to illuminate a meaning of the work as a whole.

You may select a work from the list below or another work of equal literary merit. Do not merely summarize the plot.

- *Beloved*
- *A Bend in the River*
- *Billy Budd*
- *Catch-22*
- *Cat's Eye*
- *The Crucible*
- *Frankenstein*
- *A Gesture Life*
- *Great Expectations*
- *Heart of Darkness*
- *Invisible Man*
- *The Last of the Mohicans*
- *Lord of the Flies*
- *Mansfield Park*
- *Medea*

- *The Merchant of Venice*
- *Mudbound*
- *The Odyssey*
- *Oliver Twist*
- *One Flew Over the Cuckoo's Nest*
- *Othello*
- *The Poisonwood Bible*
- *The Scarlet Letter*
- *Sister Carrie*
- *Sophie's Choice*
- *The Tempest*
- *Tess of the d'Urbervilles*
- *To Kill a Mockingbird*
- *Who's Afraid of Virginia Woolf?*
- *Wuthering Heights*

CHAPTER REVIEW

Let's outline what you have learned in this chapter about how to approach the Literary Argument question effectively.

1. Read the prompt carefully to make sure you understand the topic and your task.

2. Select a work of literary merit.

3. Brainstorm ideas for each part of the prompt and make note of specific scenes you could include to support your ideas.

4. Craft a thesis statement that answers the prompt and provides an overall interpretation of the work (a thematic statement).

5. Refer back to your brainstorming notes to plan your essay.

6. Write a well-developed introduction that includes the thesis statement.

7. Write body paragraphs introduced with strong topic sentences, each focusing on a specific scene for evidence that is explained with commentary. Remember to tie back to the prompt or the theme in each body paragraph.

8. Read back over what you have written so far to make sure you have addressed all parts of the prompt.

9. Finish your essay with an in-depth discussion of the theme, and possibly an additional conclusion paragraph.

10. Reread to catch any errors and make quick fixes to spelling and grammar.

6

Test-Taking Strategies

The AP® Literature class is all about the exam, and yet it is not at all about the exam.

AP® Literature is far more than an exam covering essential skills and enduring understandings. Through the course, we read texts that validate who we are as individuals and that challenge the beliefs we hold about other people and cultures. We become members of an academic learning community exploring how to work with different personalities, assess our own learning, and live in community with those around us. These things cannot be measured on an exam but instead coalesce to make us better students of life—not just AP® Literature.

However, there is an exam at the end of the course, and having a plan and strategies for exam day will be beneficial. This chapter will not tell you what to do on exam day but rather offer strategies and ideas for you to consider so you can put together your personal testing plan. The main thing that you should remember during the exam is that you as the test taker have choice and agency over the exam. Or to quote AP® instructor Lisa Boyd, "You are taking the exam; don't let the exam take you." To a certain extent, you can choose the order and the amount of time you spend on different sections of the exam.

Here's the basic exam overview:

Section	Format	Number of questions	Weighting	Timing
I	Multiple-choice	55	45%	1 hour
II	Essay	3: poetry, prose, literary argument	55%	2 hours

Source: CED, p. 135.

Skill category	Exam weighting
1: Explain the function of character	16–20%
2: Explain the function of setting	3–6%
3: Explain the function of plot and structure	16–20%
4: Explain the function of the narrator or speaker	21–26%
5: Explain the function of word choice, imagery, and symbols	10–13%
6: Explain the function of comparison	10–13%
7: Develop textually substantiated arguments about interpretations of part or all of a text	10–13%

Source: CED, p. 137.

Note that the essays are weighted more heavily than the multiple-choice questions, but both sections of the exam are important.

SECTION I: MULTIPLE-CHOICE QUESTIONS

The multiple-choice exam will consist of five different passages with ten to twelve questions per passage for a total of fifty-five questions. This averages to approximately twelve minutes per passage and roughly one minute per question. The multiple-choice section will have at least two poetry passages and two prose passages which vary in difficulty. Knowing this information will help you gauge time throughout the exam and check your pace.

Some general information about the construction of the multiple-choice test:

- Questions generally go in order of the passage.
- Some questions will be big-picture questions while others will be line specific.
- The complexity of the questions varies.
- The difficulty of the texts also varies.
- Texts will represent different time periods.

Here are some best practices for answering questions successfully on the multiple-choice portion of the exam:

- Read the entire passage. Read poems at least twice (if not three or four times) before answering questions. You cannot answer context questions without reading the full passage.
- Read everything on the page—including the title and footnotes. Every little piece of information helps and can make a difference.

- Do not spend too much time on one question. Every question is weighted the same so the longer you spend on a very difficult question, the less time you will have to answer easier ones.
- Leave no answers blank. You are not penalized for guessing, so narrow down as far as you can and make your best guess.
- Read at least three lines above and three lines below the line referenced in the question.
- Trust your gut. Unless you have a new insight or new information on the text, don't second-guess previous answers. Keep moving forward and trusting your close-reading skills.
- Write in your test booklet. The multiple-choice questions and answers booklet will not be viewed after the exam so don't worry about messiness, clarity, or what others may think of your notes.

Multiple-Choice Strategies

These test-taking strategies are tools you can use for the multiple-choice portion of the exam. Not all strategies will work for everyone; choose which strategies, if any, work best for you in order to have more control and confidence while working through the exam. Whatever strategies you use, be sure to practice them before the day of the exam. There are many ways to take a test, and you should know your plan. Whatever you do, don't try anything new or different on exam day.

Strategy 1: Read the question stems before reading the passage or the poem.

Briefly reviewing the question stems before reading the text accomplishes two things: context and purpose for reading. Since there is very limited time to read each text, the question stems can provide some basic information about what you are looking for before reading it for the first time. This information will help you gain more understanding during the first read through. In addition, question stems can focus your attention on relevant portions of the text.

Strategy 2: Bracket lines of the text referenced in the questions.

Putting brackets around lines referred to in a question or an arrow before a noted line will chunk that portion of the text so you can specifically focus on that portion while reading. The marking may save you time when answering questions.

Strategy 3: Mark answers for each section in the test booklet, then bubble those answers on the answer sheet at the end of each section.

Marking answers in the booklet will allow you to stay focused on the questions and text and save time by not going to the answer sheet after each question. Be sure to pay attention to question numbers when bubbling.

Strategy 4: Mark IT!

Read the question stems (not answers) before you read the text, and mark each question stem either *I* for *inference* (whole-text questions) or *T* for *text dependent* (line-specific questions). Once the question stems have been quickly scanned and marked, read the text in its entirety. When you have read it and are ready to answer the questions, answer the *text-dependent questions* first; then answer the *inference questions*. This means that you will not be answering the questions in numerical order. Answering the text-dependent questions first allows you to look at the passage a few more times before answering whole-text questions. Mark the answers in the test booklet and then transfer the answers after that section is complete.

Strategy 5: Annotate with a specific marking system.

You will not have time to fully annotate each passage or poem, but some quick annotations can not only aid with understanding but save time when answering questions. Here are a few suggestions:

- Mark positive words with a plus sign and negative words with a minus sign. This will help you quickly scan the text to determine if the tone or a character is positive or negative.
- Note shifts in the passage with a backslash. The shift can signal a change in tone, perspective, time, or any number of other things.
- Underline phrases and circle key words that connect to larger ideas.

Strategy 6: Tackle passages out of order.

Most students choose to tackle the texts in sequential order. Some students, however, will do the prose passages back-to-back and then the poetry passages or vice versa. Some students may complete the modern passages first and the older passages last. This allows you to warm up with passages that you are more comfortable with; this strategy can also build your confidence at the beginning of the exam so you're focused and confident going into the texts you find more difficult. If you choose to work out of order, be sure to bubble each section when complete and not save all bubbling to the end.

Strategy 7: Eliminate answers.

Taking time to thoroughly read all answers and work through the process of eliminating wrong answers is a strategic and systematic approach to answering questions. Answers can be eliminated if they:

- Do not match the overall tone or characterization within the text.
- Are too broad or too narrow for the question.
- Contain some information that is true, but the information is not fully true.
- Contain some accurate information but it is not in context.
- Contradict answers you know to be correct.
- Don't align with the overall central or controlling idea of the passage.

Strategy 8: Cross off incorrect answers.

Literally striking through incorrect answers can save you time if you are re-reading portions of the text or checking work at the end. This will allow you to quickly read back through the questions and correct answers if you have time to review.

Strategy 9: Use previous questions and answers to choose answers.

Answers from a single text selection will align to support an interpretation of the text. This is particularly helpful if you are stuck on a question. Eliminate choices that do not fit into a central or controlling idea supported by other question stems or answers you have chosen. A correct answer will not contradict other correct answers.

Strategy 10: Identify key words and phrases in answers.

Identifying key words and phrases within an answer will help you quickly eliminate choices that are not correct. Specifically identifying *adjectives* and *verbs* as either positive or negative will help narrow answer possibilities quickly. For example, if you know a character is portrayed negatively throughout a selection, answers with a very positive description can be eliminated. Remember you are looking for the best answer, and this choice often depends on interpretations of specific words.

Your Turn

Choose the strategies that could help you with multiple-choice questions and try them out on the practice exams included in this book (pages 189–238). Which ones worked? Why? Which ones didn't? Why?

SECTION II: FREE-RESPONSE QUESTIONS

The free-response section consists of three essays written in two hours. This averages to forty minutes per essay. The essays will appear on the exam in the following order:

Free-response question 1: Poetry Analysis
Free-response question 2: Prose Analysis
Free-response question 3: Literary Argument

You can, however, write the essays in any order you want. Readers will go through the booklet looking for the essay they are assigned to read so your essays do not even need to be in order in the booklet as long as they are labeled (1, 2, and 3). There are four basic approaches to choosing the order in which to write essays.

Approach 1: The order they appear in the test booklet

Many people prefer working in order and get stressed out if they don't. Writing essays in the order they appear takes all the guesswork out of which one comes first, second, or third. You open the book and start working.

Approach 2: Strongest essay first

Writing your strongest essay first—whether it be poetry, prose, or the open-ended, or Literary Argument, question—will ensure that you don't run out of time on an essay you know you will do well on. Starting with your strongest essay will also allow you to build your confidence before moving to an essay that you may not feel as comfortable with.

Approach 3: Weakest essay first

Writing your weakest essay first will let you do your predetermined hardest work while your mind is fresh. Getting the most difficult essay out of the way first will help with anxiety as time winds down near the end of the exam.

Approach 4: Question 3 first

Since the Literary Argument essay is the only one that you can prep for by reading novels and plays, writing this one first can be helpful. This allows you to unload the information that's fresh in your mind at the beginning of the essay section and then approach the other two essays undistracted.

Timing for Essays

The suggested time for each essay is forty minutes which is indicated under each question number. You can, however, spend as much or as little time on each essay as you like; this is another way you have choice and control during the exam. Here are some ideas to consider for the essay portion of the exam:

- Spend thirty minutes on question 3 (Literary Argument) since you have prepared for this essay. (Be sure to review chapter 5 for specific ways to prepare for this question.) This will leave you forty-five minutes each for the prose and poetry essays which require a cold reading of a text. That extra five minutes will go a long way when reading and thinking about a passage you've never seen.
- If you do not understand a passage and are not sure how to write an essay on the prompt, write a thesis, a brief summary of what you read, and move on to the next prompt. You should avoid summarizing and always try to provide evidence and commentary, but if you are having a mental block, a quick summary will help you gain one point which is better than none. You can always come back if time allows, but you don't want to take time away from a passage that you might find easier to understand and write about.
- If you find yourself in a situation where you only have a few minutes for an essay, write a thesis and as much evidence and commentary as you can. You may need to forgo taking time to outline and plan, which is recommended, but getting as much as you can on the page is important.
- Don't leave any essays blank. Write something for each prompt—no matter how little.

Your Turn

Write out your plan for how you will approach the essay portion of the exam. In what order will you do the essays? How much time do you plan to spend on each one? Review this plan with your teacher or a friend.

GENERAL REMINDERS

Get some rest.

Chances are you may be nervous the night before the exam so plan on prioritizing a good night's sleep two and three nights before exam day. Since this is a skill-based exam, there's no real last-minute cramming, so staying up late studying won't help. The brain operates and performs best when it is well rested.

Eat breakfast.

The exam will last a few hours and a growling stomach will be a big distraction. This is the time for something healthy so you won't crash during the middle of the exam.

Plan ahead of time.

Think through how you will get to the exam site, what you will have for breakfast, and even what you will wear on exam day. The goal is to have no surprises the morning of the exam. Anything you can handle ahead of time, you should.

Get in the right frame of mind.

Set a few minutes aside the morning of the exam to get in the right headspace before you walk into the exam. This will look different for everyone but do whatever makes you feel relaxed and confident. You may choose to listen to some inspiring or energizing music, do some yoga poses, meditate, or take a few deep breaths.

CLOSING THOUGHTS

Rather than viewing the exam as a test of your knowledge, shift your mindset to one where this is an opportunity to show and celebrate what you have learned during the course. You have ideas about the world around you, and this exam will give you an opportunity to share what you see and know. You have just as much right to read and have thoughts on what you read as any English teacher or professor. This is the time and place for you to share those thoughts in your own unique voice. Show what you know!

Practice AP® English Literature and Composition Exams

Full AP® Exam 1

Section I: Multiple-Choice

Total time: 1 hour

55 questions

Questions 1–11 refer to the passage.

The following passage is excerpted from a novella first published in 1991.

> I make no bones about it, I am not a woman of the
> world; I am not an educated woman; what I know I have
> taught myself. Rumour and speculation—even downright
> lies—have abounded since I was sixteen years old. In any
> 5 person's life that side of things is unavoidable, but I believe
> I have suffered more than most, and take this opportunity to
> set the record straight. Firstly, my presence on the S.S. *Hamburg*
> in my less affluent days was as a stewardess, nothing more.
> Secondly, it is a mischievous fabrication that at the time of
> 10 the Oleander Avenue scandal I accepted money in return for
> silence. Thirdly, Mrs Chubbs was dead, indeed already buried,
> before I met her husband. On the other hand I do not deny
> that men have offered me gifts, probably all of which I
> accepted. Nor do I deny that all my years in Africa are
> 15 marked, in my memory, with personal regret. Unhappiness

breeds confusion and misunderstanding. I was far from
happy in Ombubu, at the Café Rose.

In the summer of which I now write I had reached
my fifty-sixth year—a woman carefully made up, eyes a
greenish-blue. Then, as now, my hair was as pale as sand, as
smooth as a seashell, the unfussy style reflecting the roundness
of my face. My mouth is a full rosebud, my nose classical; my
complexion has always been admired. Naturally, there were
laughter lines that summer, but my skin, though no longer
the skin of a girl, had worn well and my voice had not yet
acquired the husky depths that steal away femininity. In
Italy men who were strangers to me still gave me a second
look, although naturally not with the same excitement as
once men did in other places where I've lived. I had, in
truth, become more than a little plump, and though
perhaps I should have dressed with such a consideration in
mind this is something I have never been able to bring
myself to do: I cannot resist just a hint of drama in my
clothes—though not bright colours, which I abhor. 'I never
knew a girl dressed herself up so prettily,' a man who sat on
the board of a carpet business used to say, and my tendency
to put on a pound or two has not been without admirers.
A bag of bones Mrs Chubbs was, according to her husband,
which is why—so I've always suspected—he took to me in
the first place.

Having read so far, you'll probably be surprised to
learn that I'm a woman who prays. When I was a child
I went to Sunday school and had a picture of Jesus on a
donkey above my bed. In the Café Rose in Ombubu
I interested Poor Boy Abraham in praying also, the only
person I have ever influenced in this way. 'He's retarded,
that boy,' Quinty used to say in his joky way, careless as to
whether or not the boy was within earshot. Quinty's like
that, as you'll discover.

I am the author of a series of fictional romances,
composed in my middle age after my arrival in this house.
I am no longer active in that field, and did not ever presume
to intrude myself into the world of literature—though, in
fairness to veracity, I must allow that my modest works
dissect with some success the tangled emotions of which
they treat. That they have given pleasure I am assured by
those kind enough to write in appreciation. They have
helped; they have whiled away the time. I can honestly state

that I intended no more, and I believe you'll find I am an
60   honest woman.

1.   The opening sentence ("I make no bones . . . myself" in lines 1–3)
      establishes the narrator as

      (A) a braggart who other people find overbearing.

      (B) an uneducated woman.

      (C) a self-made woman who has learned through her experiences.

      (D) a dishonest woman who is truly educated.

2.   The second and third sentences (lines 3–7) of the passage ("Rumour . . .
      record straight") suggest that the narrator

      (A) wants to explain why she has been the target of rumor and speculation.

      (B) wants her reader to understand what she has endured throughout
          her life.

      (C) has been the target of jealous women ever since she turned sixteen.

      (D) wants readers to appreciate her suffering.

3.   Which of the following statements best represents the narrator's argument
      in lines 1–17?

      (A) A rambling account of past events.

      (B) A request for mercy.

      (C) A detailed refutation of the rumors, speculations, and lies told
          against her.

      (D) A misguided attempt to clear her name.

4.   In lines 15–16, the narrator's claim that "[u]nhappiness breeds confusion
      and misunderstanding" suggests that she

      (A) might be mistaken in some of her recollections concerning her time in
          Africa because she was unhappy.

      (B) forgives those who have attacked her over the years.

      (C) is trying to avoid blame concerning her past life.

      (D) has a faulty memory because her health is failing.

5. The tone of lines 1–17 can be described as

    (A) apathetic.

    (B) self-justifying.

    (C) diplomatic.

    (D) optimistic.

6. In context, the adverb "carefully" in line 19 is understood to mean

    (A) fearlessly.

    (B) inappropriately.

    (C) foolishly.

    (D) meticulously.

7. The narrator's self-descriptions in lines 18–40 suggests all of the following EXCEPT

    (A) The narrator is confident that she is still appealing.

    (B) The narrator is justifying why men are attracted to her.

    (C) The narrator is seeking sympathy because her looks are fading.

    (D) The narrator has not been affected by time as much as other women of her age.

8. Lines 41–49 serve primarily to

    (A) allow the narrator to reveal her spiritual side in hopes of softening her image.

    (B) allow the narrator to express what a difficult time she had in Ombubu.

    (C) allow the narrator to show she is better than those who spread rumors about her.

    (D) allow the narrator to show how she is willing to help the less fortunate.

9. The word "veracity" (line 54) is understood to mean

    (A) mendacity.

    (B) deceit.

    (C) fairness.

    (D) integrity.

10. In context, the final sentence (lines 58–60) is best viewed as

    (A) ironic.

    (B) confessional.

    (C) sarcastic.

    (D) authentic.

11. Taken as a whole, the passage is best characterized as

    (A) a plea for understanding.

    (B) an extended introduction.

    (C) an extended reply to critics.

    (D) a justification.

Questions 12–21 refer to the passage.

The following poem was published in 1594.

Since there's no help, come let us kiss and part

Since there's no help, come let us kiss and part.
Nay, I have done, you get no more of me;
And I am glad, yea glad with all my heart,
That thus so cleanly I myself can free.
5   Shake hands for ever, cancel all our vows,
And when we meet at any time again,
Be it not seen in either of our brows
That we one jot of former love retain.
Now at the last gasp of Love's latest breath,
10   When, his pulse failing, Passion speechless lies;
When Faith is kneeling by his bed of death,
And Innocence is closing up his eyes—
Now, if thou wouldst, when all have given him over,
From death to life thou might'st him yet recover!

12. The tone of the first four lines of the poem can best be described as

(A) exasperated.

(B) bitter.

(C) relieved.

(D) ecstatic.

13. The use of the pronoun "I" in lines 2–4 serves primarily to

(A) indicate the personal nature of the speaker's argument.

(B) make sure the woman understands their relationship is over.

(C) highlight the immediacy of the breakup.

(D) emphasize the speaker's freedom.

14. Lines 5–8 convey the speaker's strong desire to

(A) never look upon his love again.

(B) pretend that their vows were illegitimate.

(C) return to a state of platonic friendship.

(D) move ahead as though their passion never existed.

15. The literary technique most prevalent in lines 9–12 is

    (A) imagery.

    (B) irony.

    (C) metaphor.

    (D) personification.

16. The overall effect of lines 9–12 can best be described as

    (A) an attempt to persuade the speaker's lover to reconsider the breakup.

    (B) a definitive ending of the relationship.

    (C) a figurative expression of all that had once been at the heart of the speaker's feelings for his beloved.

    (D) a plea for Love, Passion, Faith, and Innocence to restore the couple to their former bliss.

17. The use of the word "his" in line 12 refers to which of the following?

    (A) Innocence.

    (B) Love.

    (C) Faith.

    (D) Passion.

18. The final two lines of the poem (lines 13–14) accomplish all of the following EXCEPT

    (A) showing the speaker's beloved has the power to save the relationship.

    (B) suggesting that the speaker will be saved from death.

    (C) hinting at the possibility of saving the relationship.

    (D) seeming to contradict the previous twelve lines.

19. Lines 7–8 ("Be it not seen . . . love retain") are the only enjambed (no end punctuation) lines in the poem. The effect of this move suggests that

    (A) the first section of the sonnet is drawing to a conclusion.

    (B) the poet wanted to balance these lines for rhetorical effect.

    (C) there is no hope left for the reconciliation.

    (D) the speaker is in despair.

20. The speaker's attitude can best be described as

    (A) complacent but angry.

    (B) contemplative but insulting.

    (C) impassioned but hopeful.

    (D) scornful but dreamy.

21. Which of the following statements best characterizes the meaning of the poem as a whole?

    (A) Vows are the cornerstone of all relationships, and once broken, trust can never be recovered.

    (B) Even if love seems lost, there is always time to recover its previous vitality.

    (C) Independence is realized when one is free from attachments.

    (D) It is better to part ways as friends than to hold on to bitterness.

Questions 22–31 refer to the passage.

The following passage is excerpted from a novel first published in 1985.

For a short while during the year I was ten, I thought
only people I did not know died. At the time I thought this
I was on my summer holidays and we were living far out
on Fort Road. Usually, we lived in our house on Dickenson

5   Bay Street, a house my father built with his own hand, but
just now it needed a new roof and so we were living in a house
out on Fort Road. We had only two neighbors, Mistress
Maynard and her husband. That summer, we had a pig that had
just had piglets; some guinea fowl; and some ducks that laid

10   enormous eggs that my mother said were big even for ducks.
I hated to eat any food except for the enormous duck eggs,
hard-boiled. I had nothing to do every day except to feed the
birds and the pig in the morning and in the evening. I spoke
to no one other than my parents, and sometimes to Mistress

15   Maynard, if I saw her when I went to pick up the peelings of
vegetables which my mother had asked her to save for the pig,
which was just the thing the pig really liked. From our yard,
I could see the cemetery. I did not know it was the cemetery
until one day when I said to my mother that sometimes in the

20   evening while feeding the pig, I could see various small,
sticklike figures, some dressed in black, some dressed in
white, bobbing up and down in the distance. I noticed, too,
that sometimes the black and white sticklike figures appeared
in the morning. My mother said that it was probably a child

25   being buried, since children were always buried in the
morning. Until then, I had not known that children died.

I was afraid of the dead, as was everyone I knew. We
were afraid of the dead because we never could tell when
they might show up again. Sometimes they showed up in

30   a dream, but that wasn't so bad. Because they usually only
brought a warning, and in any case you wake up from a
dream. But sometimes they would show up standing under
a tree just as you were passing by. Then they might follow you
home, and even though they might not be able to come into

35   your house, they might wait for you and follow you wherever
you went; in that case, they would never give up until you
joined them. My mother knew of many people who had died
in such a way. My mother knew of many people who had
died, including her own brother.

40   After I found out about the cemetery, I would stand
       in my yard and wait for a funeral to come. Some days, there
       were no funerals. "No one died," I would say to my mother.
       Some days, just as I was about to give up and go inside,
       I would see the small specks appear. "What made them so
45   late?" I would ask my mother. Probably someone couldn't
       bear to see the coffin lid put in place, and so as a favor the
       undertaker might let things go on too long, she said. The
       undertaker! On our way into town, we would pass the
       undertaker's workshop. Outside, a little sign read "STRAFEE
50   & SONS, UNDERTAKERS & CABINETMAKERS." I could always
       tell we were approaching this place, because of the smell of
       pitch pine and varnish in the air.

22. The first sentence (lines 1–2) of the passage foreshadows which of the
    following?

    (A) The narrator's naivety.

    (B) The narrator's loneliness.

    (C) The narrator's obsession with death.

    (D) The narrator's complex relationship with her mother.

23. Annie John is the young narrator of the passage and is best characterized by

    (A) her colorful descriptions.

    (B) an immature attitude.

    (C) a mature attitude.

    (D) moralistic judgments.

24. The setting of the passage primarily serves to

    (A) reveal Annie's love of nature.

    (B) isolate Annie from her normal surroundings.

    (C) provide Annie and her mother time to grow in their relationship.

    (D) position Annie close to a cemetery.

25. The first paragraph (lines 1–26) serves primarily to convey

    (A) Annie's boredom.

    (B) Annie's curiosity.

    (C) Annie's concern for animals.

    (D) Annie's love for her mother.

26. The tone of the passage is best described as

    (A) lighthearted.

    (B) curious.

    (C) whimsical.

    (D) tender.

27. The pronoun "they" in line 35 refers to

    (A) Annie's family.

    (B) Mr. and Mistress Maynard.

    (C) the undertaker.

    (D) the dead.

28. Annie's mother can be characterized by all of the following EXCEPT

    (A) deceitfulness.

    (B) truthfulness.

    (C) voraciousness.

    (D) forthrightness.

29. In lines 40–44, "After I found out . . . small specks appear," Annie's attitude can be characterized as one of

    (A) relief.

    (B) anger.

    (C) understanding.

    (D) disappointment.

30. The final sentence (lines 50–52) in the passage establishes

    (A) a sense of Annie's growing knowledge.

    (B) a feeling of fear and uncertainty.

    (C) a feeling of Annie's growing interest in death.

    (D) an image that haunts Annie's mind.

31. Taken as a whole, the passage is best characterized as

    (A) a young girl's developing relationship with her mother.

    (B) the beginning of an obsession.

    (C) a series of unrelated events.

    (D) a coming-of-age story.

Questions 32–45 refer to the passage.

The following poem was published in 2008.

Rest before you sleep

Requiem after Fauré, for my father

Rest before you sleep   You'll be walking for hours
then   as usual   away from home   your shoes
in your hand   your feet not yet used to the road
Perhaps they need to feel the gravel
5   to know where they're headed

A woman I knew   who lived mostly in the woods
mentioned the danger in presuming to know
what an animal thinks   The fox   for example
stopping by her open tent and looking in

10   I suppose she would've felt this way about your feet
She would've said how could anyone know
what a pair of tired feet need along the way

I would've asked her how she knew the feet
were tired   Such discourse produces nothing
15   but anything less would be silence
and that would be intolerable
I wish I knew why I was telling you this

It's easier to read the mind of a fox than to guess
what a man's about to say when he returns
20   from the woods   head full of roots   veins
more like branches   shoes in one hand   feet
blistered   and none of this necessarily
an indication of how the feet feel   what miles
uphill and back have done to the soles
25   and to the small bones that propel a man

It's safe now   I think   to speak for the fox
who is only as cunning as we say it is
We're the only creatures that claim to be anything
then build a house of facts around the claim

30   I've come for vindication   No point in trying
to disguise it as a lesser wish   Wake up   stop

> while you still know where you are   Put away
> your elusive country   Give your sleep a rest

32. Which description best characterizes the poem?

    (A) A remembrance of an old woman who lived in the woods.

    (B) A tale about the cleverness of a fox.

    (C) A tribute to the speaker's father.

    (D) A meditation on death.

33. The speaker of the poem can best be described as

    (A) disinterested.

    (B) angry.

    (C) annoyed.

    (D) reflective.

34. The lack of punctuation in the poem creates

    (A) a feeling of thoughtful meditation.

    (B) a feeling of uncertainty.

    (C) a sense of dread.

    (D) a sense of hope.

35. In the opening stanza (lines 1–5), the word "sleep" can best be defined as

    (A) death.

    (B) drowsiness.

    (C) slumber.

    (D) a beginning.

36. The woman mentioned in lines 6–12 ("A woman I knew . . . along the way")
    most likely refers to a

    (A) mythical character the speaker has read about.

    (B) deceased woman the speaker once knew.

    (C) woman who understood animal behavior since she lived in the
        woods.

    (D) wise woman who knew better than to speculate about animal
        behavior.

37. The fox mentioned throughout the poem serves as a symbol of
    (A) cunning.
    (B) death.
    (C) instability.
    (D) instinctual behavior.

38. Which of the following best represents the meaning of lines 10–16, "I suppose . . . be intolerable"?
    (A) Silence is to be avoided at all costs.
    (B) The speaker's question is unknowable.
    (C) Silence leads to confusion.
    (D) Knowledge is gained through discourse.

39. In line 17, "you" most likely refers to
    (A) the woman in the woods.
    (B) the speaker's father.
    (C) the fox.
    (D) the speaker.

40. The images presented in lines 18–25 ("It's easier . . . propel a man") imply that
    (A) the speaker is frustrated with his lack of understanding about his father's motivations.
    (B) the speaker believes that the fox is a cunning creature.
    (C) when a man returns from the woods, he is confused and disoriented.
    (D) the woods can damage a man's soul and will to continue living.

41. Lines 28–29 ("We're the only . . . the claim") suggest the speaker believes that
    (A) people use facts to support their superiority.
    (B) people's claims are unrealistic and foolhardy.
    (C) people are the only animals who use logic to support their preconceived ideas about themselves.
    (D) all other creatures understand their limitations and accept them as a part of their nature.

42. The gaps throughout the poem create a feeling of all of the following EXCEPT

    (A) mourning.

    (B) thoughtfulness.

    (C) careful consideration.

    (D) confidence.

43. In line 30, the word "vindication" most closely means

    (A) exoneration.

    (B) blame.

    (C) disapproval.

    (D) condemnation.

44. The tone of the final stanza (lines 30–33) is best described as

    (A) imploring.

    (B) grateful.

    (C) defiant.

    (D) mocking.

45. In the final stanza (lines 30–33), the speaker is

    (A) trying to convince his father to fight against his impending death.

    (B) seeking to spare his father the pain associated with dying.

    (C) trying to convince his father to wake up so they can have one final conversation before he dies.

    (D) pleading with his father to calmly allow death to ease his final pain.

Questions 46–55 refer to the passage.

The following poem was published in 1976.

Coal

I
Is the total black, being spoken
From the earth's inside.
There are many kinds of open.
How a diamond comes into a knot of flame
How a sound comes into a word, coloured
By who pays what for speaking.

Some words are open
Like a diamond on glass windows
Singing out within the crash of passing sun
Then there are words like stapled wagers
In a perforated book—buy and sign and tear apart—
And come whatever wills all chances
The stub remains
An ill-pulled tooth with a ragged edge.
Some words live in my throat
Breeding like adders. Others know sun
Seeking like gypsies over my tongue
To explode through my lips
Like young sparrows bursting from shell.
Some words
Bedevil me.

Love is a word another kind of open—
As a diamond comes into a knot of flame
I am black because I come from the earth's inside
Take my word for jewel in your open light.

Line numbers in left margin: 5, 10, 15, 20, 25

46. The first sentence, "I [i]s the . . . earth's inside," (lines 1–3) reveals the speaker's claim that

(A) she is in control over her life choices.

(B) her words, like her body, are products of the Earth.

(C) the center of the Earth is black like she is.

(D) she alone is able to share the secrets of the Earth.

47. Lines 4–7 ("There are many . . . for speaking") serve to establish that

    (A) language is dynamic and ever changing like a diamond.

    (B) speaking exacts a heavy price for those who are careless.

    (C) the sounds words make are as important as the word itself.

    (D) words are created through who is speaking, like the way diamonds are created through time.

48. The second stanza (lines 8–22) primarily serves to

    (A) illustrate the speaker's complicated relationship with words.

    (B) explain how words can hurt if used incorrectly.

    (C) convey the idea that words are often poisonous like adders.

    (D) illustrate that words, like "[a]n ill-pulled tooth with a ragged edge," are difficult to understand.

49. The speaker uses similes in the second stanza (lines 8–22) to

    (A) express her feelings about being a woman of color living in America.

    (B) compare words with coal and its ability to fuel her life with energy and light.

    (C) illustrate how her complex relationship with language often frustrates her.

    (D) suggest that words can be treated as friends or enemies.

50. Line 16 ("Some words live in my throat") primarily makes use of

    (A) personification.

    (B) metaphor.

    (C) simile.

    (D) symbol.

51. In line 17, "Others" refers to which of the following?

    (A) Adders.

    (B) The speaker's throat.

    (C) Breeding.

    (D) Words.

52. In context, the word "Bedevil" in line 22 most closely means

    (A) confuse.

    (B) trouble.

    (C) encourage.

    (D) console.

53. The final stanza (lines 23–26) is characterized by

    (A) an optimistic view that the speaker has reconciled her position in the world.

    (B) the speaker's declaration that love is the primary path to liberation.

    (C) the speaker's claim that like a diamond is born from coal, her words are born out of love and the Earth.

    (D) the idea that love, like the speaker's birth from inside the Earth, is the jewel that this life has to offer.

54. The overall tone of the poem is best described as

    (A) arrogant.

    (B) regretful.

    (C) satirical.

    (D) pensive.

55. Which of the following statements best describes the overall development of the poem?

    (A) The speaker confronts the complex challenges of a Black woman living in America.

    (B) The speaker asserts that her relationship with language is a primary driver of her repression.

    (C) The speaker suggests that as coal fuels the development of a nation, words fuel her development as a Black woman.

    (D) The speaker's contrasting images of light and dark, hard and soft, mirror her complex relationship with life as a Black woman.

Section II: Free-Response

Total time: 2 hours
3 questions

Question 1: Poetry Analysis

(Suggested time—40 minutes. This question counts as one-third of the total essay section score.)

In Eavan Boland's poem "In a Bad Light," published in 1994, a visit to a museum causes the speaker to imagine the conditions that Irish women worked under during an earlier era. Read the poem carefully. Then, in a well-written essay, analyze how Boland uses literary elements and techniques to convey the speaker's complex reaction to the museum exhibit.

In your response you should do the following:

- Respond to the prompt with a thesis that presents a defensible interpretation.
- Select and use evidence to support your line of reasoning.
- Explain how the evidence supports your line of reasoning.
- Use appropriate grammar and punctuation in communicating your argument.

In a Bad Light

> This is St. Louis. Where the rivers meet.
>   The Illinois. The Mississippi. The Missouri.
> The light is in its element of Autumn.
>   Clear. With yellow Ginkgo leaves falling.
> 5   There is always a nightmare. Even in such light.
>
>   The weather must be cold now in Dublin.
> And when skies are clear, frosts come
>   down on the mountains and first
> inklings of winter will be underfoot in
> 10   the crisp iron of a fern at dawn.
>
>   I stand in a room in the Museum.
>   In one glass case a plastic figure
> represents a woman in a dress,
>   with crepe sleeves and a satin apron.
> 15   And feet laced neatly into suede.
>
>   She stands in a replica of a cabin
> on a steamboat bound for New Orleans.

The year is 1860. Nearly war.
A notice says no comforts were spared. The silk
20   is French. The seamstresses are Irish.

I see them in the oil-lit parlours.
   I am in the gas-lit backrooms.
We make in the apron front and from
   the papery appearance and crushable
25   look of crepe, a sign. We are bent over

      in a bad light. We are sewing a last
sight of shore. We are sewing coffin ships.
   And the salt of exile. And our own
death in it. For history's abandonment
30   we are doing this. And this. And

this is a button hole. This is a stitch.
   Fury enters them as frost follows
every arabesque and curl of a fern: this is
   the nightmare. See how you perceive it.
35   We sleep the sleep of exhaustion.

      We dream a woman on a steamboat
parading in sunshine in a dress we know
   we made. She laughs off rumours of war.
She turns and traps light on the skirt.
40   It is, for that moment, beautiful.

Question 2: Prose Fiction Analysis

(Suggested time—40 minutes. This question counts as one-third of the total essay section score.)

The following excerpt is from Margaret Atwood's novel *Cat's Eye*, published in 1988. Read the passage carefully. Then, in a well-written essay, analyze how Atwood uses literary elements and techniques to characterize the complex relationship between the sister and brother.

In your response you should do the following:

- Respond to the prompt with a thesis that presents a defensible interpretation.
- Select and use evidence to support your line of reasoning.
- Explain how the evidence supports your line of reasoning.
- Use appropriate grammar and punctuation in communicating your argument.

My brother has a hammer and some wood, and his own jackknife. He whittles and hammers: he's making a gun. He nails two pieces of wood at right angles, with another nail for the trigger. He has several of these wooden guns, and

5 daggers and swords also, with blood colored onto the blades with red pencils. Some of the blood is orange, from when he ran out of red. He sings:

Coming in on a wing and a prayer,
Coming in on a wing and a prayer,
10 Though there's one motor gone
We will still carry on,
Coming in on a wing and a prayer.

He sings this cheerfully, but I think it's a sad song, because although I've seen the pictures of the airplanes on
15 the cigarette cards I don't know how they fly. I think it's like birds, and a bird with one wing can't fly. This is what my father says in the winters, before dinner, lifting his glass when there are other men there at the table: "You can't fly on one wing." So in fact the prayer in the song is useless.
20 Stephen gives me a gun and a knife and we play war. This is his favorite game. While our parents are putting up the tent or making the fire or cooking, we sneak around behind the trees and bushes, aiming through the leaves. I am the infantry, which means I have to do what he says.

25   He waves me forward, motions me back, tells me to keep my
head down so the enemy won't blow it off.
    "You're dead," he says.
    "No I'm not."
    "Yes you are. They got you. Lie down."

30   There is no arguing with him, since he can see the
enemy and I can't. I have to lie down on the swampy
ground, propped against a stump to avoid getting
too wet, until it's time for me to be alive again.

    Sometimes, instead of war, we hunt through the

35 forest, turning over logs and rocks to see what's underneath.
There are ants, grubs and beetles, frogs and toads, garter
snakes, even salamanders if we're lucky. We don't do
anything with the things we find. We know they will die if
we put them into bottles and leave them by accident in the

40 sun in the back window of the car, as we have done before.
So we merely look at them, watching the ants hiding their
pill-shaped eggs in panic, the snakes pouring themselves
into darkness. Then we put the logs back where they were,
unless we need some of these things for fishing.

45   Once in a while we fight. I don't win these fights:
Stephen is bigger and more ruthless than I am, and I want
to play with him more than he wants to play with me. We
fight in whispers or well out of the way, because if we're
caught we will both be punished. For this reason we don't

50 tell on each other. We know from experience that the
satisfactions of betrayal are scarcely worth it.

    Because they're secret, these fights have an extra
attraction. It's the attraction of dirty words we aren't
supposed to say, words like *bum*; the attraction of

55 conspiracy, of collusion. We step on each other's feet,
pinch each other's arms, careful not to give away the pain,
loyal even in outrage.

Question 3: Literary Argument

(Suggested time—40 minutes. This question counts as one-third of the total essay section score.)

In many works of fiction, characters make decisions that have a lasting impact. As Eleanor Roosevelt noted, "In the long run, we shape our lives and we shape ourselves. The process never ends until we die. And the choices we make are ultimately our own responsibility."

Either from your own reading or from the list below, choose a work of fiction in which a character decides to take on a meaningful responsibility. Then, in a well-written essay, analyze how the complex nature of the character's decision and responsibility ultimately illuminates the meaning of the work as a whole. Do not merely summarize the plot.

In your response you should do the following:

- Respond to the prompt with a thesis that presents a defensible interpretation.
- Provide evidence to support your line of reasoning.
- Explain how your evidence supports your line of reasoning.
- Use appropriate grammar and punctuation in communicating your argument.

- *All Quiet on the Western Front*
- *The Awakening*
- *Beloved*
- *The Bluest Eye*
- *Brave New World*
- *Brideshead Revisited*
- *Candide*
- *The Catcher in the Rye*
- *Death of a Salesman*
- *East of Eden*
- *Great Expectations*
- *The Great Gatsby*
- *The Handmaid's Tale*
- *Homegoing*
- *The Importance of Being Earnest*
- *Invisible Man*
- *Johnny Got His Gun*
- *King Lear*
- *The Leavers*
- *The Mill on the Floss*
- *Native Son*
- *No Country for Old Men*
- *The Odyssey*
- *Pachinko*
- *Pride and Prejudice*
- *Purple Hibiscus*
- *The Road*
- *Salvage the Bones*
- *The Sun Also Rises*
- *The Tempest*
- *To Kill a Mockingbird*
- *When the Emperor Was Divine*

Full AP® Exam 2

Section I: Multiple-Choice

Total time: 1 hour
55 questions

Questions 1–11 refer to the passage.

The following poem was published in 1633.

The Canonization[1]

For God's sake hold your tongue, and let me love,
    Or chide my palsy, or my gout,
My five gray hairs, or ruined fortune flout,
With wealth your state, your mind with arts improve,
        Take you a course, get you a place,
        Observe his honor, or his grace,
Or the king's real, or his stampèd face
    Contemplate; what you will, approve,
    So you will let me love.

Alas, alas, who's injured by my love?
    What merchant's ships have my sighs drowned?
Who says my tears have overflowed his ground?
    When did my colds a forward spring remove?
        When did the heats which my veins fill
        Add one more to the plaguy bill?
Soldiers find wars, and lawyers find out still
    Litigious men, which quarrels move,
    Though she and I do love.

Call us what you will, we are made such by love;
    Call her one, me another fly,
We're tapers[2] too, and at our own cost die,
    And we in us find the eagle and the dove.
        The phœnix riddle hath more wit
        By us; we two being one, are it.
So, to one neutral thing both sexes fit.
    We die and rise the same, and prove
    Mysterious by this love.

Line numbers: 5, 10, 15, 20, 25

---

1. Declaration that a deceased person is recognized as a saint.
2. Long, narrow candles.

We can die by it, if not live by love,
      And if unfit for tombs and hearse
30   Our legend be, it will be fit for verse;
         And if no piece of chronicle we prove,
            We'll build in sonnets pretty rooms;
            As well a well-wrought urn becomes
      The greatest ashes, as half-acre tombs,
35   And by these hymns, all shall approve
               Us canonized for Love.

And thus invoke us: "You, whom reverend love
      Made one another's hermitage;
You, to whom love was peace, that now is rage;
40   Who did the whole world's soul contract, and drove
               Into the glasses of your eyes
               (So made such mirrors, and such spies,
      That they did all to you epitomize)
         Countries, towns, courts: beg from above
45   A pattern of your love!"

1. The speaker's admonition to "For God's sake hold your tongue, and let me love" (line 1) indicates his

    (A) reverence for God's name.

    (B) exasperation for being interrupted.

    (C) longing to return to his love.

    (D) insecurities about his love's intentions.

2. Lines 2–3, "Or chide . . . fortune flout," serve primarily to

    (A) plead for the chance to love freely despite his age.

    (B) point out the speaker's physical flaws.

    (C) emphasize the speaker's fear of dying.

    (D) illicit sympathy from readers.

3. The tone of the rhetorical questions in the second stanza (lines 10–18) suggests that the speaker is

    (A) angry.

    (B) wistful.

    (C) content.

    (D) frustrated.

4. In line 22 ("And we . . . the dove") the speaker makes a comparison in order to best represent his love as

    (A) one that easily takes flight.

    (B) dangerous but exciting.

    (C) a mixture of both birds' qualities.

    (D) one that can last an eternity.

5. The phoenix metaphor in lines 23–27 ("the phœnix . . . this love") shows the speaker making an argument that

    (A) their love is earthbound but hoping for rebirth.

    (B) unlike the eagle and the dove, the phoenix is a mythical creature.

    (C) much like the phoenix, the beloved is a mystery to the speaker.

    (D) the phoenix riddle illustrates a merging of their love into one eternal life.

6. In line 24 "it" refers to

    (A) tapers.

    (B) the dove.

    (C) the eagle.

    (D) the phoenix riddle.

7. Lines 28–30 ("We can . . . for verse") includes all the following ideas EXCEPT

    (A) the couple is willing to die for their love.

    (B) they believe their love is worthy of verse.

    (C) they believe that their love is attainable for ordinary people.

    (D) they believe that although they may be barred from a proper burial, their love is legendary.

8. When the speaker claims that "And by these hymns, all shall approve / Us canonized for Love" (lines 35–36), he is suggesting that

    (A) their love should be considered for sainthood.

    (B) songs will be sung about the lovers for generations to come.

    (C) he wishes that he and his beloved could be buried together.

    (D) sonnets are the only true way to express their love.

9. In lines 28–32 ("We can . . . pretty rooms") the speaker contemplates which of the following possible outcomes?

    (A) People will want to bury the pair in a grand mausoleum.

    (B) Even verse will not be able to convey the lovers' passion.

    (C) Their love will be remembered for generations to come.

    (D) Their legendary love will engender material for timeless verse.

10. In line 37 the word "invoke" most directly means

    (A) petition.

    (B) worship.

    (C) answer.

    (D) forget.

11. The poem as a whole can best be described as

    (A) a pompous statement about love.

    (B) a satiric call for the couple's love to be elevated to sainthood.

    (C) a final lament of an old man's lost love.

    (D) a passionate, final testament about love.

Questions 12–21 refer to the passage.

The following passage is a short story first published in 1976.

She was standing by the river looking at the stepping
stones and remembering each one. There was the round
unsteady stone, the pointed one, the flat one in the middle—
the safe stone where you could stand and look round. The
next wasn't so safe for when the river was full the water
flowed over it and even when it showed dry it was slippery.
But after that it was easy and soon she was standing on the
other side.

The road was much wider than it used to be but the
work had been done carelessly. The felled trees had not
been cleared away and the bushes looked trampled. Yet it
was the same road and she walked along feeling
extraordinarily happy.

It was a fine day, a blue day. The only thing was that the
sky had a glassy look that she didn't remember. That was the
only word she could think of. Glassy. She turned the corner,
saw that what had been the old *pavé* had been taken up, and
there too the road was much wider, but it had the same
unfinished look.

She came to the worn stone steps that led up to the
house and her heart began to beat. The screw pine was
gone, so was the mock summer house called the *ajoupa*, but
the clove tree was still there and at the top of the steps the
rough lawn stretched away, just as she remembered it. She
stopped and looked towards the house that had been added
to and painted white. It was strange to see a car standing in
front of it.

There were two children under the mango tree, a boy
and a little girl, and she waved to them and called 'Hello'
but they didn't answer her or turn their heads. Very fair
children, as Europeans born in the West Indies so often
are: as if the white blood is asserting itself against all odds.

The grass was yellow in the hot sunlight as she walked
towards them. When she was quite close she called again
shyly: 'Hello.' Then, 'I used to live here once,' she said.

Still they didn't answer. When she said for the third
time 'Hello' she was quite near them. Her arms went out
instinctively with the longing to touch them.

It was the boy who turned. His grey eyes looked straight
into hers. His expression didn't change. He said: 'Hasn't it

gone cold all of a sudden. D'you notice? Let's go in.' 'Yes
let's,' said the girl.
   Her arms fell to her sides as she watched them running
across the grass to the house. That was the first time she knew.

12. The passage as a whole can best be described as which of the following
    EXCEPT?

    (A) A moment of personal struggle.

    (B) A moment of personal sadness.

    (C) A moment of personal revelation.

    (D) A moment of personal anxiety.

13. Which feature is most prominent in the passage?

    (A) Imagery.

    (B) Metaphor.

    (C) Symbol.

    (D) Juxtaposition.

14. In the opening paragraph (lines 1–8), the woman is characterized mainly as

    (A) overly cautious.

    (B) determined.

    (C) intentional.

    (D) fearful.

15. Which of the following statements best describes the central role that the
    stones play in the opening paragraph (lines 1–8)?

    (A) The stones serve as metaphors for her new life.

    (B) The stones provide a path to a new life.

    (C) The stones serve as a reminder of the protagonist's past life.

    (D) The stones illustrate the dangerous nature of her crossing.

16. In lines 14–16 ("It was a fine . . . Glassy"), the narrator claims that the woman "didn't remember" the sky having a "glassy look." In context, the word "glassy" can best be defined as

    (A) clear.

    (B) lifeless.

    (C) unfocused.

    (D) crystalline.

17. In lines 20–27 ("She came . . . front of it"), the narrator comes upon the house she once inhabited. Her reaction can best be described as

    (A) disgusted.

    (B) agitated.

    (C) perceptive.

    (D) confused.

18. The woman's reaction to the children in lines 36–44 ("Still they . . . she knew") can best be described as

    (A) determined, but confused.

    (B) confused, but resigned.

    (C) disturbed, but eager.

    (D) hopeful, but alarmed.

19. In lines 33–44 ("The grass . . . to the house") the woman's mood shifts from

    (A) hopeful to realistic.

    (B) purposeful to disappointed.

    (C) realistic to self-pitying.

    (D) idealistic to frustrated.

20. In lines 37–38 ("Her arms . . . them") the woman instinctively "longs" to touch the children mainly because

    (A) she desires human acknowledgment and human connection.

    (B) she is angry at being ignored by the children.

    (C) after being ignored for the third time, she wants to get their attention.

    (D) she wants to make sure the children know that she "used to live here once."

21. Throughout the passage, the narrator views the woman primarily with

   (A) disdain.

   (B) sympathy.

   (C) confusion.

   (D) detachment.

Questions 22–34 refer to the passage.

The following poem was published in 1978.

Integrity

the quality or state of being complete: unbroken condition: entirety
—*Webster's*

A wild patience has taken me this far

as if I had to bring to shore
a boat with a spasmodic outboard motor
old sweaters, nets, spray-mottled books
5   tossed in the prow
some kind of sun burning my shoulder-blades.
Splashing the oarlocks. Burning through.
Your fore-arms can get scalded, licked with pain
in a sun blotted like unspoken anger
10   behind a casual mist.

The length of daylight
this far north, in this
forty-ninth year of my life
is critical.

15   The light is critical: of me, of this
long-dreamed, involuntary landing
on the arm of an inland sea.
The glitter of the shoal
depleting into shadow
20   I recognize: the stand of pines
violet-black really, green in the old postcard
but really I have nothing but myself
to go by; nothing
stands in the realm of pure necessity
25   except what my hands can hold.

Nothing but myself? . . . My selves.
After so long, this answer.
As if I had always known
I steer the boat in, simply.
30   The motor dying on the pebbles
cicadas taking up the hum
dropped in the silence.

Anger and tenderness: my selves.
And now I can believe they breathe in me
35   as angels, not polarities.
Anger and tenderness: the spider's genius
to spin and weave in the same action
from her own body, anywhere—
even from a broken web.

40   The cabin in the stand of pines
is still for sale. I know this. Know the print
of the last foot, the hand that slammed and locked that door,
then stopped to wreathe the rain-smashed clematis
back on the trellis
45   for no one's sake except its own.
I know the chart nailed to the wallboards
the icy kettle squatting on the burner.
The hands that hammered in those nails
emptied that kettle one last time
50   are these two hands
and they have caught the baby leaping
from between trembling legs
and they have worked the vacuum aspirator[3]
and stroked the sweated temples
55   and steered the boat here through this hot
misblotted sunlight, critical light
imperceptibly scalding
the skin these hands will also salve.

22. Which of the following statements best describes the structure of the
poem?

(A) The first half of the poem chronicles a difficult journey, and the second
half describes a return to a family cabin in the woods.

(B) It begins with a reluctant journey, then becomes deeply self-reflective,
and concludes with a series of complex memories.

(C) It begins with a long trip north, then focuses on a description of the
landscape, and concludes with a melancholy reunion.

(D) A stream of consciousness moves from a dreamlike state to end with
harsh reality.

3. Tool used in conducting abortion procedures.

23. In the first two stanzas, the speaker can best be characterized as

    (A) angry but controlled.

    (B) excited but concerned.

    (C) casual but determined.

    (D) contemplative but burdened.

24. In lines 3–6 ("a boat . . . shoulder-blades"), the primary effect of listing the various items is to

    (A) demonstrate the speaker's unorganized life.

    (B) establish the speaker's diverse interests.

    (C) emphasize the speaker's complicated past.

    (D) highlight the speaker's chaotic relationships.

25. The word "critical" is used in line 14 and line 15. Which statement best describes the meaning of each usage of the word?

    (A) The meaning of "critical" in both lines is *crucial*.

    (B) The meaning in line 14 is *crucial*, and the meaning in line 15 is *serious*.

    (C) The meaning in line 14 is *serious*, and the meaning in line 15 is *crucial*.

    (D) The meaning in line 14 is *crucial*, and the meaning in line 15 is *judgmental*.

26. The claim that "nothing stands in the realm of pure necessity except what my hands can hold" (lines 23–25) is meant to suggest that

    (A) the speaker is aware that her surroundings are peaceful.

    (B) the speaker understands her situation is fixable.

    (C) the speaker is aware that all she needs is herself.

    (D) the speaker has dreamed of a safe place to live.

27. The primary purpose of the rhetorical question "*Nothing but myself?*" (line 26) is to provide the speaker an opportunity to

    (A) acknowledge her multifaceted self.

    (B) acknowledge her part in her failed relationship.

    (C) confess what she has always known about herself.

    (D) acknowledge that her life has been one of avoidance.

28. The claim that "they breathe in me as angels, not polarities" (lines 34–35) is meant figuratively to express the speaker's

    (A) acceptance of her seemingly contradictory traits.

    (B) understanding of positive and negative traits.

    (C) realization that her anger is not as important as tenderness.

    (D) acceptance of her different selves despite her initial rejection of them.

29. In lines 36–39 ("the spider's . . . broken web"), the speaker uses a metaphor to

    (A) emphasize her ability to create a new life anywhere, even if her situation seems broken.

    (B) display her resilience in the face of adversity.

    (C) compare her genius to the spider's.

    (D) describe a path of recovery from her current situation.

30. In the context of the poem, the title "Integrity" can best be defined as

    (A) virtue.

    (B) honesty.

    (C) morality.

    (D) trust.

31. The images present in lines 41–45 ("Know the print . . . its own") convey the

    (A) oppression the speaker faced during the relationship.

    (B) anxiousness of the moment.

    (C) the speaker's deep understanding of her partner's contradictory qualities.

    (D) the speaker's powerful memories of the moment.

32. Which of the following statements best interprets the symbol of the boat in lines 3, 29, and 55?

    (A) The boat is a symbol of connectedness.

    (B) The boat is a symbol of love.

    (C) The boat is a symbol of the journey.

    (D) The boat is a symbol of control.

33. The overall tone of the poem can best be described as

    (A) concerned and determined.

    (B) reflective and melancholy.

    (C) determined and angry.

    (D) grateful and appreciative.

34. The poem as a whole presents a contrast between

    (A) memory and reality.

    (B) love and hate.

    (C) pain and hope.

    (D) joy and conflict.

Questions 35–44 refer to the passage.

The following passage is excerpted from a novel first published in 1994.

I was eighteen and going to start college in the fall. My
mother continued working her two jobs, but she put in even
longer hours. And we moved to a one-family house in a tree-
lined neighborhood near where Marc lived.

5   In the new place, my mother had a patch of land in the
back where she started growing hibiscus. Daffodils would
need more care and she had grown tired of them. She had
grown tired of daffodils.

We decorated our new living room in red, everything
10   from the carpet to the plastic roses on the coffee table. I had
my very own large bedroom with a new squeaky bed. My
mother's room was even bigger, with a closet that you could
have entertained some friends in. In some places in Haiti,
her closet would have been a room on its own, and the
15   clothes would not have bothered the fortunate child who
would sleep in it.

Before the move, I had been going to a Haitian Adventist
school that went from elementary right to high school. They
had guaranteed my mother that they would get me into
20   college and they had lived up to their pledge. Now my first
classes at college were a few months away and my mother
couldn't have been happier. Her sacrifices had paid off.

I never said this to my mother, but I hated the
Maranatha Bilingual Institution. It was as if I had never left
25   Haiti. All the lessons were in French, except for English
composition and literature classes. Outside the school, we
were "the Frenchies," cringing in our mock-Catholic-school
uniforms as the students from the public school across the
street called us "boat people" and "stinking Haitians."

30   When my mother was home, she made me read out
loud from the English Composition textbooks. The first
English words I read sounded like rocks falling in a stream.
Then very slowly things began to take on some meaning.
There were words that I heard often. Words that jump out of
35   New York Creole conversations, like the last kernel in a
cooling popcorn machine. Words, among others, like *TV*,
building, feeling, which Marc and my mother used even
when they were in the middle of a heated political
discussion in Creole. Mwin gin yon feeling. I have a feeling
40   Haiti will get back on its feet one day, but I'll be dead before
it happens. My mother, always the pessimist.

There were other words that helped too, words that
looked almost the same in French, but were pronounced
differently in English: nationality, alien, race, enemy, date,
45   present. These and other words gave me a context for the
rest that I did not understand.

Eventually, I began to hear myself that I read better. I
answered swiftly when my mother asked me a question in
English. Not that I ever had a chance to show it off at school,
50   but I became an English speaker.

"There is a great responsibility that comes with
knowledge," my mother would say. My great responsibility
was to study hard. I spent six years doing nothing but that.
School, home, and prayer.

35. In lines 1–7 ("I was eighteen . . . them"), the mother is characterized as all of
the following EXCEPT

(A) hard-working.

(B) dedicated.

(C) indolent.

(D) pragmatic.

36. By using the term "fortunate child" in line 15, the narrator is implying that

(A) children in Haiti live in squalid conditions.

(B) her mother is being extravagant.

(C) Haitian children were grateful for any gifts.

(D) some Haitian children lived without space of their own.

37. In lines 23–24, the narrator states that "I never said this to my mother, but I
hated the Maranatha Bilingual Institution" because

(A) the narrator understands the sacrifices her mother has made to send her
to the school.

(B) the narrator understands that her mother would be disappointed in her.

(C) the narrator didn't want her mother to know how much she hated
speaking French.

(D) the narrator's mother was pessimistic by nature and she didn't want to
add to her burden.

38. In context, the word "mock" in line 27 most nearly means

    (A) ugly.

    (B) disappointing.

    (C) contemptible.

    (D) mimic.

39. The simile in line 32 ("like rocks falling in a stream") is employed primarily to suggest that

    (A) the narrator could hear the sounds English words make, but they didn't make sense.

    (B) the narrator felt frustrated with the English language due to her mother's tutoring.

    (C) the narrator felt her pronunciation of English words was only understood by her mother.

    (D) the narrator's mother's tactics for teaching English were ineffective.

40. The simile in lines 35–36 ("like the last kernel in a cooling popcorn machine") contrasts with the simile in line 32 ("like rocks falling in a stream") in order to convey what?

    (A) The Creole language the narrator heard at home helped her to become proficient in English.

    (B) The Creole language the narrator heard at home contained enough English to help her learn new words.

    (C) The "last kernel in a cooling popcorn machine" is more linguistically coherent than "rocks falling in a stream."

    (D) The comparison between a naturally developing system and a man-made system is similar to learning a new language.

41. The narrator's list of words in lines 44–45 ("nationality . . . present") primarily serves to

    (A) illustrate English words that looked like French words.

    (B) demonstrate how challenging it is to learn English as a second language.

    (C) convey the specific struggles the narrator was facing in her new circumstances.

    (D) illustrate how pronunciation is the most important factor when learning a new language.

42. The primary strategy employed in lines 30–46 is

    (A) simile.

    (B) listing.

    (C) metaphor.

    (D) repetition.

43. The passage as a whole is best described as

    (A) a mother's dedication to her daughter's education.

    (B) a first-person account of escaping poverty.

    (C) an exposé on the value of proper education.

    (D) a story of personal sacrifice.

44. Throughout the passage, the narrator views her mother primarily with

    (A) dread.

    (B) derision.

    (C) respect.

    (D) fear.

Questions 45–55 refer to the passage.

The following poem was published in 1989.

Green Chile

I prefer red chile over my eggs
and potatoes for breakfast.
Red chile *ristras*[4] decorate my door,
dry on my roof, and hang from eaves.

5 They lend open-air vegetable stands
historical grandeur, and gently swing
with an air of festive welcome.
I can hear them talking in the wind,
haggard, yellowing, crisp, rasping

10 tongues of old men, licking the breeze.

    But grandmother loves green chile.
When I visit her,
she holds the green chile pepper
in her wrinkled hands.

15 Ah, voluptuous, masculine,
an air of authority and youth simmers
from its swan-neck stem, tapering to a flowery
collar, fermenting resinous spice.
A well-dressed gentleman at the door

20 my grandmother takes sensuously in her hand,
rubbing its firm glossed sides,
caressing the oily rubbery serpent,
with mouth-watering fulfillment,
fondling its curves with gentle fingers.

25 Its bearing magnificent and taut
as flanks of a tiger in mid-leap,
she thrusts her blade into
and cuts it open, with lust
on her hot mouth, sweating over the stove,

30 bandanna round her forehead,
mysterious passion on her face
as she serves me green chile con carne
between soft warm leaves of corn tortillas,
with beans and rice—her sacrifice

35 to her little prince.
I slurp from my plate

---

4. Dried chile pepper arrangements, sometimes used for decoration but often for later consumption.

with last bit of tortilla, my mouth burns
and I hiss and drink a tall glass of cold water.

All over New Mexico, sunburned men and women
40   drive rickety trucks stuffed with gunny-sacks
of green chile, from Belen, Veguita, Willard, Estancia,
San Antonio y Socorro, from fields
to roadside stands, you see them roasting green chile
in screen-sided homemade barrels, and for a dollar a bag,
45   we relive this old, beautiful ritual again and again.

45. The overall tone of the poem can best be described as

(A) kind.

(B) respectful.

(C) disillusioned.

(D) ironic.

46. The first two sentences of the poem (lines 1–4), establish the speaker's

(A) knowledge and preference for red chiles.

(B) large supply of red chile *ristras* available for his family.

(C) many uses of red chile peppers.

(D) economic situation.

47. Lines 5–10 ("They lend . . . licking the breeze") make particular use of which of the following literary techniques?

(A) Simile.

(B) Metaphor.

(C) Personification.

(D) Symbol.

48. Lines 11–14 ("But Grandmother . . . hands") serve to

(A) create a conflict between the speaker and his grandmother.

(B) establish the speaker's respect for his aging grandmother.

(C) establish the grandmother's contrary personality.

(D) establish the red-versus-green-chile debate.

49. The imagery in the second stanza (lines 11–38) serves primarily to

    (A) illustrate the grandmother's obsession with green chile peppers.

    (B) introduce readers to the speaker's "well-dressed gentleman."

    (C) establish the grandmother's understanding of her grandson's tastes.

    (D) convey the grandmother's passion for cooking for her grandson.

50. "Its" (line 25) refers to which of the following?

    (A) "A well-dressed gentleman."

    (B) A "rubbery serpent."

    (C) A "green chile pepper."

    (D) The "swan-neck stem."

51. The second stanza (lines 11–38) is characterized by all of the following EXCEPT

    (A) detailed descriptions of green chile peppers.

    (B) the speaker's sacrifice for his grandmother's well-being.

    (C) the personification of green chile peppers.

    (D) descriptive language of the grandmother's meal preparations.

52. The speaker claims that his grandmother makes a "sacrifice to her little prince" (lines 34–35). This statement seems to suggest that

    (A) the speaker is central in the grandmother's life.

    (B) the speaker is a spoiled child.

    (C) the speaker is the only male in the grandmother's life.

    (D) the grandmother is poor and can only afford to feed the speaker.

53. The shift at the beginning of the third stanza (line 39) indicates a change from

    (A) fantastic to realistic.

    (B) self-absorbed to community minded.

    (C) personal to general.

    (D) personal to hopeful.

54. The final stanza (lines 39–45) reveals the speaker's understanding that

    (A) the cultural significance of green chile peppers is geographic.

    (B) his grandmother's obsession was widespread.

    (C) green chile peppers are a symbol of hope.

    (D) many people earn their living from selling peppers.

55. Which of the following statements best represents the meaning of the poem as a whole?

    (A) Family and culture are inseparable.

    (B) Dedication to the family is the foundation of every culture.

    (C) Passion and service are the heart of a family.

    (D) Cultural and familial foundations are often found in the seemingly insignificant.

Section II: Free-Response

Total time: 2 hours

3 questions

Question 1: Poetry Analysis

(Suggested time—40 minutes. This question counts as one-third of the total essay section score.)

In the poem "Love Calls Us to the Things of This World," published in 1956, Richard Wilbur explores how human beings struggle to maintain balance in a difficult and challenging world. Read the poem carefully. Then, in a well-written essay, analyze how Wilbur uses literary elements and techniques to convey the speaker's complex reactions to waking to a new day.

In your response you should do the following:

- Respond to the prompt with a thesis that presents a defensible interpretation.
- Select and use evidence to support your line of reasoning.
- Explain how the evidence supports your line of reasoning.
- Use appropriate grammar and punctuation in communicating your argument.

Love Calls Us to the Things of This World

The eyes open to a cry of pulleys,
And spirited from sleep, the astounded soul
Hangs for a moment bodiless and simple
As false dawn.
     Outside the open window
The morning air is all awash with angels.

Some are in bed-sheets, some are in blouses,
Some are in smocks: but truly there they are.
Now they are rising together in calm swells
Of halcyon feeling, filling whatever they wear
With the deep joy of their impersonal breathing;

Now they are flying in place, conveying
The terrible speed of their omnipresence, moving
And staying like white water; and now of a sudden
They swoon down into so rapt a quiet
That nobody seems to be there.
     The soul shrinks

5

10

15

From all that it is about to remember,
From the punctual rape of every blessèd day,
20   And cries,
                "Oh, let there be nothing on earth but laundry,
Nothing but rosy hands in the rising steam
And clear dances done in the sight of heaven."

Yet, as the sun acknowledges
25   With a warm look the world's hunks and colors,
The soul descends once more in bitter love
To accept the waking body, saying now
In a changed voice as the man yawns and rises,
                "Bring them down from their ruddy gallows;
30   Let there be clean linen for the backs of thieves;
Let lovers go fresh and sweet to be undone,
And the heaviest nuns walk in a pure floating
Of dark habits,
                keeping their difficult balance."

Question 2: Prose Fiction Analysis

(Suggested time—40 minutes. This question counts as one-third of the total essay section score.)

The following excerpt is from Toni Morrison's novel *Home*, published in 2012. In this passage, a brother and sister secretly observe wild horses and a burial. Read the passage carefully. Then, in a well-written essay, analyze how Morrison uses literary elements and techniques to convey the brother's complex reactions as he recalls the events of that day.

In your response you should do the following:

- Respond to the prompt with a thesis that presents a defensible interpretation.
- Select and use evidence to support your line of reasoning.
- Explain how the evidence supports your line of reasoning.
- Use appropriate grammar and punctuation in communicating your argument.

> *They rose up like men. We saw them. Like men they stood.*
> *We shouldn't have been anywhere near that place. Like most farmland outside Lotus, Georgia, this one here had plenty of scary warning signs. The threats hung from wire*
> 5 *mesh fences with wooden stakes every fifty or so feet. But when we saw a crawl space that some animal had dug—a coyote maybe, or a coon dog—we couldn't resist. Just kids we were. The grass was shoulder high for her and waist high for me so, looking out for snakes, we crawled through it on our*
> 10 *bellies. The reward was worth the harm grass juice and clouds of gnats did to our eyes, because there right in front of us, about fifty yards off, they stood like men. Their raised hooves crashing and striking, their manes tossing back from wild white eyes. They bit each other like dogs but when they stood,*
> 15 *reared up on their hind legs, their forelegs around the withers of the other, we held our breath in wonder. One was rust-colored, the other deep black, both sunny with sweat. The neighs were not as frightening as the silence following a kick of hind legs into the lifted lips of the opponent. Nearby, colts*
> 20 *and mares, indifferent, nibbled grass or looked away. Then it stopped. The rust-colored one dropped his head and pawed the ground while the winner loped off in an arc, nudging the mares before him.*
> *As we elbowed back through the grass looking for the dug-*
> 25 *out place, avoiding the line of parked trucks beyond, we lost our way. Although it took forever to re-sight the fence, neither*

*of us panicked until we heard voices, urgent but low. I grabbed
her arm and put a finger to my lips. Never lifting our heads,
just peeping through the grass, we saw them pull a body from a*
30 *wheelbarrow and throw it into a hole already waiting. One
foot stuck up over the edge and quivered, as though it could get
out, as though with a little effort it could break through the
dirt being shoveled in. We could not see the faces of the men
doing the burying, only their trousers; but we saw the edge of a*
35 *spade drive the jerking foot down to join the rest of itself.
When she saw that black foot with its creamy pink and mud-
streaked sole being whacked into the grave, her whole body
began to shake. I hugged her shoulders tight and tried to pull
her trembling into my own bones because, as a brother four*
40 *years older, I thought I could handle it. The men were long
gone and the moon was a cantaloupe by the time we felt safe
enough to disturb even one blade of grass and move on our
stomachs, searching for the scooped-out part under the fence.
When we got home we expected to be whipped or at least*
45 *scolded for staying out so late, but the grown-ups did not
notice us. Some disturbance had their attention.*

*Since you're set on telling my story, whatever you think
and whatever you write down, know this: I really forgot about
the burial. I only remembered the horses. They were so*
50 *beautiful. So brutal. And they stood like men.*

Question 3: Literary Argument

(Suggested time—40 minutes. This question counts as one-third of the total essay section score.)

In many works of fiction, characters respond to situations in seemingly irrational or careless ways. As poet Ehsan Sehgal notes, "your behavior is the mirror for your mental state."

Either from your own reading or from the list below, choose a work of fiction in which a character's careless or irrational actions lead to positive or negative outcomes. Then, in a well-written essay, analyze how the author's portrayal of the character's complex behavior helps illuminate the meaning of the work as a whole. Do not merely summarize the plot.

In your response you should do the following:

- Respond to the prompt with a thesis that presents a defensible interpretation.
- Provide evidence to support your line of reasoning.
- Explain how your evidence supports your line of reasoning.
- Use appropriate grammar and punctuation in communicating your argument.

- *Americanah*
- *Antigone*
- *The Awakening*
- *Beloved*
- *The Bluest Eye*
- *Brave New World*
- *Brideshead Revisited*
- *The Brief Wondrous Life of Oscar Wao*
- *The Catcher in the Rye*
- *Death of a Salesman*
- *Don Quixote*
- *East of Eden*
- *A Gesture Life*
- *Great Expectations*
- *The Great Gatsby*
- *The Handmaid's Tale*
- *The House of Mirth*
- *The Importance of Being Earnest*
- *Invisible Man*
- *King Lear*
- *The Leavers*
- *Lolita*
- *The Mill on the Floss*
- *Native Son*
- *No Country for Old Men*
- *The Odyssey*
- *Pachinko*
- *Pride and Prejudice*
- *The Road*
- *The Sun Also Rises*
- *The Tempest*
- *To Kill a Mockingbird*
- *When the Emperor Was Divine*

Permissions Acknowledgments

CHAPTER 1

"AP® English Literature and Composition Skills" table (pp. 2–3): AP® English Literature and Composition. Copyright © 2021 The College Board. Reproduced with permission. www.collegeboard.org.

CHAPTER 2

Tiana Clark: "My Therapist Wants to Know about My Relationship to Work" from *Poetry* (November 2018). Reprinted by permission of the author.

Kyle Dargan: "A House Divided" excerpted from *Honest Engine*, pp. 12–13. Reprinted by permission of University of Georgia Press.

Question 2 (p. 41): 2017 AP® English Literature and Composition Free-Response Questions on AP® Exam. Copyright © 2017 The College Board. Reproduced with permission. www.collegeboard.org.

Question 2 (p. 52): 2019 AP® English Literature and Composition Free-Response Questions on AP® Exam. Copyright © 2019 The College Board. Reproduced with permission. www.collegeboard.org.

CHAPTER 3

Joshua Bennett: "Ode to the Equipment Manager" from *The Sobbing School* by Joshua Bennett, copyright © 2016 by Joshua Bennett. Used by permission of Penguin Books, an imprint of Penguin Publishing Group, a division of Penguin Random House LLC. All rights reserved.

Gwendolyn Brooks: "We Real Cool" from *Selected Poems*. Reprinted by consent of Brooks Permissions.

Rita Dove: "Daystar" from *Thomas and Beulah* (Carnegie Mellon University Press, Pittsburgh, PA). © 1986 by Rita Dove. Reprinted by permission of the author.

Robert Frost: "Out, Out—" from *Complete Poems of Robert Frost*. Non-U.S. and non-CA rights held by Henry Holt & Company.

Aimee Nezhukumatathil: "On Listening to Your Teacher Take Attendance" from *Oce-anic*. Copyright © 2018 by Aimee Nezhukumatathil. Reprinted with the permission of The Permissions Company, LLC on behalf of Copper Canyon Press, coppercanyonpress.org.

Matthew Olzmann. "Mountain Dew Commercial Disguised as a Love Poem" from *Mezzanines*. Copyright © 2013 by Matthew Olzmann. Reprinted with the permission of The Permissions Company, LLC on behalf of Alice James Books, alicejamesbooks.org.

Question 1 (p. 58): 2009 AP® English Literature and Composition Free-Response Questions on AP® Exam. Copyright © 2009 The College Board. Reproduced with permission. www.collegeboard.org.

Jon Sands: Excerpt from "Workshop on Anaphora" featured on Elisabet Velasquez's 60 Second Workshops on Instagram. Reprinted by permission of Jon Sands.

R. A. Villanueva: 2-line excerpt from "Annus Mirabilis" from Poets.org, Poem-a-Day 2018. Reprinted by permission of R. A. Villanueva.

CHAPTER 4

Question 2 (p. 110): 2007 AP® English Literature and Composition Free-Response Questions on AP® Exam. Copyright © 2007 The College Board. Reproduced with permission. www.collegeboard.org.

Question 2 (pp. 102, 115, 135): AP® English Literature and Composition Course and Exam Description, 2020. Copyright © 2020 The College Board. Reproduced with permission. www.collegeboard.org.

Dalton Trumbo: Excerpt from *Johnny Got His Gun* published by Citadel Press Books. Citadel Press Books are published by Kensington Publishing Corp., 850 Third Avenue, New York, NY 10022. Copyright © 1939, 1959, 1991 Dalton Trumbo. Introduction copyright © 1991 Ron Kovic. Foreword copyright © 2007 Cindy Sheehan. All rights reserved. Reprinted by arrangement with Kensington Publishing Corp. www.kensingtonbooks.com.

CHAPTER 5

Question 3 (pp. 154, 158): 2018 AP® English Literature and Composition Free-Response Questions on AP® Exam. Copyright © 2018 The College Board. Reproduced with permission. www.collegeboard.org.

Question 3 (p. 155): 2017 AP® English Literature and Composition Free-Response Questions on AP® Exam. Copyright © 2007 The College Board. Reproduced with permission. www.collegeboard.org.

CHAPTER 6

Exam overview table (p. 181): AP® Literature and Composition Course and Exam Description, p. 135, Fall 2020. Copyright © 2020 The College Board. Reproduced with permission. www.collegeboard.org.

Exam skill category breakdown table (p. 182): AP® Literature and Composition Course and Exam Description, p. 137, Fall 2020. Copyright © 2020 The College Board. Reproduced with permission. www.collegeboard.org.

PRACTICE AP® EXAM 1

Margaret Atwood (pp. 210–11): Excerpt from *Cat's Eye* by Margaret Atwood, copyright © 1988 by O. W. Toad, Ltd. Used by permission of Doubleday, an imprint of the Knopf Doubleday Publishing Group, a division of Penguin Random House LLC and Emblem/McClelland & Stewart, a division of Penguin Random House Canada Limited. All rights reserved.

Eavan Boland (pp. 208–9): "In a Bad Light" from *In a Time of Violence* by Eavan Boland. Copyright © 1994 by Eavan Boland. Used by permission of W. W. Norton & Company, Inc.

Jamaica Kincaid (p. 197–98): Excerpt from "Gwen" from *Annie John* by Jamaica Kincaid. Copyright © 1985 by Jamaica Kincaid. Reprinted by permission of Farrar, Straus and Giroux. All rights reserved.

Audre Lorde (p. 205): "Coal." Copyright © 1968, 1970, 1973 by Audre Lorde. Copyright © 1997 by The Audre Lorde Estate.

From *The Collected Poems of Audre Lorde* by Audre Lorde. Used by permission of W. W. Norton & Company, Inc.

Dionisio D. Martinez (p. 201–2): "Rest before you sleep" from *Poetry* (September 2008). Reprinted by permission of Dionisio D. Martinez.

William Trevor (pp. 189–91): Excerpt from *Two Lives* by William Trevor, copyright © 1991 by William Trevor. Used by permission of Viking Books, an imprint of Penguin Publishing Group, a division of Penguin Random House LLC. All rights reserved. © The Estate of William Trevor, 1991. Reproduced with kind permission of Johnson & Alcock Ltd.

PRACTICE AP® EXAM 2

Jimmy Santiago Baca (pp. 230–31): "Green Chile" from *Black Mesa Poems*, copyright © 1989 by Jimmy Santiago Baca. Reprinted by permission of New Directions Publishing Corp.

Edwidge Danticat (pp. 226–27): Excerpt from *Breath, Eyes, Memory* copyright © 1994, 2015 by Edwidge Danticat. Reprinted by permission of Soho Press, Inc. All rights reserved.

Toni Morrison (pp. 236–37): Excerpt from *Home: A Novel* by Toni Morrison, copyright © 2012 by Toni Morrison. Used by permission of Alfred A. Knopf, an imprint of the Knopf Doubleday Publishing Group, a division of Penguin Random House LLC. All rights reserved.

Adrienne Rich (pp. 221–22): "Integrity." Copyright © 2016 by the Adrienne Rich Literary Trust. Copyright © 1981 by Adrienne Rich, from *Collected Poems: 1950–2012* by Adrienne Rich. Used by permission of W. W. Norton & Company, Inc.

Jean Rhys (pp. 217–18): "I Used to Live Here Once" by Jean Rhys. From *Sleep It Off, Lady*. Copyright © 1976 by Jean Rhys. Used by permission of Robin Straus Agency, Inc.

"Love Calls Us to the Things of This World" from *Collected Poems 1943–2004* by Richard Wilbur. Copyright © 2004 by Richard Wilbur. Used by permission of HarperCollins Publishers.

Answer Key, AP® Exam 1

Section I: Multiple-Choice

MCQ	Correct Answer	Skill	Essential Knowledge	Answer Explanations
1	C	4.A	NAR-1.J	The narrator wants to make sure that her readers understand her lack of formal education isn't an impediment. She is trying to establish credibility. Therefore the best answer is C.
2	A	4.B	NAR-1.K	The narrator feels abused by rumors and false speculations and wants to explain her side of the story to set the record straight. Therefore the best answer is A.
3	C	4.C	NAR-1.M	The narrator presents a step-by-step explanation of her past actions in order to clear her name. Therefore the best answer is C.
4	A	3.D	STR-1.S	By claiming that she was unhappy in Africa, she is qualifying her previous argument. If unhappiness breeds confusion, how can readers be sure her memories are valid? Therefore the best answer is A.
5	B	4.C	NAR-1.O	The narrator reflects on her earlier life in a serious manner. Her introspection leads to her trying to justify her past actions. Therefore the best answer is B.
6	D	5.D	FIG-1.AD	In the context of the second paragraph, the word "carefully" is best understood to mean *meticulously*. The narrator goes into depth about her looks as she carefully describes her process. Therefore the best answer is D.
7	C	1.C	CHR-1.Q	The narrator is arguing that despite her age she is still beautiful, especially when it comes to her attractiveness to men. Aging has become an internal conflict for her. Therefore the best answer is C.
8	A	3.A	STR-1.R	After discussing the hardships of her life, the narrator changes her focus in the third paragraph. She is placing herself in a positive light. This paragraph seems to soften her image momentarily. Therefore the best answer is A.

MCQ	Correct Answer	Skill	Essential Knowledge	Answer Explanations
9	D	1.A	CHR-1.P	"Integrity" is a synonym of "veracity." "Fairness" doesn't rise to the intended meaning and all other choices are antonyms. Therefore the best answer is D.
10	D	4.C	NAR-1.M	After revealing her past, as she sees it, the last sentence in the passage is an authentic plea to see the narrator as an honest woman. Therefore the best answer is D.
11	B	3.A	STR-1.A	The passage serves as a long introduction to the narrator. She glosses over several areas of her life but doesn't go into any depth. The final line reveals the true purpose of her introduction: "you'll find I am an honest woman." Therefore the best answer is B.
12	C	5.B 3.D	STR-1.G FIG-1.D	In the first four lines, the speaker is expressing a sense of relief and frustration as he parts with his beloved. Therefore the best answer choice is C.
13	A	1.A	CHR-1.E	The speaker repeats the pronoun "I" three times in lines 2–4 as well as "myself." This indicates the personal nature of the speaker's argument. Therefore the best answer choice is A.
14	D	1.A	CHR-1.E	The speaker exhibits an understanding that the relationship is over, so it is better to walk away and not display any feelings they once held. Therefore the best answer choice is D.
15	D	6.C	FIG-1.V	As the speaker describes the slow death of his love, he personifies Love, Passion, Faith, and Innocence. Therefore the best answer choice is D.
16	C	3.C	STR-1.G	The speaker is starting to qualify the ending of the relationship, and he indicates that love, passion, faith, and innocence are dying, but are not dead yet. Therefore the best answer is C.
17	B	5.B	FIG-1.A	The antecedent of "his" in line 12 is "Love." All the other personified feelings serve Love's recovery. Therefore the best answer is B.

MCQ	Correct Answer	Skill	Essential Knowledge	Answer Explanations
18	B	5.B	FIG-1.N	In the final two lines, the speaker indicates that the beloved can still save their love, which adds a surprise twist to the poem. The one answer choice that is not present is B. Therefore the best answer is B.
19	D	3.D	STR-1.G	The enjambment of lines 7 and 8 creates an urgency not found in any other lines of the poem. This urgency can be associated with the speaker's despair. Therefore the best answer is D.
20	C	5.B	FIG-1.C	The speaker's attitude throughout the poem changes. For most of the poem, his feelings are impassioned, angry, and hopeful. Therefore the best answer is C.
21	B	1.A	CHR-1.E	Even though the poem begins with a breakup, by the end of the poem, the speaker suggests that there is still time to save the relationship, if the beloved so desires. Therefore the best answer is B.
22	C	4.B	NAR-1.F	The narrator begins the passage with a description of her surroundings, but once she understands what is happening at the cemetery, her obsession begins to grow. Therefore the best answer is C.
23	A	1.A	CHR-1.O	Annie's voice is curious and controlled, and her descriptions are colorful. Therefore the best answer is A.
24	D	2.C	SET-1.D	Annie and her mother move to a house on Fort Road while a new roof is installed on their primary house. By changing the setting, the author places Annie near a cemetery, which fuels her growing obsession with death. Therefore the best answer is D.
25	B	3.D	STR-1.S	The first part of the opening paragraph characterizes Annie as a typical 10-year-old girl, but once she understands the purpose of the cemetery, she starts to change. This contrast helps to convey Annie's curiosity about death and dying. Therefore the best answer is B.

MCQ	Correct Answer	Skill	Essential Knowledge	Answer Explanations
26	B	4.C	NAR-1.O	Annie's wonder and curiosity about the cemetery and the dead in general informs the primary tone throughout the passage. Other tone words may apply for certain sentences, but not overall. Therefore the best answer is B.
27	D	3.D	STR-1.T	The antecedent of the pronoun "they" is "the dead." It seems that Annie is distancing herself from dead people by repeatedly referring to them as "they." Therefore the best answer is D.
28	A	1.A	CHR-1.P	Annie's mother is a plainspoken woman, and in the passage, she answers all her daughter's questions in an honest manner. The character trait that is not seen is deceitfulness. Therefore the best answer is A.
29	D	1.A	CHR-1.P	When Annie tells her mother that "[n]o one died" and when she says she "was about to give up and go inside" after not seeing any funerals, a sense of disappointment is conveyed. Therefore the best answer is D.
30	C	5.D	FIG-1.AD	Annie's growing interest in death has sharpened to the point of recognizing the smell of the undertaker's business. The recurring images of death are starting to form a motif in the passage. Therefore the best answer is C.
31	B	3.D	STR-1.T	The passage starts in innocence and ends with an obsession with death by a 10-year-old. Therefore the best answer is B.
32	C	3.C	STR-1.W	The poem has an unusual structure, but the dedication and the content indicate a tribute to the poet's father. Therefore the best answer is C.
33	D	1.A	CHR-1.E	The dedication of the poem, "*Requiem ... for my father*," indicates the speaker/poet has lost his father. This reality creates a reflective tone. Therefore the best answer is D.
34	A	3.D	STR-1.J	The lack of any punctuation creates a continuous flow of the speaker's reflections about his father. Therefore the best answer is A.

MCQ	Correct Answer	Skill	Essential Knowledge	Answer Explanations
35	A	5.B	FIG-1.C	The traditional use of the word *sleep* indicates natural resting with eyes closed, but in this case, the traditional meaning does not apply. Therefore the best answer is A.
36	D	1.A	CHR-1.E	The woman is characterized as someone who lives in the woods and communes with the animals to the point of understanding that animal behavior is unpredictable. Therefore the best answer is D.
37	D	5.C	FIG-1.AH	The fox serves as a symbol for the instinctual behaviors of animals. All the other attributes assigned to the fox are created by people. Therefore the best answer is D.
38	B	3.D	STR-1.G	The abrupt shift from a proposed question to the idea of intolerable silence indicates the speaker's understanding that such questions are unknowable. Therefore the best answer is B.
39	B	5.B	FIG-1.A	The speaker is referencing his father. The entire poem is a tribute to him, so the only logical antecedent for "you" is his father. Therefore the best answer is B.
40	A	5.D	FIG-1.Q	The speaker is trying to understand his father's motivations. The natural images throughout the stanza (e.g., "head full of roots") help to explain the speaker's frustrations trying to understand his father. Therefore the best answer is A.
41	C	3.D	STR-1.AF	By setting all "creatures" in juxtaposition with human animals, the illogic of building facts to support preconceived ideas seems foolish. Therefore the best answer is C.
42	D	3.C	STR-1.AE	The gaps throughout the poem create momentary pauses that indicate the speaker's careful consideration of his words and thoughts. Therefore the best answer is D.
43	A	5.B	FIG-1.L	In the last stanza, the speaker admits that his true aim is vindication. A close synonym of "vindication" is "exoneration." All the other answer choices are antonyms of the feelings the speaker is expressing. Therefore the best answer is A.

MCQ	Correct Answer	Skill	Essential Knowledge	Answer Explanations
44	A	3.D	STR-1.G	In the final stanza, the speaker is pleading with his father to "Wake up stop while you still know where you are." These and other phrases create an imploring tone. Therefore the best answer is A.
45	C	6.B	FIG-1.H	In the final stanza, the speaker encourages his father to wake up and engage in one more conversation. Sleep is again used as a metaphor for death as the time for death approaches. Therefore the best answer is C.
46	B	1.A	CHR-1.E	The poet opens with the speaker as the "I" of the poem and that her voice, as well as she, is "from the earth's inside." Therefore the best answer is B.
47	D	5.D	FIG-1.Q	Lines 3–7 offer many striking images of diamonds, flames, and words being colored by those speaking. Through these connections, the poet adds importance to words being spoken. Therefore the best answer is D.
48	A	6.B	FIG-1.S	Figurative language is used extensively in the second stanza to further the speaker's interesting, but complicated, relationship with words. Therefore the best answer is A.
49	C	6.A	FIG-1.F	The similes in the second stanza, such as "Like a diamond," "Breeding like adders," "like gypsies," and "Like young sparrows," all work to illustrate the diverse comparisons the poet uses to explain her relationship with words. Therefore the best answer is C.
50	A	5.A	FIG-1.L	The speaker claims that "words live in my throat." In this instant, words are being personified to illustrate how words are living things. Therefore the best answer is A.
51	D	5.B	FIG-1.A	The word "Others" in line 17 refers directly to "words" in line 16. Therefore the best answer is D.
52	B	5.B	FIG-1.AG	In the two-word line "Bedevil me" the word "bedevil" most closely adheres to the definition of trouble. The speaker is not confused, and the remaining choices represent antonyms of "bedevil." Therefore the best answer is B.

MCQ	Correct Answer	Skill	Essential Knowledge	Answer Explanations
53	C	3.C 6.B	STR-1.F FIG-1.R	The final four-line stanza draws upon comparisons between the speaker, love, diamonds, and the Earth. The speaker argues that like a diamond her words are created through love and the Earth. Therefore the best answer is C.
54	D	3.D	STR-1.G	Throughout the poem, the speaker is involved in a serious meditation on her identity, language, and the power of truth. The only answer choice that meets this definition is "pensive." Therefore the best answer is D.
55	D	3.D	STR-1.AH	Through the use of contrasting elements, the overall development leads to a better understanding of the sometimes paradoxical relationship the speaker has with her life as a strong Black woman as well as with language. Therefore the best answer is D.

Section II: Free-Response

FRQ	Question Type	Skill	Good Answers Will
1	Poetry Analysis	1.A 3.C 3.D 5.A 5.B 5.D 6.B 7.A 7.B 7.C 7.D	• demonstrate an understanding of the different time periods the speaker occupies in the poem. • demonstrate an understanding of the speaker's relationship to the past and present events of the poem. • use 2 to 3 literary elements or techniques to support and explain the speaker's complex reaction to the museum exhibit. • establish a clear line of reasoning that supports a defensible thesis statement that directly answers the prompt. • demonstrate effective control over the conventions of written communication.
2	Prose Fiction Analysis	1.A 1.C 1.D 4.B 4.C 5.B 5.D 7.B 7.C 7.D 7.E	• demonstrate an understanding of the unique characteristics of the sister and the brother. • demonstrate an understanding of the differences and similarities of the sister and the brother. • explore the significance of the excerpt being told from the sister's point of view. • explore the nuanced relationship between the siblings, and what makes the relationship complex. • use appropriate evidence from the excerpt to support a defensible thesis statement that answers the prompt. • establish a clear line of reasoning that supports a defensible thesis. • demonstrate effective control over the conventions of written communication.
3	Literary Argument	1.A 1.B 1.E 2.A 3.F 4.C 4.D 7.B 7.C 7.D 7.E	• clearly address a meaningful decision and responsibility a specific character undertakes. • provide commentary that explores a character's complex motivations for assuming a meaningful responsibility. • explore why the decision and responsibility is complex in nature. • clearly analyze how the complex nature of the decision and responsibility helps to develop a larger meaning of the work as a whole. • use appropriate evidence from the work to support a defensible thesis statement that answers the prompt. • establish a clear line of reasoning that supports a defensible thesis. • demonstrate effective control over the conventions of written communication.

Answer Key, AP® Exam 2

Section I: Multiple-Choice

MCQ	Correct Answer	Skill	Essential Knowledge	Answer Explanations
1	B	5.B	FIG-1.AG	The speaker is irritated by an interruption when he exclaims "hold your tongue" to an unknown person. All he wants to do is love. Therefore the best answer is B.
2	A	5.D	FIG-1.O	The descriptive words "palsy," "gout," and "gray" create an image of old age from the speaker's point of view. Therefore the best answer is A.
3	D	3.D	STR-1.G	The speaker is asking rhetorical questions which emphasize the harmlessness of his love, as well as offset any additional arguments that might interfere with the fullness of his love. Therefore the best answer is D.
4	C	6.B	FIG-1.R	The speaker compares his love with the power of the eagle and the gentleness of the dove. His comparison represents his and his beloved's love for each other. Therefore the best answer is C.
5	D	6.B	FIG-1.H	By comparing his relationship to the riddle of the phoenix, the speaker is utilizing an unusual metaphor to elevate his relationship to mythic levels. Therefore the best answer is D.
6	D	5.B	FIG-1.A	The antecedent of the pronoun "it" is the phoenix riddle. Therefore the best answer is D.
7	C	3.D	STR-1.AH	The speaker believes that their love is legendary, although it may not be understood by all. The couple may even die for their love. All answers speak to some aspect of this legendary love except C. Therefore the best answer is C.
8	A	5.B	FIG-1.N	By suggesting that their love will be canonized, the speaker is exaggerating their relationship to a hyperbolic level. Therefore the best answer is A.

MCQ	Correct Answer	Skill	Essential Knowledge	Answer Explanations
9	D	3.D	STR-1.AG	The speaker is suggesting that their love will become the material of poetry, creating an ironic situation considering the message is shared through a poem. Therefore the best answer is D.
10	A	5.B	FIG-1.M	The word "invoke" in line 37 asks readers to petition the speaker and his beloved to share with the world the secrets of their great love. Therefore the best answer is A.
11	B	5.B	FIG-1.N	The poet's representation of love worthy of sainthood must be taken as satire or at least hyperbole. Therefore the best answer is B.
12	C	7.B	LAN-1.D	This short story begins with a woman's journey back to her home. During her journey, she experiences several emotions. These conflicting emotions lead to confusion, nostalgia, sadness, and anxiety, but there is no indication of a revelation. Therefore the best answer is C.
13	A	5.D	FIG-1.AD	The author creates the drama the woman faces through detailed imagery. Readers "see" the same things the woman sees and arrive at her epiphany along with her. Therefore the best answer is A.
14	C	1.A	CHR-1.P	The woman is standing and looking at the river and the stepping stones she needed to navigate for a safe trip to the other side. She is quite intentional in her choices. Therefore the best answer is C.
15	A	6.B	FIG-1.AK	The various descriptions of the stones as "unsteady," "pointed," and "slippery" are comparisons for the new, confusing journey the woman is on. Therefore the best answer is A.
16	D	4.B	NAR-1.H	The third-person narrator describes the woman's observations and thereby colors readers' understanding of the events of the story. The sky takes on a crystalline view the woman never remembered seeing before. Therefore the best answer is D.
17	C	4.D	NAR-1.W	As the woman comes upon her old home, she recognizes specific differences, including a car, that only one familiar with the property would notice. Therefore the best answer is C.

MCQ	Correct Answer	Skill	Essential Knowledge	Answer Explanations
18	B	1.A	CHR-1.P	The confusion the woman feels after being ignored by the children is quickly reversed after she puts together all the clues she gathered earlier in the passage. This final realization brings a sense of resignation to her new reality. Therefore the best answer is B.
19	A	3.D	STR-1.G	When the woman sees the children, she calls out to them three times in hopes of recognition, but she feels ignored when she doesn't get a response. Her hopes are dashed and her mood shifts to a realistic understanding of her new reality. Therefore the best answer is A.
20	A	4.B	NAR-1.H	At this point in the passage, the woman is dismayed by the children's lack of awareness of her presence. By choosing the word "longing" the narrator is suggesting that the woman has a deep desire for acknowledgment and connection with the children. Therefore the best answer is A.
21	D	4.B	NAR-1.K	The narrator stays objective for most of the passage. The narrator doesn't take readers into the woman's inner conflicts but does allow us to see and sense her feelings and actions without judgment. Therefore the best answer is D.
22	B	7.B	LAN-1.D	The poem begins with the speaker returning to a home she once shared with someone she cared for. The third, fourth, and fifth stanzas establish the speaker's internal reflections about her growth. The final stanza explores her contradictory memories of her relationship in the cabin. Therefore the best answer is B.
23	D	1.A	CHR-1.E	The speaker claims that a "wild patience" has brought her to this point, but the imagery in the opening stanza also points to a heavy burden. Therefore the best answer is D.
24	C	3.C	STR-1.F	The speaker is reminiscing about a past struggle that she likens to a malfunctioning outboard motor. Therefore the best answer is C.
25	D	4.C	NAR-1.N	In line 14 the speaker is claiming the setting is crucial for her, while in line 15 the light is judgmental of her. Therefore the best answer is D.

MCQ	Correct Answer	Skill	Essential Knowledge	Answer Explanations
26	C	4.C	NAR-1.O	After arriving at her destination, the speaker comes to the stark realization that the only real necessity in life is herself. Therefore the best answer is C.
27	A	4.B	NAR-1.K	The speaker asks a question only she can answer. Her response acknowledges her many selves that have been unacknowledged. Therefore the best answer is A.
28	A	6.A	FIG-1.F	As the speaker gains a better understanding of her multifaceted personality, she likens her traits of anger and tenderness to angels and not as simple polarities. Therefore the best answer is A.
29	A	6.B	FIG-1.S	The speaker compares herself to a spider because, like a spider, she can create even when situations seem broken. Therefore the best answer is A.
30	B	4.C	NAR-1.M	While all choices are related to integrity, the speaker is on a journey of discovery which leads to honest reflections and revelations about her life. Therefore the best answer is B.
31	C	5.D	FIG-1.O	The images the speaker describes are those that only someone with intimate knowledge would know about her partner. Even though it seems they are no longer together, the memories remain. Therefore the best answer is C.
32	D	5.C	FIG-1.AH	Throughout the poem the boat is controlled either by the speaker or the partner. The speaker is seeking personal control as she navigates memories of her lost relationship. Therefore the best answer is D.
33	B	4.C	NAR-1.O	Throughout the poem, the speaker is either reflecting on her life, her life with her partner, or the cabin they shared. Often her reflections are filled with a sense of melancholy. Therefore the best answer is B.
34	C	7.B	LAN-1.D	The poem toggles between painful memories and personal realizations. Therefore the best answer is C.
35	C	4.C	NAR-1.O	In the first two paragraphs, the mother is not characterized as indolent, which would indicate that she is lazy or averse to hard work. Therefore the best answer is C.

MCQ	Correct Answer	Skill	Essential Knowledge	Answer Explanations
36	D	2.A	SET-1.A	The narrator's new home stands in stark relief to the average conditions in Haiti. This juxtaposition of the setting illustrates the improved conditions of the narrator. Therefore the best answer is D.
37	A	1.A	CHR-1.D	The narrator shows a deep understanding of her mother's character and how she will react to an ungrateful child, so the narrator keeps her feelings to herself. Therefore the best answer is A.
38	D	5.B	FIG-1.M	The narrator says the Haitian students were "cringing" in their uniforms which imitated genuine Catholic-school uniforms, and in essence, making the narrator feel like an imitation student. Therefore the best answer is D.
39	A	6.A	FIG-1.AE	The narrator claims that when her mother tried to help her learn English, she struggled because her understanding of English was limited; therefore, the words her mother uttered were similar to the sounds of rocks in a stream. Therefore the best answer is A.
40	B	6.A	FIG-1.AE	Learning English was a struggle for the narrator, and at first, she was just making incoherent sounds, but pulling some English-type words from the mixed Creole/English she heard at home helped new English words to pop into her understanding. Therefore the best answer is B.
41	C	4.C	NAR-1.N	The words the narrator lists are intentional. As a migrant, the narrator is not only learning a new language and culture, but she is also learning the words that partially define her new existence. Therefore the best answer is C.
42	D	3.D	STR-1.S	With each repetition of "words," the narrator explores several challenges she faced learning English and the reality of certain words in her life. Therefore the best answer is D.
43	A	7.B	LAN-1.D	The focus of the excerpt is the mother's sacrifices and dedication to her daughter's education. Therefore the best answer is A

MCQ	Correct Answer	Skill	Essential Knowledge	Answer Explanations
44	C	4.C	NAR-1.O	The narrator discusses several aspects of her mother's personality. She speaks of her mother's sacrifices and pessimism, but also that at times she withheld information from her. Despite the critical observations, the narrator always shows respect for her mother. Therefore the best answer is C.
45	B	4.C	NAR-1.O	The speaker's tone throughout the poem is respectful of his grandmother and the place chile peppers play in his culture. Therefore the best answer is B.
46	A	1.A	CHR-1.C	The opening sentences establishes the speaker's deep knowledge and personal preference for red chile peppers, which helps set the contrast with his grand-mother's preference for green chile peppers. Therefore the best answer is A.
47	C	6.C	FIG-1.V	The speaker claims that "I can hear them talking in the wind," personifying the red chile *ristras*. Therefore the best answer is C.
48	B	5.D	FIG.1.P	When the speaker's aging grandmother holds out the green chile pepper, the speaker doesn't express his preference for red chile peppers. Instead, he moves into an exploration of his grandmother's love of the peppers. Therefore the best answer is B.
49	D	5.D	FIG-1.Q	The imagery and diction choices throughout the second stanza convey the deep passion the grandmother has for cooking for her grandson. This "mysterious passion" is in ser-vice to him. Therefore the best answer is D.
50	C	5.B	FIG-1.A	"Its" refers back to the green chile pepper in line 13. Therefore the best answer is C.
51	B	4.C	NAR-1.N	The second stanza is filled with passionate descriptions and literary techniques that describe the grandmother's passion for cook-ing, but it does not focus on the speaker's sacrifices for his grandmother. Therefore the best answer is B.
52	A	4.A	NAR- 1.B	The speaker's detailed descriptions of his grandmother's cooking ultimately center on his grandmother's nearly royal treatment of her grandson. Therefore the best answer is A.

MCQ	Correct Answer	Skill	Essential Knowledge	Answer Explanations
53	C	3.D	STR-1.G	The first two stanzas focus on the speaker and the speaker's grandmother. The third stanza shifts from the personal to a broader cultural view of green chile peppers. Therefore the best answer is C.
54	A	2.A	SET-1.A	The setting of New Mexico and small towns within New Mexico provides a broader cultural understanding of the importance of green chile peppers. Therefore the best answer is A.
55	D	7.B	LAN-1.D	The meaning of the work as a whole centers around the love and passion of the grandmother as she prepares a culturally significant meal for the speaker. The speaker connects this family meal to a larger tradition in the final stanza. Therefore the best answer is D.

Section II: Free-Response

FRQ	Question Type	Skill	Good Answers Will
1	Poetry Analysis	3.C 3.D 4.C 5.A 5.B 5.C 5.D 6.A 6.B 6.C 7.B 7.C 7.D 7.E	• demonstrate an understanding of the literal situation the speaker is experiencing. • demonstrate an understanding of the speaker's moments of astonishment upon first awakening. • explore the speaker's developing observations of the laundry. • use 2 to 3 literary elements or techniques which support a defensible thesis that directly addresses the prompt. • establish a clear line of reasoning that supports a defensible thesis. • demonstrate effective control over the conventions of written communication.
2	Prose Fiction Analysis	1.D 2.B 3.B 4.B 4.C 5.C 5.D 6.A 7.B 7.C 7.D 7.E	• demonstrate an understanding of what is literally happening in the excerpt. • demonstrate an understanding of the narrator's complex reactions to witnessing the burial of a lynched African-American man. • explore how the final paragraph adds to the narrator's complex memories of the day. • use appropriate evidence from the excerpt to support a defensible thesis statement that answers the prompt. • establish a clear line of reasoning that supports a defensible thesis. • demonstrate effective control over the conventions of written communication.
3	Literary Argument	1.A 1.B 1.E 3.B 3.D 3.E 3.F 4.C 4.D 7.B 7.C 7.D 7.E	• clearly focus on a specific character and why his or her actions are irrational or careless. • explore how the character's irrational or careless actions result in positive or negative outcomes. • demonstrate why the character's irrational or careless actions are complex. • clearly analyze the complex nature of the character's actions, and how they help develop a larger meaning of the work as a whole. • use appropriate evidence from the work to support a defensible thesis statement that answers the prompt. • establish a clear line of reasoning that supports a defensible thesis. • demonstrate effective control over the conventions of written communication.

Glossary/Index

Bolded terms in the book are defined here.